RAISING A SECURE CHILD

Also Available

For Professionals

The Circle of Security Intervention:
Enhancing Attachment in Early Parent–Child Relationships
Bert Powell, Glen Cooper, Kent Hoffman, and Bob Marvin

Visit the authors' website, *www.circleofsecurity.com*,
for more information.

RAISING A SECURE CHILD

How **Circle of Security Parenting**
Can Help You Nurture Your Child's
Attachment, Emotional Resilience,
and Freedom to Explore

**Kent Hoffman, Glen Cooper,
and Bert Powell,**
with Christine M. Benton

Foreword by Daniel J. Siegel

THE GUILFORD PRESS
NEW YORK   LONDON

Copyright © 2017 The Guilford Press
A Division of Guilford Publications, Inc.
370 Seventh Avenue, Suite 1200, New York, NY 10001
www.guilford.com

Printed in the United States of America

This book is printed on acid-free paper.

Last digit is print number: 9   8   7   6   5   4   3

Library of Congress Cataloging-in-Publication Data

Names: Hoffman, Kent, author.
Title: Raising a secure child : how circle of security parenting can help you
    nurture your child's attachment, emotional resilience, and freedom to
    explore / Kent Hoffman, Glen Cooper, Bert Powell, and Christine M. Benton.
Description: New York, NY : Guilford Press, [2017] | Includes bibliographical
    references and index.
Identifiers: LCCN 2016049134| ISBN 9781462527632 (pbk. : alk. paper) | ISBN
    9781462528134 (hardcover : alk. paper)
Subjects: LCSH: Parenting. | Parent and child. | Security (Psychology) |
    Child psychology.
Classification: LCC HQ755.8.H595 2017 | DDC 649/.1--dc23
LC record available at https://lccn.loc.gov/2016049134

With respect and gratitude to Jude Cassidy, PhD—
mentor, colleague, and friend

CONTENTS

Part II

CREATING AND MAINTAINING THE CIRCLE

*How to Be Bigger, Stronger, Wiser, and Kind—
and Good Enough*

Purchasers of this book can download and print enlarged
versions of the Shark Music Checklist and Your Core Sensitivity
in Adult Relationships at *www.guilford.com/hoffman2-forms* for personal
use or use with individual clients (see copyright page for details).

FOREWORD

If you are looking for a practical, wise, science-based, and accessible guide to creating the kind of attachment your child needs to optimize development, you've come to the right place! Kent Hoffman, Glen Cooper, and Bert Powell are highly gifted and experienced clinicians whose Circle of Security approach has been proven in research to be a practical and effective way to help parents nurture their children well.

I first met these three masters of human relationships years ago and was immediately impressed with their sensitivity, kindness, and humanity. As they worked to develop their Circle of Security approach, they continually based their creative endeavors on the scientific studies of attachment—how children connect with their caregivers—to be sure their foundations were solidly established. Then they went further and tested their model to see if it worked, not only for their own programs but also for those who had learned to use it around the world. Building on the newest findings of neuroscience, this approach can offer you the latest and best on how to raise your children.

Attachment refers to how we as mammals rely on our caregivers for nurturance as we grow toward maturity. A selective few attachment figures will naturally shape our growth by the ways in which they communicate with us from our earliest days. Attachment research has shown that those children who are fortunate to develop what is called "secure" attachment are most likely to grow into caring, thoughtful, reflective, emotionally and socially intelligent, resilient individuals who thrive.

If this is what you are looking for in your child's future, the Circle of Security approach to parenting will show you how to optimize growth toward these life-affirming traits. You may be wondering, however, why anyone would need to read a book about something that is so natural. Why doesn't everyone just have secure attachments?

Research has shown that many factors influence how we parent our children and that offering ways for children to be seen, soothed, safe, and secure provides a gateway to their well-being. But many things can get in the way. One of those factors is our own childhood experiences. Yet the research is robust and clear: It isn't what happened to us in our childhood by itself that is the crucial factor in predicting how our children will become attached to us, but rather the way we've made sense of how our childhood experiences have influenced us. Careful studies on over 10,000 individuals have shown that how we've been able to reflect on those things that were not so good and make sense of how they impacted our development and affect our current parenting is what matters most (see my book *The Developing Mind* [2012] for a summary of these findings). And even if our attachments to our own parents and other caregivers were secure, any of us can benefit from deepening our awareness of how we provide nurturance for our children. There is always room for learning and growth! The great news is that it is never too late to make sense of your life and learn to enhance your connections with those you love.

As you learn about how to reflect on your relationship with your child now, you'll see more clearly that how you communicate with your child can create, as our wonderful authors suggest, a way to "Be-With" your child in deeply rewarding ways. You'll be given the opportunity in the course of these magnificent pages to make sense, for example, of how "shark music" (a brilliantly evocative name these authors have given to the echoes of our own childhood attachments) can arise from implicit forms of memory. We all have a storehouse of emotions, images, bodily sensations, and beliefs we may not even feel are coming from the past that may be directly limiting our ability to connect with our child in these important and learnable ways that support the cultivation of secure attachment. We usually don't even know that shark music is interfering with how we connect with our children. This book will show you how to approach such experiences and free yourself from how they may be hindering your parenting.

Relationships are never perfect. If you have perfectionism in your strategy, you can actually start creating tension in your parenting by being too hard on yourself. This is a book filled with practical suggestions for how to be kinder with yourself and in turn model a receptive approach for your child. The great news from attachment research is that we can set a certain intention and make healing repairs when we experience the inevitable ruptures in those attuned, contingent connections. This book will show you how to identify and heal such ruptures through the powerful examples and clear descriptions of this important process of repair.

As I was reading these words of wisdom, I was impressed again and again with the exquisite sensitivity, clarity, and outright brilliance of these humble and dedicated guides. What a gift *Raising a Secure Child* is for us, for our children, and for the world. Thank you, Kent, Glen, Bert, and your associate, Christine Benton, for composing such a masterpiece. And thank *you* for having the insight, courage, and love to take in these pages and bring security into your child's life. Enjoy the journey ahead!

DANIEL J. SIEGEL, MD
author of *The Developing Mind, Brainstorm, Mindsight,*
and *Mind*; coauthor of *Parenting from the Inside Out,*
The Whole-Brain Child, and *No-Drama Discipline*

ACKNOWLEDGMENTS

To say that the three of us have been fortunate would be a stunning understatement.

Through the past three decades, as we've built this approach for parents and children, we have been offered gifts of support and guidance far beyond what we expected possible. Fellow clinicians, researchers, and early intervention specialists from around the world have consistently responded with clarity, constructive criticism, and added insight, all in the direction of honing the message we are seeking to offer families.

Primary among those offering support is Jude Cassidy at the University of Maryland. She has, from the beginning, been mentor, colleague, and friend. Without her clarity, scientific rigor, and deep understanding of attachment research, the Circle of Security would not exist as it does today.

Most certainly, John Bowlby and Mary Ainsworth—the founders of attachment theory and research—are at the foundation of this entire approach. Similarly, James Masterson and Ralph Klein—our early teachers of object relations theory—offered the blueprint to the core sensitivities that deeply influence the thinking presented here. In addition, we are grateful to Daniel Stern and Susan McDonough, whose influence was essential to the building of an early intervention model for parents. We are also thankful to Bob Marvin, who was helpful in the early phases of designing the research, certain aspects of the

Circle, and helping us more systematically understand parental themes of interaction based on attachment research.

Our gratitude will always extend to Dave Erb for offering the initial metaphor of the boat-and-dock out of which the Circle graphic emerged. His capacity for and modeling of Being-With is at the foundation of this work.

We want to thank Sandy Powell, one of our original guides in how to better understand and honor the intensity and promise within families. In addition, we are grateful for the ongoing support of Stig Torsteinson, Ida Brandtzaeg, Caroline Zanetti, Joe Coyne, Anna Huber, Susan Woodhouse, Per Götberg, Jenny Peters, Clare Gates, Francesca Manareisi, Megumi Kitagawa, Brigitte Ramsauer, Charlie Slaughter, Camelia Maianu, Andreea Peca, Oana Budacu, Sonya Vellet, and Charles Zeanah.

We are grateful, daily, for the great support and guidance offered by Gretchen Cook, Andy Cook, Bill Bloom, Angie Dierdorff, Neil Boris, Deidre Quinlan, Deborah Harris, and Carlos Guerrero at Circle of Security International. Their commitment, consistency, creativity, and kindness are the heart of how this approach is finding its way into the world.

We want to thank Dan Siegel for his gracious foreword. We also thank all of the parents throughout the world who submitted stories and quotes. Even though we were able to use only a small number, all were helpful in the writing of this book.

This publication of our work has required the immense support of The Guilford Press's Editor-in-Chief, Seymour Weingarten, who, from early on, believed in our vision and trusted that it could be made available in printed form in a way that would be supportive to parents, and, especially, Senior Editor Kitty Moore, who not only believed in the project but offered unfailing guidance throughout. At the heart of this support has been their suggestion that we utilize the writing expertise of Christine Benton. Through the writing of our first book for professionals and this book for parents, Chris has become a remarkable resource and friend. Her capacity to bring both coherence and simple clarity has been invaluable in the writing of each book. Through the last 6 years Chris has become deeply versed in our approach, and her sense of how to frame our thinking has been invaluable. In addition, her sense of humor throughout both writing projects has been a joy. We are so pleased that Chris's name is on the cover of this book. It could not have been written without her.

Our gratitude also to Rae Swenson for her helpful support throughout and to Hannah Flint and Nick Stewart at Hands Up Digital for their creative illustrations.

Finally, we continue to offer our gratitude and love to our own families for their steadfast presence through the years. Sandy, Chelsea, and Travis; Christine, Erin, Erik, Sara, Scott, Benjamin, and Zachary; Kim, Kai, and Sarah—you are at the heart of the Circle we have come to know in this life. Your tender presence and commitment are the reasons we could even begin to consider a career based on security and love.

AUTHORS' NOTE

We are pleased that you have found your way to our work with parents. It is our hope that this material will be shared with parents and professionals. We are aware that the written word is not a substitute for training and supervision, and we do not imply or endorse the notion that reading this material will adequately offer preparation to provide any form of Circle of Security® intervention.

It is extremely important to us to maintain the fidelity of the Circle of Security protocols. To this end, the name Circle of Security is registered and the graphics included in this book are copyrighted. For further information on this work for professional purposes, please reference our book *The Circle of Security Intervention: Enhancing Attachment in Early Parent–Child Relationships*. For permission to use the name Circle of Security or Circle of Security Parenting in any promotional material or for research, please go to our website: *www.circleofsecurity.com*. Thank you for your help in protecting the fidelity of the Circle of Security.

This book is richer thanks to the generous contributions of many individuals who have taken our training around the world. You will find quotations from them scattered through the book, and their input has informed the text as well.

Anecdotes and illustrations of attachment interactions in this book are based on families we have known both personally and professionally. They either are thoroughly disguised to protect the individuals' privacy, are composites, or are representations of common themes in attachment.

INTRODUCTION

As parents (or expectant parents) we all want to do the best for our children. We read up on the latest child-rearing theories and practices, find the best pediatricians and teachers, figure out which foods will promote healthy growth, and vow to avoid making the mistakes we see other parents make—or those our own parents made.

As it turns out, however, there's one big mistake that a well-meaning parent can make, and that's trying to be a perfect parent—or at least one whose primary focus is on trying not to make mistakes.

The underlying message of this book is that we already have what we need to be good parents. As human beings, we come equipped with positive intentions for our sons and daughters and a hardwired drive to form a close and lasting attachment with them. We can use those endowments to teach our children what it means to be human—filled with confusing needs and uncomfortable emotions, hapless and flawed, stumbling about in an ever-learning state of glorious imperfection. Through a secure attachment, our children can feel safe and cared for in the tough internal experiences that we all share. With the trust that they can count on someone else to help soothe the sting of life's inevitable hardships, they gain the confidence they need to go out and find out who they are—and who they can become—in the big wide world.

Over the last 30 years, the three of us have become increasingly convinced that a secure attachment is the most important foundation we can offer to our children. It's every bit as vital as nutrition, health care, and education. In fact, it just might be more potent than any of those necessities, because a child whose earliest experience is centered on a secure attachment can figure out what he needs not just to survive but to thrive, feel comfortable asking for it, and trust that he'll get the help he seeks.

Research evidence shows that children who have a secure attachment with at least one adult do better in school, have better friendships, enjoy greater physical health, and go on to have more intimate, fulfilling, and enduring relationships throughout life. In our work as clinicians helping people with all sorts of difficulties, we started to recognize that at the root of many struggles was the lack of a secure attachment in childhood. When no one had been there for them often enough as children, satisfying intimate relationships eluded them as adults. They wrestled with self-doubt and underachieved or overachieved at work. They suffered stress-related health problems or felt chronically dissatisfied with their lives and close relationships. It's hard to regulate your thirst for success, know what you want, and explore your options with ease when no one helped you manage and make sense of your needs during childhood. And when our clients began to have children of their own? You guessed it: They were aching to do their best as parents and felt a deeply instinctive urge to form a bond with their babies. *They just didn't know how.* Or they thought they knew how (they had read all the books, after all), but then problems that mirrored their own during childhood arose in their relationship with their beloved son or daughter.

We wrote this book to offer a map to secure attachment. Thirty years ago we set out on a quest to bring the benefits of attachment into homes, to bring simplicity and accessibility to the groundbreaking theory formulated by psychiatrist John Bowlby and psychologist Mary Ainsworth starting in the 1950s and refined over the next few decades. This theory, that a secure, trust-based emotional bond between parent and child holds the key to healthy development, had long been applauded as valid and important, but it had yet to be applied in a practical, parent-friendly way. Scientists hailed secure attachment as providing no less than "psychological immunity" for developing children and the adults they became, but the remarkable clarity of thousands of studies showing the necessity and benefit of security remained hidden inside journals without access to parents. We were captivated by the potential to bring these insights to those who can make the best use of them: parents and other caregivers.

That was the beginning of the story of an intervention we call the Circle of Security. It took shape as a 20-week group program for parents struggling with their relationship with their toddlers and pre-schoolers, and since then has been adapted for individual therapy and other uses—in schools, by social service agencies, in foster homes, throughout the world. It has undergone painstaking revision and in fact continues to evolve every day as we plumb the depths of this profound and primal relationship.

In research, the Circle of Security approach has been shown to help parents dealing with even the most overwhelming obstacles—poverty, incarceration, undereducation, abuse histories, and more—form a secure attachment with their children. Many of these adults had had no model for healthy parenting at all. As clinicians and scientists, these results were immensely gratifying to us. But they could not compare with what we gained in our own relationships, with the personal insights reported by therapists we trained in the Circle of Security, or with what we have witnessed virtually every time someone has been introduced to the map and the story of the Circle of Security. The Circle of Security map for attachment seems to speak to everyone—regardless of their culture—on a deeply instinctual level about how we relate to one another and who we are as a species. For the three of us, the lens of the Circle of Security has magnified and deepened our understanding of our marriages, our children, and our colleagues. It has informed our foster parenting and our friendships, our counseling and volunteer work. For us and many others, it has renewed faith and hope in a benevolent and a more positive world.

That parents were able to overcome the most daunting challenges to bond with their children confirmed again and again our conviction that we *all* have what we need to be good parents. Sometimes we just have to be given a map to find our way back to it. Maybe our own upbringing left gaps in our emotional fluency. Or the unavailability of caregivers to help us with our fundamental needs—often through no fault of their own—left us lacking trust. Or the vagaries of our own adult lives have drawn us away from the connection with our children that we so dearly desire right now. This book is our humble attempt to take you back to—or keep you on—the Circle of Security. We trust you'll do the rest.

And most of the time you will. Research has shown that about 60% of parents form a secure attachment with their child. Security can't be measured rigidly, and so sometimes a bond will be considered "mostly secure," or "somewhat" secure, with qualifications. Security can also be learned, as we've discovered through our own research. And it's important to know that even secure attachments aren't always pretty. Even when things are going well, parents whose children are securely attached make mistakes and respond sensitively to their child's needs only much of the time, not *all* of the time.

"Good-enough parenting" is our mandate.

Developing the trust that she can count on a loved one to *try* to be there for her is critical to a child's having good relationships for the rest of her life. As the world is increasingly acknowledging, relationships are where we actually live. They're the fiber of our families, our communities, our careers. If you've ever had a demanding, perfectionist boss, or you've expected your partner or spouse to unfailingly anticipate all your needs, you know that "perfect" doesn't work in relationships. What works is flexible, responsive sensitivity and availability. What works is acknowledging lapses and mistakes and doing what we can to make up for them—and certainly to learn from them.

In the crucible of our closest relationships, we learn not only that we can entrust another person with our deepest needs but also that even the most empathic among us will have those lapses and disconnects—often, in fact—*and that these daily ruptures can be repaired*. If we aim for mistake-free, "perfect" parenting, we're sending a message to our children that our performance is more important than meeting their needs. We're also setting them up for unrealistic expectations throughout life. No one *is* perfect, so a relationship that expects perfection is doomed to fail. A relationship in which two individuals use their understanding of human needs and inevitable struggles to try to get to know their similarities and differences has limitless potential for growth and fulfillment. Aren't those the kinds of friendships, work relationships, partnerships, and marriages we want our children to grow up and have?

It all starts with us. Imagine your 6-year-old coming home from school looking dejected. Would you simply give him a snack and hope that will make him feel better? (How would you feel if you'd been turned down for a promotion or been rejected by a close friend and your partner tried to help by giving you a cookie?) It doesn't take a psychologist or a seasoned parent to know that this child needs more than a snack to give him a boost. But we sometimes need a reminder that a young child needs validation of how sad and confusing it feels to have the classmate who was his "best friend" yesterday choose someone else to play with today. He needs a hug or a touch and maybe some quiet time with you to regroup. He needs your help in figuring out exactly how he feels and your affirmation that his difficult feelings belong—to him and within your relationship.

All of those aspects of responding might very well come naturally to you as a parent. But what you might not realize is how deeply important that response is to your child. You're not just making him feel better in this moment so he can go out and play or focus on homework (although you are doing that). You're teaching him what he's feeling when all he might be able to identify is "Ouch." You're telling him that it's OK to feel emotions like sadness even though they hurt—that these emotions carry important messages. You're teaching him that pain can be worked through with the help of another person. You're helping him learn something about who he is—a person who values friendship and appreciates loyalty. In other words, you're helping him grow, promoting the development of a healthy self, helping him figure out how to navigate the choppy waters of all relationships.

But what if you didn't respond with understanding and affection and some time with your son? Let's say you were busy working on your family's finances when your child sulked into the house. He came over and pulled at your sleeve to divert your attention from the computer. You kept your gaze on the screen and impatiently said, "Not now, honey. I have to finish this." Your son walked into the living room, and it wasn't until half an hour later that you found him curled up on the couch, sniffling quietly.

Now you have the chance to impart what may be an even more important lesson: You shake off your exhaustion and impatience (bills and taxes aren't fun, after all), go over to sit next to your child, and as you rub his back gently you ask him what's wrong. It takes a little work to get it out of him, and he doesn't respond immediately to your apologies and your slightly delayed offer of comfort, but he comes around. A simple happy ending with a much more serious consequence: You've taught your child that even adults make mistakes, but they try. You've taught him that he can still trust you to be there for him and that, some of the time, he might have to be patient with you. You've established the foundation of a healthy relationship—one that includes struggles and resolution, ruptures and repairs—for the rest of his life.

How to Use This Book

This is a book written to honor your innate capacity and your deeply wired positive intentions as a parent. It is also a book designed to offer clear, memorable, research-based learning that will stay with you through each day, offering support and balance whenever you begin to feel confused or in need of guidance. Our commitment is to keep what we have to say simple because parenting in the heat of the moment requires an "I know what to do next" kind of simplicity instead of a "What did they say on page 217?" kind of complexity. Hopefully, as you venture through these pages, our words will become a supportive, no-nonsense, and easy-to-make-sense-of companion as you continue on as the parent you are privileged to be.

We've divided this book into two sections. Some of you will find Part I is all you need to gain a new perspective on parenting. It's here that we explain why attachment is so important—what decades of research have revealed—and why security can be elusive yet relatively easy to reclaim. We all stray from the close connection to our children (and other loved ones) at times. Life is demanding. Crises arise. Attention is diverted, of necessity. It's at these times that we can lose sight of our child's needs and let shared connection weaken. With the map of the Circle of Security firmly ingrained in the mind, however, it's easy to find our way back to the simple goodness of our most important relationships.

The Circle of Security shows us that the developing young child has two groups of needs: needs for comfort and safety on one side and needs for exploration on the other. Children travel between these needs over and over throughout the day, but we don't always understand what they're after. What we see is their behavior, and if that behavior is difficult for us to deal with, that's what we react to. There are dozens of ways we can be blinded to these needs, and the Circle of Security map is intended to open our eyes to what is hidden in plain sight in everything our children do and what they need from us. Chapter 3 illustrates the Circle and describes these fundamental needs in ways that parents around the globe have found resonant and memorable.

In our age of achievement, it's a lot harder to sit with emotional experience—our own and others'—than to try to have an answer for and quickly fix whatever problem is causing discomfort. This is certainly true of us as parents. (A Google search for "helicopter parents" turns up almost 6 million results as of late 2015.) But a key part of creating a secure attachment for our children is what we call "Being-With" the child. This doesn't mean just maintaining a physical presence, sitting by approvingly, sharing "quality time" while your child vaporizes a monster in a favorite video game or demonstrates a well-practiced soccer move. It means creating a shared emotional experience through which your child learns that all humans have key feelings in common (while also learning that every individual also experiences feelings uniquely). An emphasis on Being-With your child helps you prioritize seeing needs that are often hidden in plain sight. Your Being-With your child helps her develop empathy while also building confidence in her own emotional competence as she learns, with you, how to regulate emotions and manage difficult ones. Being-With is the topic of Chapter 4.

When we said you already have what you need to be a good parent, we did not mean, of course, that your own instincts are immune to negative interference or operate in a vacuum. How your parents or other caregivers raised you will affect your attachment style just as how you raise your children will affect theirs. This is true for all of us, and every single one of us will have some modicum of insecurity about particular emotional, attachment-type needs. You won't necessarily be aware of these influences, because they are stored in memories formed before you learned to talk, but amazingly, your baby is wired to sense them and may try to help protect you from what makes you uncomfortable by pretending not to have certain needs. These will be areas where you'll struggle, and these inclinations have a way of being passed down to the next generation. Bringing them to the surface with the help of Chapters 5 and 6 can protect your children and grandchildren from struggling with the same aspects of parenting. When you know what's pulling your strings, you can actively choose security for your child.

Many people introduced to the Circle of Security find that their new understanding of the important bond between parents and children is the core of what they need to choose security. They simply pull out their mental Circle map (or look at the one they have posted on their refrigerator) when stress threatens or confusion sets in. But some of us find the process a bit more difficult (and all of us will find it difficult at certain times, in particular situations). We know we came from backgrounds where security wasn't fully available. For us it becomes important to be more curious about what gets in the way—and, truthfully, knowing what gets in the way can be enormously illuminating for all of us. Building this curiosity and a willingness to explore the hidden alarms set off by our own upbringing will be supported by venturing into Part II. There you'll find questionnaires for self-exploration and additional descriptions of what attachment in its many variations looks like. We introduce you to many parents and children engaged in the important business of attachment from infancy into adolescence. You'll see how we all struggle, we all make mistakes, and how it's possible to repair our mistakes and help our children thrive.

Welcome to the club.

ALL AROUND THE CIRCLE

Understanding Attachment and the Importance of Security

You think, because one and one make two, that you understand two.

But to truly comprehend the nature of two, you must first understand . . . and.

—JALALUDDIN RUMI, 13th-century poet and scholar

ATTACHMENT

Why It Matters

Something extraordinary happens in the most ordinary moments between parent and child:

> Danny waits for his mother's reassuring smile and nod before climbing into the sandbox with the other children.
>
> Emma instantly calms when her dad lifts his 1-year-old daughter onto his lap even though he's tapping away at his phone and barely looks at the little girl.
>
> Jake stops clobbering his toy drum when his mom switches from demanding that he put it down to exclaiming, "Wow, that's some sense of rhythm you've got, buddy."

Moments like these are so ordinary as to be forgettable, even unnoticeable. Yet what accrues to children as those moments accumulate is nothing short of profound. Every time you answer your child's need for comfort or confidence, you're building a bond of trust. Every time you show that you understand how your child feels and what your child wants, you're demonstrating the power of a primal connection that all of us are born seeking. Every time you help your baby or toddler manage the discomfort and frustration of being a newcomer to the human condition, you're teaching your child acceptance of emotions (even the "ugly" ones), of himself, and of others.

These are the gifts of attachment. A secure attachment forms naturally for a child when a parent or other primary caregiver can:

- Help the child feel safe when frightened or uncomfortable
- Help the child feel secure enough to explore the world, essential to growth and development
- Help the child accept and manage his or her emotional experience

Both parents and children are hardwired for attachment. You start forming a bond with your child even before birth, and miraculously, your newborn emerges with a powerful instinct to be close to you. Not just any adult will do, even though plenty of adults can provide the food, warmth, and protection necessary to the baby's physical survival. Decades of research suggest that babies immediately fall in love with a parent's face because even when they can barely focus on it, they can already sense the parent's love and devotion. This is the person, a baby intuits, who is going to be here for me. This is someone who will help me figure out this confusing new world and find the goodness in it.

Our common bond as parents is that we all want goodness—love and compassion, understanding and acceptance, meaning and fulfillment—for our children. And children come into the world wanting and needing goodness from us. One of our most important mentors, developmental psychologist Jude Cassidy (along with social psychologist Phillip Shaver), recently defined attachment security as "confidence in the possibility of goodness." From our perspective, this is precisely the issue. We want what's good, deeply necessary, and fulfilling for our children. And they come to us in their unique, miraculous, ever-fresh, and often demanding way with that exact request. "Please help me trust in the goodness of you, the goodness of me, the goodness of us." Of course, this is what we're here to offer.

The Critical Importance of "And"

We all begin life more integrated with another person than separate. This is not just an acknowledgment that sharing a body before birth creates a bond for mothers and babies that often endures after it. Babies also become attached to their fathers, their grandparents, or anyone else whose gaze says "I am here for you," and who then makes good on

that promise much of the time. The very youngest babies seem to recognize this devotion and start to respond in kind during their first days
of life. They follow us with their eyes, flap their arms in excitement
when we return from work, and their first smiles come in response
to our smiles at them—a gift that few parents ever forget. In the Circle of Security program, when we are trying to convey to parents how
very important they are to their children, we play Joe Cocker's song
"You Are So Beautiful" as we show video clips of attachment moments
between parent and child.

As pediatrician and psychoanalyst Donald Winnicott once said, "If
you set out to describe a baby, you will find you are describing a baby
and someone." He was referring to how essential we are to our infants.
Baby Gino or Sasha or Hiroto may have separate arms and legs and
face but really doesn't fully exist yet as an individual. We tend to view
babies as completely formed little creatures who know deep down what
they're feeling and needing and who they are but simply lack the language to express it. In actuality, newborn babies have no clarity about
what they're feeling except that there are many times when something
unknown and difficult starts happening to them (they need *something*)—
an unformed longing begins to grow. When Mom or Dad gazes into a
distressed baby's eyes and coos "There, there" and magically figures
out what the baby needs—and even provides it!—the parent is telling
the baby "I'm here with you. We share the same kinds of feelings, and
we'll figure this out together." As this exchange is repeated again and
again, the baby learns that human emotions are natural, acceptable,
and shareable. She learns that this special adult can manage them for
her and gradually help her learn to manage them for herself—a process
called "coregulation of emotions." She learns that although she and her
parent(s) have many important things in common, each of them is also
unique. She learns that the relationship—the *"and"*—is critical to the
formation of the self.

Up until the middle of the 20th century, the self—a being separate
from other humans—was the focus of developmental psychology. In
Western society, this emphasis informed many attitudes and expectations about how we should conduct ourselves over the lifespan. As
soon as we were able, we were expected to take care of ourselves, and
social policies—in the United States at least—often favored individual
rights over community needs. In our work with the Circle of Security,
we've come around to the opposite view: it's the "and" that matters.
We would even go so far as to say this: Self-sufficiency is a myth. From

birth through old age, our ability to act with some sense of autonomy is directly related to our capacity for connectedness. What does this mean for parents raising a young child? *If we want our children to be independent, to go out and take on the world, we have to give them full confidence that they can come back to us as needed.* Autonomy *and* connection: That's secure attachment.

Here's what it might look like:

Lei is 3 years old. She's vibrant, playful, and full of curiosity. She and her father have just walked to the park that's two blocks from their home and, typically for them, as they approach the climbing structure, Lei briefly looks back at her father (not more than a millisecond) and then rushes off to climb her version of Mt. Everest. What the casual observer might not notice is that in that millisecond of checking in with her dad, Lei gets precisely the permission and support she needs—Is it a glance? Is it something in his eyes?—to know it's perfectly OK to risk this new adventure.

Fourteen seconds later she's already atop the structure, looking back at her father, pride flowing from every pore, as she calls out her sense of accomplishment: "I'm a big girl."

"Yes, you are, Lei," her dad responds, "Yes, you are!" (What Lei doesn't know is that her father has to work very hard not to interfere, to hover, because some part of him is afraid she might fall. But, based on their previous experiences on this structure, ones where he's felt the need to stay close and protective, he's found that his daughter has the strength and the balance and the enthusiasm to find her own way on this particular part of the playground.)

Twenty more seconds pass, and Lei is now climbing down. She's still having fun, she's still enjoying her increasing sense of competence, but she finds herself running back to her father, smiling and remarkably proud of her accomplishment. She's delighted. He's delighted. She looks in his eyes, they briefly touch, and then—bam!—she's off, running toward the slide, ready for yet another round of excitement.

Again, that's secure attachment. In that simple moment, Lei's father is right there with her, responding to the shifting needs that his daughter experiences as she goes about the somewhat scary task of exploring her world. Significantly, Lei also *knows* that her dad will respond, because he has done so many times in the past. This is one reason the entire sequence appears so seamless, so unplanned. Lei's expression of basic psychological needs and her father's answering them have become the fabric of their relationship.

Attachment: A Lasting Legacy

Lei and her dad may not have had to think consciously about interacting this way, but the benefits of their secure attachment certainly had staying power, as they do for all of us. That first relationship, so close as to make "two" almost indistinguishable from "one," isn't something we shrug off the way a butterfly shrugs off its chrysalis and flies off to live happily ever after. It's something we carry with us into all relationships, all work, all communication, and if it is a secure attachment, it just *might* lead to "happily ever after."

Decades of research have now shown that having a secure attachment with a primary caregiver leaves children healthier and happier in virtually every way we measure such things—in competence and self-confidence, empathy and compassion, resilience and endurance . . . in the ability to regulate emotions, tap intellectual capacity, and preserve physical health . . . in pursuing our life's work and having a fulfilling personal life.

Perhaps most important, a secure attachment in a child's first relationship lays the foundation for good relationships throughout life. And we now know without a doubt that relationships are the engine and the framework for satisfaction and success in all domains of life. Research has shown that social relationships promote mental and physical health and even lower the risk of death: In studies of many countries, analyses have shown over and over that the more people were involved in social relationships, the less likely they were to die prematurely—in fact, the

> **Fifty years of research has shown that children with a secure attachment:**
>
> - Enjoy more happiness with their parents
> - Feel less anger at their parents
> - Get along better with friends
> - Have stronger friendships
> - Are able to solve problems with friends
> - Have better relationships with brothers and sisters
> - Have higher self-esteem
> - Know that most problems will have an answer
> - Trust that good things will come their way
> - Trust the people they love
> - Know how to be kind to those around them

most isolated individuals were twice as likely to die as the most social. Western society seems to be making a shift toward understanding the importance of the "and," with books and TED Talks on topics like the value of vulnerability enjoying growing popularity. We're beginning to recognize that our relationships aren't just "extras." Those who get along best with coworkers often get promoted first—and not just because they've formed smart alliances; they're often the most productive. And although we understand that hovering obsessively over our children isn't helpful, we do recognize these days that consistently soothing babies isn't hovering and won't ruin them for life. The relationships we form sustain us—even define us—because in every "and" we form we become something more than we would be alone.

> *"I reassured myself that he has always been resourceful, resilient, and confident. Two days later, he . . . called me full of exuberance and delight at his success. I told him, 'Good luck with your adventure,' knowing that this is exactly what he needed to hear. I was able to hold him from afar, knowing that he had all the tools, love, attachment, and resources resulting from years of experience with secure attachment. It was because of his secure attachment that he was able to explore further and further away."*
> —Heidi S. Roibal, Albuquerque, New Mexico, after her
> 23-year-old son left on a solo cross-country journey

Attachment: It Really Does Matter

Intuitively, you already know about the importance of the "and." Trust and a feeling of security with others can transform relationships—deepening a friendship when you confide a shameful childhood secret, cementing an intimate relationship when you risk proposing marriage, creating collegiality and mutual respect when you ask for the promotion you deserve. Even the major achievements—painting your best picture ever; coming up with a great, if radical, innovation on the job; writing a great speech—that don't seem to involve others are often made possible by security. When we trust in the openness and acceptance of others in general, creativity, competence, wisely chosen risks, and clear thinking become more available to us because we expect our offerings to get an understanding, welcoming reception, in an environment of safety. And when they do, and we succeed, the importance of attachment is reinforced by the fulfillment of sharing the joy with others.

A secure attachment is like a virtual teddy bear. When you have confidence and trust in the goodness of me, you, us, you carry that trust with you through important transitions and passages in daily life. In fact, we adults generally measure how our lives are going by how our relationships are going. If our relationships are going well, life goes well. When love is in place, we do well.

> *Secure attachment is knowing that someone has your back,* and knowing someone has your back opens a world of new possibilities.*

If you've experienced secure attachment's beneficial effects, you won't be surprised that the total absence of attachment can be devastating. As far back as the 13th century, Roman emperor Frederick II decided to conduct an experiment to see whether newborn children would speak the language of Adam and Eve if they weren't exposed to another language by the adults around them. He ordered caregivers not to talk or gesture to a group of babies, and they all languished. Seven hundred years later, the same association showed up in the alarming 30% death rate of children in orphanages during the 1930s and 1940s. Provided with the apparent necessities of life—food, shelter, clothing—many still could not survive without an attachment to a primary caregiver.

With this kind of evidence, how could it have taken so long for attachment to be valued? These things take time, and as is so often the case, embracing a new theory often means displacing others that have become entrenched. The two dominant schools of thought regarding child development during the early 20th century were the psychoanalytic theories of Sigmund Freud and company and the behaviorist theories of John B. Watson and later B. F. Skinner and others:

• Freud decided that the psychological problems he saw in his adult patients might have their roots in various unconscious thought processes that started humming along during infancy and continued to exert their effects as a baby matured. These processes drove how a

---

*Thanks to Jude Cassidy for this insight.

baby interacted with his parents and what the baby appeared to need in addition to food and other care. These theories kept the focus of some developmental psychologists (and psychoanalysts treating adults) on arcane concepts regarding the unconscious mind that didn't resonate with people living in the real world.

• In another camp resided the behaviorists, who believed babies had one thing on their mind when they reserved a special smile just for Mom, cried when she left their sight even though other willing caregivers were handy, or settled miraculously into Mom's arms. That thing was a reward: If they smiled, Mom seemed happy and would come closer. If they cried, Mom often came back. If they snuggled into Mom's arms, she'd let Baby stay there. As far as Watson was concerned, babies were driven to attach so that Mom would stay nearby, where she could dispense the food, warmth, or dry diaper they needed. Few today would deny that we humans respond positively to rewards. The trouble with adhering strictly to these early forms of behaviorism, however, was that Watson advised mothers not to show too much loving care for their children, *or children would grow up expecting the world to treat them the same way, which would make them all invalids.*

Enter the voice of reason: British psychologist John Bowlby. It was after World War II, and Bowlby was participating in research for the World Health Organization involving institutionalized World War II orphans and hospitalized children. The children were all receiving optimal care: they were well fed, clothed appropriately, and had warm beds and attentive health care, just like the prewar orphans. What they didn't have was Mom or Dad. And just like the orphans of earlier decades, all suffered terribly without the comfort, love, and closeness of a primary caregiver. Similarly, in the 1950s Bowlby and colleague John Robertson filmed a 2-year-old who spent 10 days in a hospital and saw her parents for only a half hour once a day. The little girl was transformed from vivacious to completely despondent.

Bowlby's observations changed visiting rules for hospitals forever and have informed professional child care ever since as well. And they spawned his efforts to answer the million-dollar question that should have been asked since the dawn of the human race: *Why* did the lack of a parent or other caregiver matter so much when everything the children seemed to need to thrive was provided?

As is typically the case with scientific advances, the answers came from a confluence of evidence from different fields of study, summed up in the box on pages 20–21.

As Bowlby surmised, babies may be driven to attach to their primary caregiver because of a deeply instinctual evolutionary drive designed to help the species survive. *Out of the mouths of babes*: On a nonverbal level, babies may understand a lot more than we adults do about how important attachment is, and that's why they pursue it with such determination. Bowlby and Ainsworth already had plenty of evidence that the absence of attachment in early life can be harmful to the child, so they dedicated themselves to studying it during the second half of the 20th century. They identified three subsystems that fall under the attachment umbrella:

- Careseeking: the instinct to stick close to someone who can comfort, protect, and organize one's feelings
- Exploration: the instinct to act on one's curiosity and to pursue mastery
- Caregiving: the instinct to provide the care sought and bond with the baby

As you'll see in Chapter 3, these three drives form the landscape for the Circle of Security. These drives explain why babies need a secure attachment to survive and grow, to become individuals, *and* thrive in relationships. Ironically, many people today still focus on behavior in child rearing, perhaps because it's something we can see, and if we can change it, we feel confident that we've addressed any problems that are arising. Behavior, however, is merely an expression of a child's needs. Behavior is a message—a message about the attachment needs that are hidden in plain sight.

Hidden in Plain Sight: Why Behavior Management Is Not Enough

Let's get real: As parents or expectant parents, our concerns are much more immediate than the enhancement of the species into a future too distant to imagine. We all have so much on our plate, and trying to ensure the healthy development of our own children is overwhelming enough. This is, of course, why so many caregivers and caretakers of children rely on behavior management to corral children into feeling

The Development of Attachment Theory

If babies provided with all of the apparent necessities of life still failed to thrive, John Bowlby speculated, maybe a deeper instinctual drive was at work in the urge to attach: Was an evolutionary drive behind it? Could something that parents provide beyond the body's survival needs be necessary for the preservation of the species?

Animal studies said yes. Konrad Lorenz, a pioneering expert in animal behavior, found that, through a phenomenon called "imprinting," goslings would follow around whatever animal or object they saw first. Psychologist Harry Harlow then explored the mother–infant bond by studying baby monkeys' behavior. First he found that the monkeys raised in the lab in isolation from other monkeys became reclusive, couldn't socialize normally with other monkeys, and displayed unnatural fear and aggression. Second, when he gave infant monkeys a choice of being with a wire monkey that doled out food and a cloth monkey that didn't, the babies overwhelmingly chose the monkeys that felt more like mother's fur even though they couldn't offer any food. Once they were introduced to these surrogate mothers, they returned to the same one over and over—showing clear signs of what has become known as "attachment."

Over the next several decades, Bowlby formulated attachment theory, a view that explains how seeking a connection with a primary caregiver not only helps the individual survive but also serves the preservation of the species. Imprinting, a sort of primitive attachment behavior, is seen as a way of introducing the newborn animal to its species—not only so that the baby could learn how to survive from an animal with the same needs and the experience to satisfy them but also so that it would know which other animals to seek out for mating and reproduction.

But to what extent were humans similar? How was the preservation of the human species being enhanced by attachment? The simplest answer is that when human babies stick close to a protective, caring adult, the chance of long-term survival for each one is improved, and the more infants who reach adulthood, the more the species is perpetuated. Yet we now know that attachment clearly enhances development and creates not just *more* adult humans but also *better* ones. With secure attachment, apparently, the species not only survives but also evolves. If it was that potent, how could we understand its formation to ensure that secure attachment happens as often as possible?

Back to the human lab. Developmental psychologist Mary Ainsworth, recruited to work on Bowlby's research team in London, became instrumental in showing that there were patterns in the way attachment happened. Based on her observations during a groundbreaking field study in Uganda and then, back in the United States, in Baltimore, Ainsworth determined that there were different attachment styles that arose between Mom (or other primary caregiver) and Baby. Later, Ainsworth also came up with an enormously valuable research procedure for studying specific parent–child duos to identify their attachment style. Ainsworth's so-called Strange Situation Procedure (SSP), described in Chapter 4, is the gold standard for assessing attachment today and a central part of our own work with families. It helps us, and others in the attachment field, understand where attachment might not be secure and how to help parents and children become attached.

---

their best, doing their best, being their best. As we said, rewards have their place in child rearing and elsewhere. But if all we do is address the behavior before us, we might as well get used to the idea of using star charts and time-outs forever. (Picture having to send your 30-year-old daughter $10 every week to get her to call you.) Targeting behavior is like treating the symptoms and ignoring the cause of an illness.

When we're confronted with a child who is "acting out" or acting distressed, it helps to think about what's hidden in plain sight: Is the child frustrated by feeling like he can't make us understand his need for comfort? Is this little girl "so emotional" because she hasn't learned to regulate her emotions with an adult's kind understanding and confident boundary setting? Is this little boy struggling to learn the alphabet because his mind is constantly caught up with trying to convey his need to be the architect of his own adventures? Is the child before you having trouble making friends because she hasn't learned to trust others' goodwill?

Over the last 50 years, researchers have been looking at what's hidden in plain sight on a broad scale. We now know

> Leading neuropsychology researcher Allan Schore found that many regulatory and survival functions in the right brain (which dominates during the first 3 years of life) depended on the baby's experiences to mature, *specifically attachment experiences with the primary caregiver.*

that attachment can tip the balance in a child's stress level, ability to manage emotional experience, capacity for learning, physical vitality, social ease, and more. The more we individual parents know about what's hidden in plain sight underneath our child's behavior, the more compelling it feels to form a secure attachment.

Secure Attachment Inoculates Children against Toxic Stress

If attachment is an insistent, primal drive, imagine how stressful it must be to have it thwarted. The stress of unmet attachment needs can certainly manifest in a child's behavior (How do *you* act when you're under a lot of stress?), but we know from a lot of research that it can also derail children's mental, emotional, social, and physical growth and development.

The kind of stress that starts in infancy when the pressures of being a helpless newborn aren't eased by a parent's comfort has been called "toxic stress," because it creates pathways in the brain that keep the child on high alert for danger, making it difficult to concentrate on learning and often prone to "shoot first and ask questions later." When a baby is hungry, wet, or frightened, the stress hormone cortisol courses through his brain; cortisol triggers a "black hole" kind of longing that a newborn can't articulate but feels intensely. (See the box on the facing page for more details on the health effects of excess stress.)

Feeling secure in the presence of a loving, dependable caregiver is like being offered a second skin that protects us during times of stress.

Security Keeps Children on a Healthy Developmental Track as They Grow

The stress of unmet attachment needs can burden a child not just in infancy but throughout growth. Although it's difficult to determine how *directly* secure attachment affects the attainment of certain developmental milestones, a landmark 30-year study at the University of Minnesota initiated in the mid-1970s found long-term patterns between secure attachment and specific aspects of development. Imagine a 9-year-old having a mother with breast cancer or a sole-breadwinner father who has lost his job. Life events like these, tragic but common,

Stress and Health

The human body comes equipped with a brilliant system for handling threats, and yet we can't always control the threats we face—ongoing worry about finances, family conflicts, dangerous living environments, *or, for an infant, whether or not a sensitive, responsive caregiver is generally available*—and this is when stress arises. Perception of a threat sets off a complicated series of neurochemical events, one of which involves the stress hormone known as cortisol. Cortisol's main job is to return the body to a state of equilibrium and stability (homeostasis) following stress. The problem is that in regulating various systems affected by stress, mainly metabolism, cortisol affects others along the way, most notably the immune system. In doing its work, cortisol tells the body to stop fighting, to return to a stable state, and thereby lowers immunity, making the body more vulnerable to disease. This is one reason that those under chronic stress seem to get sick more often than others. Unfortunately, through repeated episodes of acute stress and also chronic stress, excess cortisol is released, and it can damage memory, cognition, and even add abdominal fat, which carries cardiovascular risk. *Babies whose attachment needs aren't met start life at a physical and mental health disadvantage.*

We adults lose our grasp of how stressful these mundane problems feel to an infant, but for the baby *any* unmet need can send cortisol soaring—and the black hole expanding. Fortunately, there's an antidote: comfort from Mom or Dad. *In lab research, babies' cortisol has been seen to plummet when they are picked up and held during any stressful incident.*

impose a lot of stress. This is where security born of attachment comes to the rescue. The Minnesota researchers found, for example, that children around grade 4 who had a secure attachment history had fewer behavior problems when their families were under major stress than those who did not.

In the Minnesota study, L. Alan Sroufe, Byron Egeland, Elizabeth A. Carlson, and W. Andrew Collins looked at the development of 180 children from the last trimester of pregnancy into adulthood and found that starting out securely attached afforded measurable protection from the ravages of stress all the way through those years.

They also found links between insecurity and later psychological problems. Security comes in the form of providing a safe haven
for comfort as needed and also offering a secure base for exploration.
Lei's father provided both for his daughter in the scene described earlier. In the Minnesota study, children whose parents were emotionally
unavailable for comfort had more conduct disorders in adolescence,
and children whose parents resisted letting them explore were more
likely to have anxiety disorders as teens. The study also found an association (though not as strong) between both types of insecurity and
depression—the children felt either hopeless and alienated or helpless
and anxious.

The developmental path is filled with tasks for your baby to do,
skills to learn, capacities to develop. Here is how attachment plays a
critical role in many of them.

Learning to Regulate Emotion

Your bundle of joy can seem a lot more like a bundle of distress during
much of the newborn months. Experts in developmental psychology
widely agree that a major goal of having a reliable parent or other primary caregiver—called the "attachment figure" in the field of psychology—is to get help with all that infant angst. Obviously, babies can't
handle the intense and baffling experience of emotions all by themselves. First, Mom or Dad regulates the baby's emotions from the outside—soothing her cries, singing lullabies, smiling gently at her, rock-
ing her, and so forth. As Baby learns that someone can help make
difficult feelings acceptable and manageable, she increasingly turns to
that caregiver in times of need, and this helps her start to learn to
soothe herself. Ultimately, when all goes according to developmental
plan, the child learns to regulate her own emotions. Now she has a
budding ability to comfort herself when she is being dropped off at
preschool instead of spending the morning sobbing. Now she can
sometimes talk herself out of being afraid of the monster under the bed
instead of endlessly seeking reassurance without an ability to self-
soothe. Now she can turn away briefly when she feels shy upon meeting someone new before looking back again once she's calmed down.
(Importantly, however, she has also learned the valuable lesson that
she can turn to others for coregulation throughout life when needed.)
Being able to control emotional arousal not only frees the child to go

about the business of learning and growing but also prevents the dangerous buildup of cortisol and thus promotes physical health too. Recent and ongoing research is demonstrating that being able to regulate emotion has far-reaching benefits, because being free of the stressful arousal of prolonged or exaggerated emotion means being free to pursue life to its fullest.

Emotional regulation skills serve us in the same ways throughout life. Besides facilitating productivity at work, helping you deal effectively and kindly with that annoying neighbor, and channeling your passions to "change the world" in the way you want, emotional regulation is great for relationships. And this is not just because you won't actually "throttle" your tantrumming toddler or agonize over the "insensitivity" of friends if you can regulate your emotions but because being able to coregulate emotions is a big part of intimacy. Going to a scary medical appointment? Just having your partner or a close friend by your side might help you keep your fear (and cortisol) at a manageable level. Ever cried over a loss with someone you trust and found your anguish subsiding faster than you thought it

> The Minnesota study found that security made children less likely to get frustrated or aggressive when they faced social problems and less likely just to give up and go away. They exhibited more persistence and flexibility and less fussing and whining in general.

A Caveat: Don't mistake "emotional regulation" for rejecting or suppressing emotion. In the cradle of a secure attachment, babies and children learn that emotion is normal, acceptable, and useful. Just accepting it goes a long way toward keeping it from getting out of control or overstaying its usefulness. We help our babies learn this invaluable skill by "Being-With" them in their full experience, which is the subject of Chapter 4.

Also beware of overprivileging your child's emotions. As also discussed in Chapter 4, sometimes in the process of trying to be sensitive to our children's emotional needs, we inadvertently teach our children that every feeling they have is paramount and must be attended to "now"—which actually thwarts resilience.

could? If so, how do you feel about that person now, as you recall that moment?

Becoming an Individual—without Being Alone

The small hands of a 6-year-old child fidget and fumble with the slender wick that her father has tied to the middle of a coat hanger. Sitting in front of her is the familiar family canning pot, now holding warm water and a container half full of molten wax. Gingerly, with the nervous precision of a first grader, the girl gradually dips the wick into the gently bubbling wax. The first coat is barely discernible as she brings it up for her parents to review. Sensing her uncertainty, her father reassures her that the candle will gradually build with each repetition. The second and third rounds bring little more in the way of noticeable results. Then, in a moment of surprised delight, she begins to see that the wax is finding its way onto the thread that dangles before her. Again and again she dips. Again and again she looks over to see the smile in her mother's eyes as the candle gains in size. The reassurance she seemed to require only minutes before is now securely within her knowledge as she continues this process of candle-in-the-making. Months, even years from now, as this particular candle is lit, the reassurance, confidence, pleasure, and delight experienced in its creation will be available in each moment of its burning.

Trust learned early radiates late. This 6-year-old child has once again been bathed in the caring response of her parents, a resource she has known since the moment of her birth. What she has experienced in her early years has been an attunement and sensitivity that allow her to settle in and have confidence in her caregiving environment. Young children need to know that they can be sure of someone who is committed to caring for their physical and emotional needs. Trust in self and trust in others is invariably built on early experiences of relying on the sensitivity and availability of at least one responsive caregiver—that is, on security via attachment.

In the field of developmental psychology, the formation of a coherent sense of self—personality, identity, and so on—is of course a major goal. When a parent responds sensitively and warmly to a child's earliest needs, the self is formed with every interaction, just like the wick repeatedly dipped into wax until a candle emerges. The emphasis here should be on the *interaction*; it's in this first relationship that a baby's individuation is cultivated, and it's in all the rest of our relationships that we continue to develop throughout life. When attachment is secure, all the psychological capacities of the growing child are nurtured to form a coherent self—one where the individual's memories and self-image make sense with the history that helped form them.

It might seem paradoxical that we gain a strong sense of self only in the context of others. But maybe it's not paradoxical at all: How can a baby recognize that he is an individual person without becoming aware that there is an "I" and a "you" in this "we"? Secure attachment to a caring adult gives babies the support they need to become separate individuals by not asking them to deal with the confusion and distress of being alone and helpless. To navigate the often difficult and confusing experiences of a child's emerging sense of self, babies need an "other" who is available to understand and empathically regulate. In the many experiences of being soothed, comforted, sensitively stimulated, and calmed, it is as if the wick of a child's innate self is repeatedly being dipped into the quality of relationship provided by the caregiving environment.

For a newborn baby, not being alone is of course life preserving. But scholars of both attachment theory and object relations theory* stress that survival is more than a beating heart and a full stomach. Babies are driven to make a connection with that "other" who can help them make sense of the chaotic world in which they find themselves. Not finding that connection leaves a frightening void. Psychoanalysts like Donald Winnicott called the terror of being alone and abandoned when you can't even form words one of the "primitive agonies." Imagine a free fall from a trapeze—you reach out for the hands of your fellow acrobat and let go of the bar in time to catch them . . . and find no one is there. If we are born seeking a self in the context of other people, finding no one there *definitely* threatens our survival. Now imagine this sense of abandonment—this fearsome feeling of free fall—buzzing along in your subconscious thoughts for the rest of your life. Talk about stress!

---

*A fascinating field of psychological study with an impossibly opaque name: It's a complex but enlightening theory of how we develop a sense of self in relation to others ("objects") and how we carry our images of ourselves and others into our later relationships.

Freeing the Mind to Learn

It's no exaggeration to say that when children feel safe and supported, learning takes care of itself. We're innately curious; we don't need to be talked into it. We don't need to be quizzed into cognition ("What color is this?"). Children need to be allowed access to their own innate desire for mastery. This desire will, naturally, find its own focus and its own pace. For Jacob, age 4, it's a plastic zoo with animals all over the living room floor. By age 7, it might be Minecraft on the iPad. For another boy it might be painting and drawing at age 7 or Club Penguin in social media. For 3-year-old Lei, when she's not at the playground, it's anything she can turn into little people who can act out whatever script comes to her mind. In 10 years it might be how the world's tallest buildings are constructed or math that her parents have never even heard of.

> In the Minnesota study, secure children were found to be more open and more flexible in problem solving, to welcome novel situations, and to deal with tough learning tasks with less frustration and angst. This is no surprise to us. At the core of trying to meet a child's attachment needs is the notion that "We'll figure this out together"—that emotional struggles can be worked through within the "and."

Of course children vary in their intellectual capabilities. But with a secure attachment they can at least all be primed to fulfill their unique potential. Without that security, children are so distressed by the wasteland of unmet needs and lack of connection that they can't think about much else—at least not very efficiently. When we talk to teachers and parents about attachment and cognition, we often say:

Children can't learn when their hair is on fire.

Children who are brought up with enormous stress, due to lack of comfort, among other necessities, are so busy preparing for danger that they can't concentrate.

They also don't seem to learn as well in the absence of social connection. Who hasn't noticed the contribution to literacy of a parent reading to a preschooler or the value of a really good teacher? A secure attachment is the first social connection that helps your baby start learning. Here's how it works:

1. The parent serves as a secure base from which the child can explore—whether it's the playground, as in Lei's case, or a chemistry set.
2. Trust in the parent makes it easier for secure children to seek assistance with learning from parents.
3. Fruitful, pleasant interactions between parent and child obviously facilitate exchange of information.
4. Through attachment, children develop a coherent sense of self and others that enable them to think clearly about, well, *thinking* and to regulate their thought process efficiently.

Toddlers who are securely attached have been seen to be more active in exploration and to have longer attention spans. In one study, 2-year-olds got involved in more symbolic play when securely attached, fueling the development of a healthy, creative imagination (see the box on page 30). Researchers Corine de Ruiter and Marinus van IJzendoorn created a diagram showing that when parents form a secure attachment with their children by interacting with sensitivity, gentle, nonpunitive instruction, and scaffolding, they build the child's self-esteem and mastery of motivation, attention control, persistence time on-task, and metacognitive skills. All of these abilities contribute to academic achievement.

> The longitudinal Minnesota study showed that insecurely attached preschoolers were much more reliant on their teachers than securely attached children of the same age. The same pattern became evident at summer camps when the children were age 10.

Security → Confidence → Self-Reliance

As a species, we're not meant to be independent to the point of isolation or utter self-sufficiency, but we won't live very long if we can't become fairly independent. Just as it might on the surface seem paradoxical that we need an "other" to develop a "self," children who can rely on an adult from birth will be able to rely on themselves when they get older—*particularly because they will know when to seek the counsel or comfort of a trusted other.* Of course the converse is also true: Children without a secure attachment can end up having trouble relying on themselves when they're older (or they can end up unable to rely on anyone *but* themselves).

Does Attachment Help Develop Your Child's Imagination?

We all want our children to grow up with a firm grip on reality, but there's little doubt that a healthy imagination has benefits. Dr. Robert Emde, an expert in early social–emotional development, has called imagination an "adaptive psychological function of emotional significance." Attachment researcher and scholar Inge Bretherton ascribed creativity and learning benefits to imagination: When a child can use imagination to tell a story, he can translate the "as if" of imagination to the "what if" of cognition, creating and experimenting with alternative futures. This means imagination can enhance social interactions too, as children try to picture what their peers and caregivers might do and say and respond accordingly.

Most children develop the capacity to imagine at age 3 or 4, but research has shown that even as young as age 2 children enjoy fantasizing with parents and can often distinguish between reality and fantasy. Interestingly, though, they may become much more confused when under stress. *In reducing the child's moment-to-moment and long-term stress, the security of attachment may offer the by-product of a healthy imagination to children at an early age.*

A Foundation for True Self-Esteem

When a parent is there for us a lot of the time (not all the time—an important point that we'll delve into throughout this book), we get the message that we must be pretty deserving. Sounds silly—I mean, that's Mom or Dad's job, right? It's not an award. But imagine the thought process if the baby were verbal: "Hmm, I cried and Mom came over and picked me up. She looked into my eyes and made a sad face, then she said so softly, 'I know, I know, it's so hard. . . . ' How did she know how I felt? Well, whatever, here she is, and I'm starting to feel better." Then, the next time around: "Well, look at this: Mom's back. She was running around doing something awfully fast, but she still came over when I cried." And again: "Look! She's here! I was just starting to get a little worried—hadn't seen her in a few minutes and didn't know where she'd gone. But I didn't even cry, and here she is!" Here's the conclusion the baby draws from this pattern:

Mom is saying "I am here, and you are worth it."

I conclude "You are here, and I must be worth it."*

> The researchers in the long-term Minnesota study found that this is also a by-product of the emotional regulation learned in a securely attached relationship: Children who learned to trust that their parent would help them regulate painful emotions also accumulated confidence in their own ability to regulate emotion, and this resulted in greater self-confidence and self-esteem during preschool and by age 10.

Secure babies start life with a big advantage: They already know that, when nothing makes sense in the world, when pain and fear and sadness seem to come out of nowhere, there's someone who thinks they're worth being with—no matter what.

As you undoubtedly know, "self-esteem" has been a controversial concept. Not that many years ago, many parents and other adults dealing with children believed that self-esteem came from ensuring that children didn't feel inferior to others: a gold star for everyone! Just for showing up! The counterargument that it's competence that feeds self-esteem seems to have won out in conventional wisdom, and fortunately, as we've already seen, a secure attachment is also the foundation for the confidence and other attributes needed to develop competence. The idea that low self-esteem increases stress seems self-evident. We want our children to feel good about who they are and what they can do and not be wracked with envy or relentless competitiveness to prove their self-worth.

Another Caveat: Self-esteem comes from attachment security, not from being told you're superior to others. In a revealing longitudinal study of 500 elementary school–age children, researchers at the University of Amsterdam reported in 2015 that children who said their parents let them know they were loved had higher self-esteem 6 months later, whereas those whose parents told them they were more special than others showed more narcissism but not greater self-esteem. Self-esteem comes, at least in part, from being accepted, not from being overvalued.

---

* With thanks to Jude Cassidy.

Building Social Competence

In the Introduction to this book we noted our firm conviction that relationships—the "and" in life—are key to health and happiness in all ways these conditions can be measured. To us, therefore, the term "competence" seems too flat. Yet its meaning encompasses all the ways we can benefit from the social part of our lives: intimacy, mutual support, empathy, and getting along in all the domains of life, from school to work to home and community. In an article about how health policy can take into account the way social relationships benefit our well-being, the authors concluded that "social relationships affect a range of health outcomes, including mental health, physical health, health habits, and mortality risk."

Supportive interactions with others benefit immune, endocrine, and cardiovascular functions and reduce wear and tear on the body due, in part, to chronically overworked physiological systems engaged in stress responses. These processes unfold over the entire life course, with effects on health. In childhood, emotional support from others (like a primary caregiver) assists in the normal development of various regulatory systems, including those that govern digestion, mood, energy, and our overall response to stress. For adults, social support can keep stresses we're experiencing and those we see coming from having negative effects on our heart. People who are married have a lower risk of cardiovascular disease than those who have lost a marriage through death or divorce.

Children with secure attachments exhibited social competence in the Minnesota study "from their expectations and representations of relationships, to their engagement with others and skill in interaction, to their popularity." Sroufe and colleagues found that secure children were more actively involved in their peer groups both in preschool and middle childhood and less isolated. The preschoolers had more empathy and more mutual relationships. By age 10 they had more close friendships and were able to sustain those relationships better in the midst of larger peer groups. By the time they were teens the secure children could function well even in social arenas where they felt vulnerable and demonstrated leadership.

Better Physical Health

Speaking of health, physical development depends on a matrix of complicated factors, flowing from both nature (genetics and other biological influences, like illness) and nurture. Secure attachment has been linked with better physical health, although the pathway between the two isn't well-defined. If attachment enhances social relationships as we know it does, and social relationships promote physical health as we know they do, then we can guess that attachment may promote physical health too. We do know that the psychological immunity from secure attachment reduces the wear and tear on the body that causes all kinds of disease.

Attachment: Is It the Key to What It Means to Be Human?

Maybe there's more behind attachment than an evolutionary drive. Something about attachment strikes a deep chord in us. Perhaps this is because the interactions between a parent and an infant are a child's initiation into the essence of life, emblematic of the way we navigate the influences of nature and nurture as we move through our world. One researcher called the mother–baby relationship "the first encounter between heredity and the psychological environment." The fact that attachment happens is a reminder that we are inherently relational beings.

And because our first experience of an intimate relationship is in our contact with our first caregivers, the quality of this connection will affect our every future perception of relationship. Alan Sroufe put it this way: "The infant–caregiver attachment relationship is the core, around which all other experience is structured, whatever impact it may have. Thus, we came to a position that early experience is never lost, however much transformation occurs in later development."

That is, it takes two—to develop and to thrive, from birth to death. As Donald Winnicott implied, it's all about the "and." And that "and" is profound—and profoundly important. Robert Karen, whose 1990 *Atlantic* article "Becoming Attached" introduced the concept of attachment to the general public, said, "There is something simple and life affirming in the attachment message that the only thing your child needs in order to thrive emotionally is your emotional availability and responsiveness."

The attachment message in fact affirms the view of thinkers from psychology to philosophy and theology about the meaning and purpose of life: Many have found that our common bond as human beings is the desire to love and be loved. This need is as universal as it is beyond the bounds of science to measure it. Attachment and bonding behavior, while obviously necessary for the survival of the species, does not explain the mystery of how a parent falls in love with a child. Nor does it explain the wonder of how a child falls in love with a parent. The need to protect and be protected does not fully define the need to tenderly nurture and be nurtured. Nor does it account for a child's request to be in a relationship centered on pleasure and mutual delight.

Attachment shows us that love isn't just a warm feeling. Developmental researcher Colwyn Trevarthen says that each infant comes into the world waiting to "experience being experienced." The process of seeking and receiving help with strong emotions that is at the core of attachment contributes to the young child's belief that the relationship is stronger than any given emotion. This is a belief that can be the foundation of not only strong relationships throughout life but, more broadly, strong communities and strong nations around the world. We can speculate and debate about where this power arises, but there is little question that it may be one of the greatest gifts to humanity.

Whatever the question, learning to be connected is a big part of the answer.

"Intimate attachments to other human beings are the hub around which a person's life revolves, not only as an infant or a toddler or a schoolchild but throughout adolescence and years of maturity as well, and on into old age. From these intimate attachments a person draws strength and enjoyment of life and, through what he or she contributes, gives strength and enjoyment to others. These are matters about which current science and traditional wisdom are at one."
—JOHN BOWLBY, Attachment and Loss, Volume 3*

And now for the unavoidable, thorny question: If attachment is so deeply inborn, instinctive, so ingrained in the human operating system, why do we need to talk about it?

---

*This quotation has been paraphrased to remove gender-specific language.

SECURITY

Befriending Imperfection

The baby girl is only 6 weeks old. It's 2:00 A.M., and she's crying. Again. Her mother hasn't gotten more than 2 hours of sleep a night in, well, 6 weeks. When she walked to the corner drugstore for another package of diapers that afternoon, she was sure she was just going to crumple to the sidewalk, where everyone else out there would simply step over her and keep going. That would have been OK; maybe she would have gotten in a nap. Now her family is trying to help. Her husband and mother-in-law are taking turns trying to soothe Sophie in the living room. Sophie's cries do stop with another's presence, but only briefly. Hannah tosses and turns and then stares at the ceiling. No use. She can't sleep when her daughter's in distress.

Throwing on a robe, she heads for the darkened living room and motions to her mother-in-law to pass her the baby. The minute Sophie feels her mother's arms around her she quiets. Hannah starts her slow circuit on a well-worn path around the room.

The fact that her mother's touch instantly calmed newborn Sophie surprised her father, her grandmother (who had raised five children of her own), and most of all Sophie's mother, Hannah. "No one ever told me about that!" she exclaimed years later. That night, however, her relief at being able to soothe her baby's discomfort just by being there was followed quickly by a twinge of fear and not a little resentment.

Having this kind of power over her child's well-being imposed a terrible responsibility, didn't it? If she could ease Sophie's distress where others couldn't, what if she wasn't there every minute? What if she made a mistake?

Hannah was getting a taste of the imperfection of parenting. If you're already a parent, you've probably had the same conflicting reactions: relief and even a little awe that your mere presence can soothe your child (Where did you get *this* power?), combined with a touch of resistance and, particularly, fear. How could you remain up to this important task? How could you possibly be good enough, wise enough, patient enough, energetic enough to be the parent this wonderful child deserves? If you're expecting your first child, you undoubtedly have the same bursts of anxiety about your ability to be the best possible parent.

It is because of the prevalence of these doubts, this worry, these preconceived notions about what it takes to be a parent, that we must talk about attachment and the importance of security. The pressures on parents—both external and internal—to achieve some form of perfection (or at least to avoid making significant mistakes) in parenting sit on our hearts and minds like a well-meaning but suffocating elephant in the room. We know (and are told) that parenting is the most natural thing in the world. This should make it easy, shouldn't it? Knowing exactly how to do what's best for our children should be part of our innate programming, shouldn't it? We should love every minute of this, right? Of course we know it's not that simple or absolute; we joke about it with other new parents as well as seasoned mothers and fathers like our own parents and grandparents. Yet deep down we still expect the very best from our Mom or Dad selves—because our inborn positive intentions for our children tell us this role is just that important.

At the heart of this book is a simple observation the three of us have been able to make over the decades of our work with parents: Every parent wants what's best for her or his child, which is to say that we've come to believe that all parents are hardwired to offer love and security to their children. Even when this doesn't appear to be the case, even when we've worked with parents who have treated their children in ways that seem profoundly off-center and painfully problematic, we have never found a parent who wakes up in the morning plotting for ways to be a bad parent.

And yet many of us still worry we may turn out to be not so good (or even bad) at parenting. Why?

We know that we're only human and we live in an imperfect world. Yet our drive to be good caregivers tells us to give parenting our all. And society sets very high standards for us. These two forces collude to push us into the pursuit of perfection. We won't feel right if we don't do everything in our power to be great parents, and so we yield to the urge to measure ourselves by how well we follow child-rearing philosophy A or parenting advice B. We start treating good parenting as a destination that ends in an achievement or a product (The perfect child? The never lonely child? The always happy child? The never deeply sad child?) instead of as a process that takes care of itself (when we let it). We interpret "mistakes" as setbacks rather than as lessons for our children and ourselves that cement security and facilitate good relationships.

We can't say this often enough: *Modeling perfection and the pursuit of it does not promote healthy development. Pressuring ourselves to always get it right or to guarantee that our children never experience the pain we may have experienced growing up creates an anxiety that our little ones can't help recognizing. Working too hard actually compromises our children's need to trust in our faith in relationship, an essential foundation of security throughout their lives.*

So let's bring the elephant in the room out in the open. In this chapter, we shed some light on the various and insidious ways that the pressure to be "perfect" or "mistake-free" or "completely available" can threaten secure attachment. Time and again in our work with parents from all cultures, of all ages, in every demographic group, we've found that exposing these false expectations and the parenting practices they encourage helps people relax into raising their children.

As we describe in this chapter, when you can relax into bonding with your child, you radiate a calm, responsive confidence in your parenting that builds your child's trust that you are there for her and teaches her that she'll find others who can be trusted in the same way for the rest of her life. That's what the Circle of Security is all about. We've offered it to support parents' faith in themselves and their relationship with their child. In the following pages we show you how the Circle provides that support and what you can expect from the rest of this book.

The Pressures of an Imperfect World

Let's get this out of the way. Parenting isn't always pretty. It's a privilege and a joy. It's also a hassle and sometimes a painfully thankless job. Sometimes no matter what you do, your child is unhappy or unhealthy or suddenly over-the-top difficult, apparently insisting on being the bane of your existence. At least today. This is one reason Hannah felt a pinch of resentment when she realized that her daughter had entered the world feeling more comfortable with her mother than anyone else.

This reaction is completely normal. But if you feel you need to do everything exactly right, it might make you feel so uncomfortable that all you want is to stop feeling that way. At times you might silently blame your baby for being aggravating. A baby who wants to attach to a parent has the most positive of intentions, finding your face irresistible, just as you have positive intentions for your child. She's not trying to get attention just for attention's sake or trying to make life difficult for both of you. She just doesn't know what to do except cry for help and seek the connection her emotional life depends on. Common sense usually tells you this. But if you can't accept the imperfections and messiness of parenting (including inevitable moments of resentment, overwhelm, and a desire to run in the opposite direction), common sense might elude you.

The other option we sometimes choose is to blame ourselves, denying we feel any resentment and scolding ourselves for it.

Ambivalence about parenting is the elephant in the room: Raising children is difficult, it can make us very uncomfortable, and yet many of us feel like we're not allowed to admit that. This was never clearer than in the research method chosen for a 2015 study reporting that German adults found the first two years of parenthood more stressful than divorce, loss of a partner, or unemployment. The researchers knew that parents are afraid that complaining about the physical exhaustion, emotional turmoil, disruption of intimate relationships, and other by-products of parenthood will reflect badly on them. After all, the image of the perfect mother or father doesn't include dissatisfaction with parenthood. So instead of directly asking parents how they felt parenthood had affected their well-being, they simply asked them to rate their happiness starting before they had a child and then once the child was about age 2. Sometimes it takes a little trickery to reveal a giant pachyderm.

We Need More Help . . .

There's no denying that parenting takes effort and resources and isn't always fun. But what's the message we get when society acts like we should be able to handle it without help? In the United States, parents are expected to return to work too soon after having a child. A huge number of women are trying to subsist at the poverty level. And we're bombarded with the message that failing to give our children a competitive edge will get them left behind and rob them of the potential for a brilliant future. Whether you're subject to these pressures or not, trying to be a parent in the 21st century is challenging. The implied message: If you need support—even breathing space—to create a secure attachment for your child, there must be something wrong with *you*.

In August 2015, *Huffington Post* editor Emily Peck wrote that a 2012 U.S. Department of Labor survey revealed almost a quarter of new mothers were back at work within 2 weeks, mainly because they could not afford to stay at home. Not surprisingly, the higher the mother's education level (and, presumably, the better the job as a result), the longer the paid maternity leave. Nothing conveys the attachment consequences of this separation of mother and newborn child better than the waitress working 60 hours a week who said she would fall into an exhausted sleep with a hand on her month-old baby *because it was the only connection available to her.*

Public outcry—and, hopefully, a growing corporate conscience—has recently led to increased parental leave by some large companies, but it's notable that they tend to cluster in the white-collar work world employing college-educated workers and paying higher salaries. What about the 42 million American women said to be at the poverty level by the Shriver Report, single mothers accounting for over 50% of the babies born to women under 30, and the fact that virtually all single mothers surveyed said the biggest thing that could be done to help them would be policy-mandated paid maternity leave?

Whether mothers want to stay at home with their children or not, the choice is not always up to them. Nor is it up to fathers raising children. In our experience, it doesn't matter whether the primary caregiver is mother or father, male or female, grandparent or uncle. Children will attach to whichever adult is reliably there for them, and even when a parent can't stay home with them till they're ready for school, they do attach—often very securely—to their parents. It's not that attachment doesn't happen; it's that parents can't help feeling torn, because society tells us this is a really important job but doesn't do much to back that up.

In September 2015, Anne-Marie Slaughter called it "A Toxic Work World" in a country where 57% of women are in the labor force, many of them enduring 12- to 16-hour workdays, still making only 77 cents for every male-earned dollar, and ending up burned out and ill. Anxiety attacks and an epidemic of stress aren't the product of just trying to parent with all these competing pressures; women and men struggle constantly with care of elders, adult siblings who need help, and other extended family.

Slaughter urges all of us to "stand up for care," warning that, until our society provides for the necessity to care for others *and* hold a job, our families and communities will wither and we'll never regain our competitive edge in the world. We would add that when parents cannot afford to care for their children as they wish to, attachment suffers.

. . . And Less Advice

No wonder we think we need to try to be perfect parents. We often feel alone out here. So naturally we're tempted to look for prescriptions, rules, and guarantees. There's so much we need to accomplish and achieve that we sometimes try to skip the more time-consuming work of problem solving and seek immediate answers from outside

Stress Is High for Americans in the Parenting Years

In 2013 the American Psychological Association reported that, on a scale of 1–10, with 1 representing no stress and 10 representing a great deal of stress, so-called millennials (ages 18–33) and Gen Xers (ages 34–47) ranked their stress at 5.4—where a healthy level of stress is considered to be 3.8. Despite their stated intentions to reduce stress, adults in these age groups said they're having trouble managing stress, lying awake worrying and experiencing irritability and anger on a regular basis. Stress is one major influence on the state of mind that we take into parenting.

experts. In November 2015, the *Washington Post* told a story about the growing popularity of psychotherapy via apps and websites where the focus is on receiving something akin to a quick fix for personal problems. With millennials and Gen Xers suffering higher rates of anxiety and depression than their elders, it's no surprise that they would try to find a solution that limits both longer-term reflection and ongoing connection. But in our experience, just as with parenting, psychotherapy is a method that is grounded within an experience of connection. The Circle of Security program, in fact, is constructed to create what Donald Winnicott called a "holding environment" for parents—a safe place where they can feel understood and accepted so they can do the sometimes tough work of looking at the way they parent to see if they want to make different choices. Your secure bond with your baby is the baby's first holding environment, and it's there that your child learns that sometimes problem solving can be difficult, but it's always easier and more successful within the "and."

There are thousands of helpful parenting books out there, and numerous in-person programs to inform us on specific aspects of child rearing or provide useful principles and philosophies we can return to as a supportive foundation. As a parent who has confidence in your ability to care for your growing child in the way that is right for you and your family, you'll undoubtedly take advantage of these resources as needed. We're not here to warn you off others' advice. The key to making good use of it, however, is to be equipped with the confidence to make your own choices about which advice to follow and how to follow it. If you're trying to be the perfect parent, you may latch on to the latest parenting trend and adhere to its tenets as if it were a life-saving prescription. But then what if you "fail"? Or the tips and techniques don't deliver on their promises? Or someone comes along with what's considered to be an even "better" plan? Once again, you've been found lacking—by yourself or some formless supervisor who hovers over your parenting efforts. Maybe you'll move on to the next big parenting movement and continue the cycle. The plethora of advice out there gives you unlimited avenues to try—and their sheer number sends the implicit message that you *could* be the perfect parent, if only you would become better informed. There's nothing wrong with being knowledgeable and skillful. But why not start with what you already know? The Circle of Security is here to keep you in touch with your innate capacity for wisdom and love.

Overparenting. Hovering. Overinvolved.

These are real. These are, in part, the outcome of being given "expert advice"—all of which adds to a long list of *dos* and *don'ts* (all of which carry an underlying message of "do it right, or else . . . ").

Pressure. Pressure. Pressure.

You have likely heard the story of the centipede that was unable to walk because someone told him it was essential that he count his every step. So it goes with so much that is happening in the culture of parenting, an environment that has become incredibly stifling for parents because the implications of "the next step (potentially wrong or even disastrous for our child)" render us all but frozen in place. "If I do X, he'll end up this way, and if I don't do Y, he'll end up that way." Caught somewhere between OMG and WTF, we feel stuck without any kind of reference point we can trust.

Fortunately, within the context of half a century of developmental research, there is a quiet clarity slowly being made available to parents. It has very little to say about dos and don'ts; rather it offers us a way to begin to make sense of and eventually make our own choices regarding those dos and don'ts. Attachment theory and its practical application via the Circle of Security gives us the option of making those choices without following someone else's "10 steps to successful parenting" program.

As hard as it may be to hear, parenting in the direction of emotional health for our children does, indeed, require making healthy choices. But more important than any specific choice is who we are and how we feel as we make that choice. If I'm simply following a formula or reading a cookbook for how to raise a happy baby, my child will feel like she's being managed or manipulated, even if it's for her own good.

The problem: how to learn key aspects of parenting that will, indeed, be beneficial to my child while not becoming anxious about a "right versus wrong" approach to parenting. If, in reading these pages, you become nervous or more nervous about parenting than you currently are, we've done you a disservice. If, however, you recognize the significance of what you do and also find yourself increasingly at ease with how you have a clear path to offering what's needed for your child, we'll have accomplished precisely what we hope to offer.

The Misdirection of Behavior Management

In Chapter 1 we mentioned that the importance of attachment was downplayed in the 20th century in favor of behaviorism. It's not that behavior isn't important. It's that behavior is not the problem—even though it sure feels like it is if you're trying to get that "impossible child" into the car to go to the supermarket or the preschool. Behavior is just a message. Yet the emphasis in our society still is often on a child's behavior. Certainly behavior that's conducive to learning is important once a child is in school, and we all need to behave in ways that allow us to move through our world without intruding unnecessarily on others and their goals while we try to meet our own. But for the youngest children, behavior is not where our parenting focus should dwell.

Behavioral approaches are wonderful when they work, but they often temporarily change behaviors without addressing the underlying issues from which the behaviors emerge. That's because they're essentially another attempt at a quick or superficial fix. Successfully managing our child's behavior may make us feel good too—and we certainly need that if we're always aiming for perfection and inevitably falling short—because our well-behaved children are visible evidence of our skill as caregivers. More on the perfect parent–perfect child idea later. For now, suffice it to say that the experience of emotional connection via attaching to our child can make us feel better than "managing" any incident of misbehavior.

To get what we believe is a more accurate picture of behavior, imagine an iceberg. On the surface you see nothing but a huge outcropping of ice. What you don't see is the mass that lies below the surface, which often represents more than 80% of the whole iceberg. Now imagine that what you see on the surface is a child's behavior and that what you don't see is the child's legitimate need for our shared support and regulation of those needs. As the three of us have worked

Through the years we've come to see that all children, at the level of what's beneath the surface, are "wise and waiting." Children have an innate wisdom about what they most need and will wait, often for years, until they can find someone who will finally recognize and respond to their genuine need.

with many high-risk children in a variety of settings (schools, foster homes, family counseling), we've come to know how essential it is for caregivers to always have an awareness of the legitimate need that is often below the surface of any particular (negative) behavior. As a young foster parent, in fact, one of us recalls trying star charts, time-outs, logical consequences, and different forms of positive and negative reinforcement with little lasting result before switching to sitting down with whichever child was acting out and saying, "We are going to stick with this until we get to the other side of it." Once a relationship developed in which sharing feelings was central to their experience of being parented by us, these children's problematic behaviors dissipated. Reacting to the behavior rather than meeting the need (hidden in plain sight), all three of us have learned, may result in short-term compliance but misses an opportunity for long-term change.

From our point of view, feelings that aren't let in the front door turn into negative behaviors that will kick out the back door.

Parents or Friends?

Looking for the quick answer, following the latest prescriptions, trying to cure the symptom instead of the underlying problem—all of these parenting choices result from trying too hard. Desperate to find our way, these attempts may be the only recourse when the standard is impossible to uphold. When you believe the stakes are sky high and you're never allowed to fail, you'll naturally cast around for anything that might help.

Attachment is an emotional bond, for sure. But being there for your child in all of the child's needs is more than that. It involves taking charge whenever necessary, embracing your role as the older, wiser party in the parent–child duo. There has been a lot of talk over recent decades about parenting styles, from permissive to authoritarian, with most experts recommending that we strive for the happy middle of authoritative—being confident that we know what's right in a given situation for this particular child and not being afraid to act on that conviction. Still, the closing of the "generation gap" experienced by the baby boomers may have helped to blur the line between the parent role and the friend role, and the millennials and Gen Xers that are today's parents may have inherited this (mis)perception. In our experience, being more friend than parent is often another form of perfectionism, one that fears the messiness of struggle and inevitable times of unhappiness in children. Of course we want our children to be happy and it's wonderful to be our children's friends, but we need to do it in the context of being older and wiser, aka parents. Healthy parenting is not a democracy. To feel safe and secure, children need to know that someone cares enough to be in charge even when this includes the discord of making decisions that may be unpopular.

The Burden of Our Imperfect (Messy) Selves

Pressure to be perfect doesn't come solely from the outside world or our interpretations of society's messages. Our choices about how to be perfect parents for our children also have internal origins. We all carry memories, explicit and implicit, around with us, and they inform all of our relationships. In parenting, it's not your actions but the lens through which you see your actions that we're finding to be of most importance. If you were expected to be "perfect" growing up, for example, you take this expectation into your parenting. If you want to make sure your children never feel the pain you once felt, this may also place an unhealthy burden on you. Parenting is of course to some extent about what you do. But even more, it's who you are as you do it.

It's what is known as your state of mind that is actually being conveyed to your child as much as, if not more than, what you're actually doing. A common refrain that we use in our teaching is that children read between the lines. They pay attention to our actions, but they may pay more attention to the state of mind behind our actions. So, for example, if you're trying to calm your little one after a tumble and saying just the right words ("There, there honey, I'm sure this feels bad right now"), but inside your mind you're thinking "I'm not a very good mother, I hope I'm doing this right and I'm probably not," your child isn't likely to soothe as fully as she might.

We recognize that this kind of information can seem like a remarkable bind: "If I came from a less than ideal family background, my child will pick up my insecurities no matter how hard I try." Fortunately this isn't the case. What our children pick up on is our deep intention to offer the security they need most. Our positive intentionality is the message hidden between the lines that they most need to know: Our intention is always to offer the goodness they need within a context that is always less than perfect. Our children don't need perfection; they need to trust in our commitment to their legitimate needs, which includes a commitment to finding a clear and coherent way to understand what those needs are.

History Often Limits Vision

Sometimes the lessons we learned in childhood blind us to what our children need even when we have a map like the Circle of Security as a guide. Opening up our parenting options may be especially important and especially difficult if we didn't have the benefit of a secure attachment during our own childhood. Has the fulfillment within intimacy you want eluded you? Do you feel like something has always held you back from pursuing or achieving the life you hope for? Of course it would be a gross overgeneralization to say that an insecure attachment has created all of your life's discontents, but attachment exerts such a powerful effect on every aspect of our life that insecurity in early childhood may very well be a significant aspect of your adult disappointments. This book allows you to explore your own attachment style and its implications throughout your life thus far, if you wish to do so.

Perfect Child → Perfect Parent?

A common side effect of perfectionistic parenting is to try to have the perfect child. This phenomenon is associated with a particular attachment style and is driven by the implicit memories of our childhood attachment bond with our parents that we carry into our own parenting. How these memories become our legacy when we're not even aware they're pulling our parenting strings is discussed further in Chapter 5. But we see evidence of the perfect-child pattern all around us. Consider the reaction to Amy Chua's 2011 book *Battle Hymn of the Tiger Mother* to grasp how seriously parents view their child's success as a reflection of how well they have performed the "task" of motherhood. The book was meant as cultural commentary, but it became the subject of hot debate over whether demanding perfection from our children is the right way to parent. The common perception that "successful child equals successful parent" (whether it be a child's manners, athleticism, intelligence, or appearance) is far more pervasive—and persuasive—than we might want to admit.

Then there is the impulse to define our children as "special." This, too, flows from a particular attachment style discussed in Chapter 5. It can take the form of overprivileging a child's every emotion, as mentioned in Chapter 1, assuming our child is unable to withstand frustration or upset. As we soon make clear, attempts to overprotect our children, doing our best to keep all difficulty and struggle at bay, rob them of the capacity building necessary for resilience, a skill set that can be learned only within a context of shared problem solving and understanding support in the face of less than ideal circumstances. Or it might take the form of overvaluing the child, as if he's uniquely gifted and inherently superior to his peers. As we noted in Chapter 1, telling a child he's better than others doesn't raise his self-esteem; it raises his narcissistic qualities. A secure attachment based on a child's trusting in parental love increases self-esteem.

Of course one of the most pressing concerns of parents today is that their children might "fall behind." Many of us wouldn't even know how to answer the question "Fall behind what?" and yet some fuzzy image of a goal that will elude us if we don't push our children forward cloaks us in worry. The focal point of this worry is often cognitive development. Will our children be smart enough, well educated enough, perform well enough academically to get where they want to go (or where we want them to go) in the future? The debate rages on about what should be the emphasis of early education: social development, emotional intelligence, imagination and creativity, or intellectual prowess? In the United States we still focus mainly on the last, and yet the countries we view as our biggest competitors in the adult marketplace tend to stress play and socializing for the first couple of years of school—and produce higher cognitive and achievement scores in secondary grades. These countries recognize the importance of play to cognitive, social, and emotional development in children. Consider your relationship with your child her first playground: a place where she can safely explore her world without constrictions created by emotional intolerance or fear.

Worrying about our children's cognitive capacity is natural, but it's symptomatic of focusing on the horizon rather than on what's happening here, right now. For the youngest children, the here and now is all there is, and it's plenty for them to deal with. So much of what we focus on throughout this book has to do with this precise theme: How can parents prioritize emotional security as the "win now and win later" approach their children need? Here's a quick rule of thumb: The more children feel safe and secure within their primary relationships early in their lives, the more relaxed and resilient they will be when facing the challenges and opportunities that will emerge as they get older.

So How Do We Ensure a Secure Attachment for Our Children?

The good news for parents is that knowing how to parent doesn't have to be complicated. With our inherent capacity (already built deep within us) as a guide we can venture into the so-called task of parenting as something much more akin to the gift and privilege it actually is. Recognizing and trusting our genuine desire to offer what's best for our children and their huge capacity to bring this forth from us, parenting can become almost easy.

You probably know by now that we're not talking "sleep in, never feel overwhelmed, parenting is such a breeze" kind of easy. Rather, we're suggesting that once we can trust our positive intentionality as parents and have a simple visual image that allows us to translate our child's needs into a clear and understandable road map, the "hard work" of parenting becomes something much more comfortable.

Consider Lei and her father from Chapter 1. Think about baby Sophie and her mother. In those simple, natural interactions you can see the primal drive of the child to seek care, and you can see a similar inborn drive on the part of the parent to give care. Although it's not so obvious in a baby's first days and weeks of life, it's not long after birth that you can also see a child begin to explore. Go to any playground and you'll see the same exchange that occurred between Lei and her father: Lei wants to run out and explore her world and her capacity to interact with it; her father is there to make that possible. And here's Sophie 5 months later:

Hannah is working on her computer at the dining room table while Sophie pinballs around the room in her walker. When she coos and babbles, Hannah looks up and they grin at each other. Then the phone rings. It's Hannah's biggest client, who wants to know how his project is going. As she details her progress, Sophie's voice rises; the babbling escalates to a high-pitched squeal. The little girl isn't crying, and she isn't upset, but her voice is so commanding that Hannah immediately looks over and has to stifle a laugh as her client asks incredulously, "What *is* that, your dog?"

Sophie is secure enough at this tender age to know she can count on Hannah to be there while she zips around the room on her own.

This support for her exploratory efforts is so crucial that, when she can tell Mom's attention has turned elsewhere, she uses her "siren song" to call her back. If Mom hadn't already proven reliable over and over, Sophie may not have tried at all. (A year later, Sophie set off a car alarm while trying out her siren song from her stroller one day. Hannah was sure Sophie wanted to find out whether strangers walking by would respond in the same way as her parents. And of course they did.)

Sophie recognized her mother well before she knew her own name or understood any of the language used by the attentive family trying to calm her. She may have grasped the importance of the bond between them before her mother did. This is what a budding secure attachment looks like. It isn't always pretty (stay tuned for an update on Sophie), but the beauty of this bond has been depicted in poetry and art throughout history.

The good news for all of us is that attachment happens. It's not a matter of whether a child becomes attached, but of what the quality of that attachment is. It's not a matter of whether a parent wants to answer her child's needs and ease his discomfort but of whether she knows how (or can't see it for other reasons we discuss later). We've found that, even when the caregiver's attachment drive is disrupted, the child's can keep going strong.

Incredibly, with a little help many parents beat the worst odds. The parents in our original Circle of Security groups typically struggled with a variety of current and past problems, from poverty and limited education to a history of abuse and recent addiction to drugs. This amounts to very challenging contexts of the type that Alan Sroufe says exert such a powerful effect: "The infant's development is inextricably tied to the care that surrounds it. In the same way, the care that caregivers provide is dependent upon the nature of the surrounding stresses and supports." When those stresses and supports are enormous, as they are for single teenage mothers and others who have to try hard to make it through every day—*and also for many "average" parents today*— it's hard to meet a child's needs with sensitivity or to respond with the kind of coherence and understanding that is necessary.

For more than 20 years we've worked with teen and recently homeless parents who seemed unlikely to be able to meet the challenges of parenthood. Many came to our program in tears—terrified that they would continue the cycle of abuse and neglect they had experienced as children. With the help of a parent-friendly approach that encourages the formation of a healthy attachment, many of these teens have become highly successful parents fully capable of supporting themselves and their children on a path to what attachment researchers call "earned secure." Even when the odds are stacked against them, over and over again we have seen parents tap into the love and caregiving instincts they were born with and provide genuine and lasting security for their children.

What about those of us who aren't dealing with challenges of that magnitude? Would Lei grow up to live a long, healthy, and happy life if her father devoted his daughter-directed time to providing her with the best education, a comfortable home, and the most nutritious food and left the one-on-one contact to nannies and other adults? She very well might. A lot of variables affect child development. If Lei had a long-term nanny from infancy, or a grandparent or other relative who cared for her in the way we see in the playground scene, she might still have had the secure attachment to a primary caregiver that lays the foundation for healthy development. And, as we said earlier, she'd still be attached to her parents, but likely with less security than to the one who had been more primary in her upbringing. There is no discounting the role of an intimate and ongoing connection with another person.

Without a pattern of the kind of interaction Lei and her dad had in the park from any caregiver, Lei might end up being the child who sits off in a corner pretending to be happy while everyone else is playing. She might have difficulty making friends, because she doesn't know how to comfort someone else who's gotten hurt or understand that differences of opinion are natural. She might grow up to view herself as "too special to be bothered" or "too strange to belong." Underneath it all, she'd actually be lonely.

Fortunately, a lot of the scenes like the one in the park will just come naturally. And if things unfold that way much of the time, your child's self will develop and healthy development will ensue. For the most part, forming a secure attachment with your baby will be a no-brainer. We couldn't put it better than Robert Karen did:

> You don't need to be rich or smart or talented or funny; you just have to be there, in both senses of the phrase. To your child, none of the rest matters, except inasmuch as it enables you to give of yourself. What's more, you don't have to be an outstanding mother, just in Winnicott's famous phrase a "good-enough" mother.

As a solid rule of thumb for any parent: Good enough is, well, good enough.

Take a look at Sophie and Hannah 5 years later:

Sophie comes crashing into the house after school, yelling that she wants to get a big tattoo of a bird "just like Bella's babysitter has!" Hannah snorts and laughs, saying, "Yeah, that sounds just *great*." Sophie bursts into tears, drops her backpack, and runs to her room. Hannah sighs and picks up the backpack, where she finds an intricate (at least for a 5-year-old) drawing of a large-winged bird (or is it a dragon?) sticking out of the pocket. Going into her daughter's room, she sits on the bed and says, "Hey, honey, this is really beautiful." Silence. "Maybe we can try to find some body paint." More silence. "Bella's nanny is really cool, huh?" Sophie nods vigorously and excitedly starts to describe the stories the 25-year-old tells of the phoenix that "lives" on her arm.

Sophie has learned that Mom understands what she needs even when she can't articulate it. That's why it sometimes hurts so much when Mom *doesn't* get it right away. Fortunately, Mom usually figures it out, and all is once again right with the world.

Numerous approaches and programs have arisen that are designed to bring parents and children into a closer, more empathic relationship, and they all have strengths. We designed the Circle of Security with the specific goal of making decades of attachment research as understandable as possible so that parents can support a secure attachment with their children. Our approach was created to offer:

- A way to understand your child's legitimate needs
- A way to understand how you see those needs (how some feel more acceptable than others)
- A way to make sense of why you welcome certain needs and struggle with others
- Access to that part of you that is willing to override your discomfort in order to prioritize the needs your child has

In the following chapters, you'll find more on how to form a secure attachment and why. Everything we discuss is founded in the underlying theme of inviting you to trust: yourself, your innate wisdom, your intention to do your best, and your curiosity to find out whatever it is that may get in the way of offering your best. We've found over and over that parents' trust builds their child's trust—that you'll be there to help them with the emotional needs that are so confusing to young children and that you'll take charge at those many moments during the day when someone older and wiser needs to step in. The Circle of Security is designed to build this reciprocal trust and a secure attachment by helping you in the following ways, which provide the framework for the rest of this book.

Saying Good-Bye to Perfectionism and Self-Blame

Pretend for a moment that every parent on the planet has this one simple fact in common: We all have exactly 12 flaws as parents. Not that these flaws are the same for everyone. Many of us have similar configurations fitting into similar patterns while also being stunningly unique in how messed up we actually are.

Now pretend that someone comes along and tells you that having these flaws isn't actually a problem . . . unless you also have "the 13th parenting flaw," the one that makes the other 12 almost impossible to deal with. What's this 13th flaw? The belief that you shouldn't have the other 12. Here's the deal about the 13th flaw: It always includes blame. This blame is always built on the illusion that there is "an answer" for our imperfection or struggles as parents and we should already know it. The hidden (insidious) message: "Imperfections do not belong in parenting." (Good luck with that.)

This much we know: We all struggle as parents. All of us. No one is perfect. Indeed, any attempt to be perfect is by its very nature a sign of imperfection. When we fight our flaws as parents, they turn to stone and sit on us with a weight we can barely withstand. Then we either fall into shame and guilt, continually berating ourselves, or pretend we don't make mistakes and, inevitably, find someone else to blame (our children, our partner, our upbringing). When we honor our inevitable flaws, when we can bring kindness, acceptance, and understanding to the mistakes we make as parents, something shifts. New possibility and wonderful surprises start showing up for us and our children.

Blame has never helped a parent become a better parent. Being kind to ourselves flows from understanding that parenting is a remarkably difficult task, that we all make mistakes, and that our deep intention to do what's best for our children is what matters. As we keep saying, children are remarkably good at reading between the lines. They can tell when we're anxious and self-critical. They can also recognize when we are able to honor ourselves for doing the best we can under often difficult circumstances.

Being kind to ourselves increases our capacity to be kind to those we love most. It just may be that in our willingness to honor those 12 inevitable parenting flaws our children get what they need most of all. That's why this book has been designed as a "holding environment," which you'll read more about in Chapter 4. We hope that creating a secure base for you to explore what drives your parenting will enable you to surmount the ever-present obstacle of perfectionism.

Relaxing into Confidence

Working hard at parenting from a place of constant anxiety about whether or not you're doing it right is likely not going to help your child feel more secure. Secure parenting is actually about being relaxed—more or less—in our choices, trusting that we're good enough, willing to believe that we're within the comfort zone of what will be beneficial for our child. The question this book will help you get in the habit of asking is the question your child will be asking unconsciously: "Is this about your need to be a good parent or about your child's actual need in this particular moment?" As we never tire of saying, our children almost always know what's going on just below the surface: "Are you so anxious that you're doing whatever you're doing to make sure you don't do it wrong, or are you focusing on what is actually needed here?" or "Can you (please) chill and trust that you're OK and that we'll find our way through this difficult moment?" Which is to say, "When you trust that you're good enough, I can calm down and find the soothing I most need in my distress."

Current research from Germany shows that parents who are relaxed instead of vigilant or overfocused on their infants have infants with less anxiety. Too much focus, being hyperinvolved, actually feels overwhelming to a child. The message: Babies and young children seem capable of picking up the underlying tone of what we do as much as the actions of our doing. If we're worried, they somehow recognize this. The research implies that helping parents regulate their own emotions—so that they come to their child with confidence and ease—is very important; it may even be central.

So. From our experience this is best done by helping parents make sense of the parenting landscape and, with a simple road map (the Circle of Security, illustrated and fully described in the next chapter), realize that there are key themes that need to be recognized and responded to, but never from a position of fear or anxiety or pressure to do everything "just right." "I'm able to respond in this way because I can trust it is important, not because it feels like I'll harm my child irreparably if I don't."

Keeping Our Eye on the Circle

When daily hassles interfere with our ability to respond confidently and calmly to our children, as they will constantly, we can easily get pulled away from what's going on and not see what the child needs from us in that moment. Does she need to be held and comforted for a little while? Does she need to run with her imagination and zest for life and go out and explore with the confidence that someone is waiting for her if it all becomes too scary? In our haste to get things done and be "good" parents, we sometimes leap to "*Why* does my son need comfort right now?" or "*Why* is my daughter itching to run around when it's bedtime?" Of course it makes sense to figure out what's behind certain needs so we can go through whatever problem-solving process is called for. But first we have to know we can identify the need itself. The Circle of Security, mapped out in full in Chapter 3, can be imprinted in our minds so that we can call it up whenever we're confused about what our child is after. Acknowledging and accepting that need will go a long way toward further understanding of our child and his or her uniqueness.

Being-With: Attuning to Our Child's Emotions and Needs

For many of us, the pressure to "get it right" requires constant doing, whether it's reading up on the latest parenting advice, getting our children into the best schools, or managing their behavior. The antidote to focusing primarily on the future ("What *will* he need to succeed?") is what we call Being-With ("What does he need right now?"). This is a state of sensitive attunement where we share in (without fully adopting) our child's emotional experience, helping the child understand and regulate difficult feelings and staying with him while he gets through it. Being-With means sitting still—not trying to change your child's experience but accepting it and showing that you're here with him in it as another human being who struggles with similar feelings. Being-With takes practice for many of us achievers, but it will go a long way toward nurturing a secure attachment. It's the subject of Chapter 4.

Keeping Our Hand on the Circle: Balancing Sensitive Responding with Taking Charge

Actually, these two are not mutually exclusive. A major "rule" of the Circle of Security is, Whenever possible, follow your child's needs; whenever necessary, take charge. To figure out which is the best response at any moment, we need to Be-With the child and also remember that as parents we are bigger, stronger, wiser, and always kind. We are parents first, not friends. Emotional discomfort can be managed when we take charge and help our children find a way through current struggles. Problems can be solved—together—with trust and encouragement from us. With the map of the Circle of Security in mind, we'll become more adept at intuiting our child's needs, and with the attunement made possible by Being-With, we'll have a better idea of where our child really is on the Circle. Both Being-With and being bigger, stronger, wiser, and kind are covered in Chapter 4.

Sorting through Our Baggage

A major discovery in our work has been that parents often have trouble recognizing and responding to certain needs on the Circle. But they may not see themselves reacting in this way at all, because those reactions are rooted in their own childhood upbringing and attachment experiences. Please know that this is not an indirect way of saying that whatever you do is your own parents' fault. In fact, as we've found in our own lives, trying to explore our parents' own attachment style has opened a way of creating compassion and empathy for them and the struggles they dealt with. Do you feel driven to have the "perfect child" because being perfect was valued highly by your own parents? Do you feel uncomfortable when your child edges toward independence because your own parents didn't seem to like you to stray too far from their side when you were young? How much you want to delve into your own attachment style is up to you, but you'll be introduced to how it pulls your parenting strings in Chapter 5. You then learn in Chapter 6 how we tend to pass on these messages regarding needs to our children, who cooperate by avoiding needs we find uncomfortable as a way to keep us less anxious and available. Understanding how our children behave to try to hide needs we're uncomfortable with can help us override our unrecognized mental messages and form the secure attachment we want to create.

Wishing You Well on Your Journey to Secure Attachment

We are writing this book because the three of us know, firsthand, why attachment matters. A part of this knowing is the result of our decades of clinical work with adults who consistently needed to return to and gradually change core conclusions they had formed about themselves and others during their earliest years.

But it gets a bit more personal. As co-originators of the Circle of Security we have also been asking ourselves about our own experiences of attachment and how they impact our personal lives. As it turns out, each of us emerged from a family that struggled in small and large ways when facing the very issues we now help parents make sense of. Which is to say that this work was often created from the inside out, a way of making sense of current research within the context of our personal understanding of how essential healthy attachment actually is.

As you will find throughout this book, the focus is on the richness and value of supporting secure attachment: a capacity learned within a particular kind of relationship that allows for joy when life goes well and resilience when life gets difficult. Attachment security is its own reward: once established it offers those who experience it a depth of trust and opportunities for success at an emotional, intellectual, and interpersonal level that supports lasting fulfillment through the lifespan.

That's the good news of what you're about to read. There is no bad news, but that doesn't mean the journey to secure attachment is entirely smooth and straightforward. In the early days of our entry into attachment research it wasn't uncommon for each of us to feel a certain sense of difficulty as we recognized the implications of what was needed for a secure attachment and what might have been absent in our own upbringing. These revelations can be tough at first, although they ultimately lead to the insight that our own parents did their best but had no way of recognizing what wasn't actually working well and what might be more effective. This book is our attempt to help you recognize what does work well and where you struggle to be a truly good-enough parent. We hope you'll feel that it's also a holding environment for you as you proceed on your own journey.

In our work with street-dependent/homeless and other struggling parents, when feelings of hopelessness have threatened to overtake us, we've found that there comes a moment when we see one of the young moms—a child raising a child—reach for her little one with remarkable tenderness or smile with stunning care as her child smiles back. And it's then that we know that *at least this much is real.*

In fact, one of the greatest gifts we've received from attachment research is the confirmation that the world in which we live is actually coherent. Deeper than the complexity (and all of the crazed reactivity that we see in response to the "too much" of life) is a pure simplicity, a truth we've come to trust: No one does well without "and"; every heart is still seeking the love it was born to know.

A MAP FOR ATTACHMENT

The Circle of Security

When your newborn baby gazes at you with complete vulnerability, it's as if you have your child's heart, seeking the love it was born to know, cradled in your hand. Will you be worthy? Your baby thinks you already are. Will you know what he needs?

Believe it or not, you have very little to worry about. Your baby is right there to help you figure it all out. As parents, even brand-new ones, we have the opportunity to discover that learning is reciprocal within a secure attachment. Babies learn from us, seeking us out so we'll share what they need to know, but they also teach, reminding us that within the "and" of the parent–child bond, so much goodness and wonder are possible.

Babies are not just students. They are also our teachers.

This interdependent relationship plays an important evolutionary role and, on an individual level, has an important developmental purpose. We like to think it's even more, because no one can explain the depth of love between a parent and a child. But let's start with how this mutuality enables parents without experience and babies without language to figure out between them what's needed.

How Babies Learn within the "And"

Since the mid-20th century, we've known that babies are unbelievably efficient learners. Decades ago Daniel Stern, a pioneer in infant developmental science, called them the best researchers on the planet. At that time it wasn't easy to observe the infant learning process, but now digital video allows us to see changes in babies' expressions and actions as often as every one-twenty-eighth of a second by freezing film of their interactions with their caregivers. Each change we can see represents a shift in the baby's internal world—an amalgam of feelings, actions, and experience—as the baby takes in external information and processes it on the inside. It's as if we can actually see the mental and emotional gears turning. And, oh, how they turn when the baby is engaged with another person! Babies seem to know intuitively that they need help from someone who really cares to make any sense of their internal experience. Fortunately, this doesn't mean Mom or Dad (or whoever else functions in this role) is the only go-to person the child will accept or even seek out. At a very young age babies learn to recognize smiling, attentive adults as open to interacting and will engage with them. As developmental psychologist Edward Tronick has pointed out, they quickly learn to distinguish Mom-who-is-there-for-whatever-I-need from Uncle-Louie-who-plays-exciting-games-with-me-but-always-hands-me-off-when-I-get-too-scared. An important benefit of this learning is figuring out who is going to be a good-enough backup caregiver. Somehow babies understand that it's always good to have some spares.

The more they connect with others, the more they learn. The fact that a developing baby is designed to receive internal and external input—making the baby an "open system" in scientific terms—means the baby has great potential to grow with a lot of human contact. Over the first months of her life, Sophie learned that she could count on many others in her world—Dad, Grandma and Grandpa, Aunt Liz, her regular babysitter—to be there for her, and this gave her the confidence to interact with new people as well. She spoke her first words well before age 1, she recognized her long-distance grandmother at 1½ after not having seen her for several months, and when approached by strangers she got quiet and reached for her mother for reassurance that it was OK to engage with them, which she did when she got the go-ahead and Mom stayed close. Before she was 2 she regularly demonstrated empathy, handing her teddy bear to a crying baby at the playground and beginning to cry herself when a family member expressed upset. Hannah knew she was seeing a little girl who was going to be at ease and adept in navigating a complex world. Was all this a direct result of Sophie's earliest relationships? Maybe not completely, but they set the tone of learning for the little girl.

Our early relationships give us an arena in which to try to gain a coherent sense of who we are, who the other person is, and what we're doing together. When we're sensitive and responsive to each other, Edward Tronick has said, a connection is made, and "there is an experience of growth and exuberance, a sense of continuity, and a feeling of being in sync along with a sense of knowing the other's sense of the world." Babies learn who they are as they connect with who we are. This makes connections with others the best classroom we can ever have. That's great news: This classroom charges no tuition, and it's available everywhere we look. But it can also be a bit daunting.

It's disconcerting because it's the quality of the connection that counts. We've all experienced this phenomenon. A stranger on the bus sees that you're near tears as you think about a dear friend you just lost, makes eye contact, and gives you her seat. You learn something about kindness, about intuition, and about your value as a fellow traveler, even to someone who has never laid eyes on you before. A teenager comes home from a party after suffering a humiliating rejection by a boy she has a crush on and finds her mother, who never waits up for her, sitting in the living room. Mom takes one look at her daughter and just waits, smiling gently, until her daughter opens up. As the girl relives the offense with increasing indignation, Mom matches her resentment just enough to let her daughter get over the venting and get on with the grieving. The teen learns that when our emotions are valued, we can let them do their job and move on.

> The two-person comfort zone of attachment is known scientifically as a "dyadic regulatory system," where "dyadic" means simply that the regulation goes on between two people.

When we interact with someone we trust, we enter a kind of two-person comfort zone. Hannah senses that baby Sophie is afraid, and so she picks her up and holds her close. In response, Sophie quiets. In the same moment, Hannah gains confidence as a mother, Sophie gains confidence that her fear is manageable, and the loving bond between them grows stronger. When we respond appropriately and sensitively to each other's internal experience, and adjust our behavior accordingly, we build trust and gain meaning from the other person and develop a level of psychological complexity we couldn't have achieved on our own. In other words, babies need empathic connection to thrive. And they definitely need it to learn.

This is, tragically, nowhere more evident than in the damage done by lack of connection. Children raised in some orphanages and other settings where no such shared connection is available just don't learn and don't thrive. Even a momentary break in connection—such as where a person adopts what researchers call a "still face" (expressionless, unreacting)—is enough to make an infant angry, frustrated, or withdrawn. If the lack of connection continues, children become sad and more chronically withdrawn. When connection is virtually absent, babies not only become depressed, distressed, and listless—they don't develop at all.

Guessing versus Seeing

Fortunately, most parents respond sensitively much of the time—again, well over 50% of parent–child duos become securely attached naturally. They understand their child's needs and their child's ways of expressing them, and most of the time they answer them. But besides the many distractions that can interfere, our own internal world (known as our state of mind) can sometimes keep us from seeing what our child needs. We bring a fairly sophisticated understanding to our interactions with our children, which is a big part of why we can sensitively interpret what our baby is feeling and help her regulate those emotions well before she can do it herself. But it also leads to assumptions. We often think we know more than we actually know.

If you're within view of other people right now, take a minute to look at them. Do you immediately get an idea of their state of mind? At ease or uncomfortable? Happy or sad? Energized or tired? Angry or frustrated—and, if so, about what? There's a very good chance that, especially if you know these people well, you think you know what's going on in their minds.

We call this totally normal phenomenon "guessing versus seeing." Guessing about our children's state of mind kicks in when we're distracted by a million other things going on or have tasks to accomplish. It kicks in when we're tired or ill or annoyed. (It also gets triggered by a very deeply ingrained type of state of mind that we call "core sensitivities," but that's the subject of Chapter 5, and we won't go into it now.) And it's a natural product of what we've already learned about our own child (or other people's children if this is our first).

The problem with guessing versus seeing is that accurately "seeing" our child's internal world in any given moment is the key to dyadic or shared regulation. If we guess that our 3-year-old son is angry because he won't stop crying and gets louder the more frustrated we get, we'll react differently than we would if we stop to look more closely at what's going on (which might be simply frustration at not being able to work a toy correctly). If we guess that our 19-month-old daughter is hungry because she keeps pointing at the kitchen, we might get her something to eat when what she wants is to be carried into the kitchen so she can show us that she can fill a cup with water.

Of course responding to our children (and everyone else) always involves a certain amount of guesswork when needs aren't stated directly. And a big part of well-regulated interactions is making errors and then making up for them. We learn as much from that as from being right the first time around. That's fortunate, because very young babies often can't tell us exactly what they need and we're going to have to indulge in a certain amount of guesswork (You may feel that you're guessing not just some of the time but all of the time!). The goal is to find a way to attune to our child so that our guesses are accurate most of the time. (In Chapter 4 we talk about how we can stay attuned to our children in the midst of everyday chaos.) At the foundation of our work is the understanding that parents do better at both seeing and guessing if they have a map of what their children need.

Enter the Circle of Security.

Meeting Children's Needs around the Circle of Security

After years of working with families we've found that life can interfere with the instinctual attunement between parent and child in an infinite number of ways. Whatever the cause, we've also come to trust that a child's drive to attach and his needs within his attachment system are almost always hidden in plain sight. As parents, what we need is a

The Circle of Security.

way to bring these needs into clear view, especially in the heat of the moment when we can feel lost or overwhelmed. The Circle of Security (COS) was devised as a simple road map, a way to quickly and accurately know what need our child is exhibiting in any given moment.

The Circle depicts all three of the central or core needs within the attachment system defined by John Bowlby and Mary Ainsworth: careseeking, exploration, and caregiving. Careseeking is shown on the bottom of the Circle—the need for a safe haven (comfort in the face of vulnerability) that children turn to their parents for. Exploration is on the top of the Circle—the need for a secure base from which children can set out and launch their need for autonomy. The hands on the Circle represent parents and their caregiving. Interestingly, while attachment theory had always acknowledged both attachment behaviors (careseeking) and exploratory behaviors (building mastery), when we originally created the Circle of Security, we did not depict exploration in terms of a "need"—until Jude Cassidy stated that children need a secure base for exploration as much as they need a safe haven for comfort. Meeting both needs is critical to secure attachment and to the child's developing emotional regulation skills.

**The Circle of Security shows that little children can be
viewed as constantly "going out and coming in."***

---

*You can view an animated depiction of "going out and coming in" on our website: *www.circleofsecurity.com.*

In Chapter 1 we described a scene in which 3-year-old Lei ran back and forth between the playground equipment and her father. This scenario showed how children travel around the Circle over and over in mere minutes. They do the same thing throughout their day, exploring, then seeking comfort or reassurance or safety and, once they've filled their emotional cup, running out to explore again—at home, in child care or preschool, at the homes of relatives and friends, at the dentist's office, while shopping, and at the beach. The journey and the interaction between caregiver and child vary depending on the setting and the child's age (among other factors). A parent of a 2-year-old who is screaming in fear at having his mouth examined by a dentist will quickly try to comfort the child. A parent with a 4-year-old may have to look for more subtle signals that he's a little freaked out by having his teeth examined and give him a reassuring nod or a squeeze of his hand—just enough to let him know that he is OK. Giving him this chance to calm his fears allows him to go out and "explore" further, even if exploring means just sitting cooperatively in the chair and seeing what happens. At exciting places for children, like the beach, it might be hard to tell when a child is approaching the parent as a safe haven and when he needs a secure base: Is he running back to Dad with different shells to engage Dad in his exploration or to take a break from the slightly scary movement of the waves lapping the shore?

If you have children (rather than expecting your first), take a little time today to watch them through the lens of the Circle of Security diagram. Can you see when your child is on the top of the Circle and when on the bottom?

> *"Depending on where our daughter is on the Circle, it allows us to recognize what her needs are throughout the day. It shows us that each of Amy's actions has a purpose. The Circle also taught us that Amy needs us in every aspect of her life, whether right by our side or at a distance."*
>
> —Eric and Claudia, Florida

Why a Circle?

We chose a circle to depict secure attachment because so much about security is a matter of balance. Knowing that our children's needs for autonomy and vulnerability are of equal importance turns out to be among the most important aspects of our teaching. Once parents come

A Fairy Tale of Real Life

Once upon a time, in fact all through time, in a faraway place, and in every place, children have needed to be held in safety and security. It was in being held that our curiosity about the world was born. Because we were confident somebody was there for us, we were able to venture out across great distances, undertake amazing feats, and learn new skills. We loved exploring so much, because always—always—we knew deep in our heart that we would be welcomed back in by the ones who cared so much. Almost like drinking from a magical well, we soaked up this love and encouragement from this important person. And then, as if by surprise, we were off—out into the amazing world of new possibilities. Although these new possibilities were delightful to explore, no matter how far away we would go, we found ourselves looking back to make sure that important person was still there, because this is a story of adventure and love.

The security of knowing that we would be welcomed back into the loving arms of that important person gave us the courage and confidence to take on the world. For we were as sure as sure can be that when things were too much for us alone, the ones who loved us were willing and able to help.

Having help when help was needed made it fun for us to explore so we could learn to be successful in the world. So we would come back in and then, just like that, out we went. We knew that special someone would watch over us and was ever ready to welcome us back. This combination taught us the most important lesson of all.

The End.

Or perhaps we should say, "The Beginning."

to recognize, honor, and balance both themes, children are more likely to experience security: trust in themselves and trust in those they need most.

Different but Not Separate

As Sophie demonstrated, children start life trying to develop a healthy sense of self by seeking a connection with someone else. As noted earlier, developmental scientists have observed over and over that we learn who we are through our relation to others and how that under-standing of "us" and "them" undergirds the rest of our emotional lives. This illustrates a balancing act that we try to master throughout life: How do I have close relationships without losing my individuality? How do I maintain my individuality without losing the ability to be part of an "and"? How do I know when to rely on myself and when to turn to others? Children start learning about this balancing act in shared moments with their parents when they need help regulating their ever-changing state of mind. Children learn that when Mom is sensitive to shifts in their state of mind, she knows when to offer com-fort and when to offer encouragement. These shifts are continuous and seamless, which is why the unbroken line of a circle or an oval seemed so appropriate to us. It's also the way very young children like Lei in Chapter 1 go back and forth between a parent and their own explora-tions throughout their day.

> *When children are exploring, they need us just as much as they do when they are in our lap.*

Emotional Regulation

It's the same with emotional regulation. As Chapter 1 explained, our experience of trusting the ones to whom we're attached helps us learn to regulate our own emotions by giving us someone to regulate them for us and then regulate them with us (so-called coregulation) so that, eventually, we learn how to do this by ourselves. A big part of attach-ment throughout childhood (and the rest of the lifespan, in fact) is figuring out when to rely on ourselves and when to seek help. How do I manage my enthusiasm and curiosity unless someone sponsors and supports my intense interest in the world? How do I make sense of painful feelings unless someone helps me by offering understanding and concern when they emerge? And emerge they do, countless times each day. It's in these little moments on the top and bottom of the Circle that a child is introduced to how feelings can be regulated, both experienced and controlled. We don't learn to greet our feelings, espe-cially the difficult ones, alone. We learn to greet them in relationship. As this happens we learn to trust how we feel and our capacity grows in learning how to care for and honor the feelings of others.

A Holding Environment

Circles have been used to represent people coming together out of mutual need, empathy, and celebration throughout history—from pagan rituals to modern prayer circles, from protective borders to close-knit communities, in Native American, Celtic, ancient Chinese, and many other cultures' symbolism. No other form seems as perfect to depict the attachment relationship as a circle. Pediatrician and psychoanalyst Donald Winnicott called the atmosphere created in secure attachment a "holding environment," where parents help their young children manage difficult internal experiences by sharing them. One of our mentors, Daniel Stern, described this holding of feelings as "Being-With," a way of honoring difficulty rather than getting over it—a process of joining a child's experience and normalizing it as part of the human condition while showing that it can be managed successfully. The all-important learning: It's possible to turn to others for help when needed.

The circle is also a good graphic metaphor for the phenomenon of parent–child relationships: All parents periodically fail to recognize and meet their child's needs, and this can briefly rupture the Circle, leaving the relationship incomplete (although reparable). This also allows us to see that when we aren't meeting our child's needs around the Circle it's because we just got off balance—not that we did something terribly wrong. Relieving us of self-blame promotes self-honesty, which also frees us to look at the Circle's map of needs with a clear eye so we can discern what we might need to do to get balanced again.

In sum, we chose a circle to depict children's attachment needs because of the simple elegance and the clarity it brings.

The Top of the Circle: A Child's Need for a Secure Base

When children feel safe and secure, their curiosity automatically kicks in and they want to learn about the world. But before they set off to explore, they need to feel they have our full support to go out and discover their new world. With support from us, children head out for grand adventures. We call this full support "filling their cup." It's not unlike leaving home with enough gas to get where you want to go.

When we were devising the Circle of Security, we watched thousands of hours of children interacting with their parents, in real time and on video, to distinguish among the following four needs involved in supporting children's exploration and four needs involved in offering them comfort, shown in the full Circle of Security diagram below. The distinctions are subtle and became clearer with the ability to freeze a scene from one fraction of a second to another. We are constantly refining our observation skills and are always awed by the challenge of seeing children's subtle shifts in needs. Parents' intimate connection with their own children invariably makes them more astute, but even with that personal clarity children's needs are hard to discern all the time.

Watch Over Me

Sometimes a toddler just needs us to be there, sort of on standby. Imagine your 2-year-old sitting on the floor, concentrating hard on stacking blocks. Believe it or not, he might quit prematurely if you leave the room. Your relaxed presence isn't "doing nothing." It makes your little boy's learning and discovery possible. Babies often need little more to encourage their exploration than a parent watching over them as they turn their gaze to new sights, sounds, and touches. With a little experience you learn to recognize your infant's need for interaction, and your baby learns that you're available when needed—and therefore gains courage and confidence to stretch out a little farther.

*The Circle of Security showing the child's needs
for a safe haven and a secure base.*

The Challenge: Just being there. In our culture of high achievers, it can be incredibly hard to do nothing but watch. Parents can easily get caught up in the mandate to create "quality time," which most of us interpret as a choreographed shared activity in which we give the child our undivided attention and play an active role of nurturing, molding, shepherding, coaxing, teaching . . . you get the picture. If your child seems to be playing contentedly by himself, try holding back on joining in, waiting for some sign from him—a prolonged gaze at you, reaching out a hand, or explicitly asking for your participation—before assuming he wants you to do any more than watch.

Delight in Me

Sometimes children and babies switch from just wanting us to watch them to wanting us to show delight in who they are. If your child looks up at you during play, you smile with warmth and eye contact, and your child then wriggles in joy or smiles back and eagerly turns back to her play, you'll know what she was looking for was your delight in her. The earlier in life your baby knows you find her delightful just as she is, the more confident she'll be and the more self-esteem she'll build—because she knows the most important person in her life finds her valuable and lovable just as she is.

The Challenge: Knowing the difference between delighting in who your child is and delighting in what she does. Both are important, but it's essential that a child not grow up believing she's only as good as her last gold star, home run, or A+. Sometimes "delight in me" needs are best met nonverbally, to avoid the temptation to say "Good girl!" or "Great job!" or "Nice block building!" When you feel like verbally expressing enthusiasm for what your child is doing, ask yourself whether you're feeling pride in her reaching some developmental goal you have in mind ("She's walking so early!") and do your best to cast that off and just welcome what a delightful being you have before you. When she looks back and sees the quiet twinkle in your eyes, she'll learn something about herself that all of the praise in the world couldn't possibly teach.

Enjoy with Me

Here's where you do participate more fully in whatever your child is doing. Sometimes children want us to share their activities and adventures. Maybe your 3-year-old wants you to play make-believe with him using his stuffed animals. Maybe your 2-year-old wants you to narrate what she's doing: "I see you're putting all the animals in the barn. Maybe it's cold outside." These moments *are* often the appropriate times to say "Wow! What a nice drawing!" Children need to take joy in their achievements to take growth-promoting risks and develop competency, and your narration and supportive comments get the ball rolling for them. (Praise, however, can take on too prominent a role in parenting, as we note in Chapter 8.)

For babies, "enjoy with me" often means looking at the world through their eyes and talking to them about it. Not only does this help them develop self-worth and a sense of accomplishment—"Yes, I'm good at this and he notices"—but it also helps them develop an understanding of how minds work. When Dad says, "The bear is very soft—it feels good, doesn't it?" the baby knows that what Dad sees is what she sees but that her mind is separate; sometimes Dad is only guessing at what she's feeling. We have shared minds, the baby learns, but they aren't exactly the same. This "theory of mind" is a critical brick in the building of the self, helping babies grasp the difference (and commonality) between themselves and others. Being able to take another person's perspective is the foundation of empathy, and being able to fit together internal experience with language that is personally meaningful develops healthy individuality.

The Challenge: Knowing how to share and enjoy your child's activity without taking over. We've seen toddlers deflate in the midst of play they were enjoying when an adult not only plays along but starts to direct the activity or quiz the child without paying any attention to the child's state of mind or desires. If your child quiets and stops participating, you know you might have gone too far and it's time to show that you don't know what the child wants all the time but are always interested

> Stopping yourself when you see your child deflate because you started to take over or stepping back after noticing your child's upset when you've begun to require that he perform for you are examples of what we call "rupture and repair"—when the Circle is broken by parents' inevitable minor gaffes and then repaired by their sensitive acknowledgment that they understand they made a mistake. Even the youngest children thereby begin to learn that these "mistakes" are just part of being human—that no one is perfect and what matters is *caring enough to notice and change our behavior.*

in finding out. This honoring of separate minds will pay big dividends as your child gets older. (Part of why children push back and even rebel in their teen years is connected to their legitimate need to have their own initiative and thinking welcomed by another. If this doesn't start early, it can show up as a struggle as they mature.) Saying "Do you want to put the next block on?" or "I think you want me to watch you for a while" sends an important message that you're available but not intrusive.

Another Challenge: Being responsive to overstimulation. For babies, there is a risk that "enjoy with me" moments will become overstimulating. Even with positive emotion, an infant can have too much of a good thing. If your baby seems to be enjoying peekaboo or another game with you but suddenly looks away, she is trying to tell you that the interaction is too much and she is trying to calm herself. This is an important moment to follow the baby's need, because it conveys that you find all of the baby's emotions and needs acceptable. Trying to regain the baby's attention by stepping up the entertainment you're providing says you're not comfortable with whatever internal experience the baby is struggling with. She needs you to help her calm herself, and one important aspect of that is giving her space and time.

You can see the same thing in older children when they suddenly start hitting or pushing over toys in what had a moment before been a fun activity. If you've ever seen a toddler laughing with glee at being tickled and suddenly acting like he's in pain, you've seen this kind of overstimulation. Our subtle presence rather than a more active presence can make such a difference.

Help Me

Sometimes children need help when they're exploring. In these moments they need just enough from Mom or Dad to learn to do new tasks by themselves. Or they need help to keep going on an endeavor for long enough to experience a sense of mastery. Picture a baby who can't sit up by himself for very long. Mom might sit behind him with a hand on his back to provide stability so the baby can explore other abilities, like reaching for a toy in front of him. If he can't quite get it or it keeps slipping out of his hand, he's naturally going to get frustrated. But given a little time, he just might figure it out and learn that he can master this action with a little effort (and, for now, a little help).

Or imagine a toddler trying to complete a puzzle that belongs to her kindergarten brother. She so desperately wants to keep up with him but gets more and more frustrated at not having the fine motor skills to manipulate the wooden pieces. You could put them in for her, or you could pull out an age-appropriate puzzle and let her work at that until she has some success. And then let her try the other puzzle again, a little at a time. Teens also need this available-yet-respectful stance when they're trying to navigate all the changes that life suddenly sends their way. Sometimes an adolescent will turn to us when we make it clear we're open for a discussion but also supportive of their choice in timing a conversation to be most helpful.

The Challenge: Achieving balance between offering too much and offering too little help. Without any help, young children lose interest and self-confidence if success continually eludes them. They'll also miss out on learning that others can be a resource for learning. With too much help, they won't learn to trust in their own capacity and won't develop the creative use of frustration to learn new skills. They may also learn that they can't do important tasks without our direction. In these ways, learning is hampered. Trying things that are at the edge of their developmental ability is exactly how our sons and daughters grow. But for parents it's always difficult to decide in the moment whether to wait and let a baby or toddler struggle or to help—and if you help, whether to do it for him or help him figure out how to do it himself. Even the most talented teachers in the world can't get this right all the time, despite astute observation and sensitive responding. Sometimes we just don't have time—either to help or to let our children work it out. We all make mistakes here.

> *Scaffolding—giving just enough help to allow children to learn to do it themselves—is a major benefit of the "and" for them: When we help just enough, they gain confidence in themselves yet recognize that it has come through our support.*

The Bottom of the Circle: A Child's Need for a Safe Haven

The idea of a child's needing comfort seems pretty clear-cut. A baby cries and Mom whispers, "There, there" as she cradles her infant and gently rocks her. A 3-year-old's face crumples when her idolized older brother yells at her to stay away from his toys, and Dad says, "It's OK, honey, he's not really mad; it's just a new truck" as he pats her on the head. But children's needs for a safe haven aren't always that simple. Just like the needs on the top of the Circle, the needs on the bottom can be subtle and the shifts rapid.

Children move to the bottom of the Circle when tired, frightened, hungry, uncomfortable, or their emotional cup is empty. That's when they need us to welcome them coming to us. We need to fill their emotional cup to provide our full support for their returning to the adventure of exploring their world.

Protect Me

This need might seem too obvious to state. It is not, however, that we just need to protect our babies and older children from physical, mental, and emotional harm. We need to do it in a way that sends the message that we're committed to protecting them, that they can count on us. Imagine how you'd feel if you were defenseless and the person who was supposed to be your caregiver helped you out sometimes but not others, or protected you from aggressive dogs but smirked when you shrank from the person down the street who'd once bullied you, or acted like protecting you was a chore that the caregiver detested. If you had such a caregiver, you'd probably feel threatened, even when sitting in your safe, warm living room, because you would know that something bad could happen to you at any time. You'd be on constant high alert, cortisol racing through your bloodstream and subjecting you to all the damage of excess stress we talked about in Chapter 1.

An infant, new to this big and sometimes scary world, definitely needs someone to be right there to protect her even when her fear signals aren't loud and clear, because she hasn't yet sorted out this experience called fear. Having a caregiver who can read her subtle cues for help, offering presence in the face of seeming danger, can bring the soothing that is required for a sense of security.

The Challenge: Again, balance. It's important to help our children when fear overtakes them even if we know they have nothing to fear. So we not only have to protect them from things they can't protect themselves from and from things they haven't yet learned are dangerous but also help them manage their emotions when fear overwhelms them. Sometimes just moving closer or putting a hand on the shoulder of a toddler facing something new and/or scary (rowdy older children at the playground, being introduced to adults he's never seen in his home before, the first day of preschool, his first playdate without Mom or Dad, a checkup) can give a young child the protection he needs without sending a four-alarm warning that might make him develop a lifelong fear of novelty. We need to guard against imposing our own fears on a child, because that invalidates his own personal experience just as much as mocking his fear would. Understanding the cry that means your baby is afraid and not wet or hungry gives him the confidence that you'll be there to protect him whenever needed.

Comfort Me

Children need to be comforted for all kinds of distress. They get tired, hungry, hurt, scared, lonely, frustrated, or confused by a bewildering world and need tenderness and soothing many times during the day. The younger they are, the more important it may be to offer a little empathic comfort along with a feeding or a Band-Aid. These heartfelt gestures tell them not only that you'll be there to ease their physical discomfort but also that you accept the emotions they are feeling and can help them regulate these feelings too. This is why many child-rearing experts strongly suggest cradling your baby in your arms and making warm eye contact while you feed her instead of watching TV or checking your e-mail. Here again, the child learns that she can overcome distress with the care of another and therefore risk going out into the world where she's bound to become uncomfortable on and off but also learns that she can turn to others for comfort—a lesson that will help her form good reciprocal relationships throughout life.

  The Challenge: Keeping the "you" in "us." That is, making it clear that you understand and can resonate with your child's emotional experience without taking on that experience yourself. It's hard not to go too far in trying to convey an empathic connection, especially when your parental instinct makes you feel for your child. To help a baby or young child understand that our feelings are our own but we can get help with them from someone else who cares, it's important to display what Daniel Stern called a "feeling-shape" similar to your child's, by matching the child's feeling with your facial expression, voice, body language, and touch, and avoid imposing any distress of your own evoked by the child's feelings. A baby who is wailing in distress doesn't need a parent who wails in response but someone who makes a sad face, touches her gently, and speaks with soft understanding so the child can think, "Oh, you do understand how I feel, and I'm not alone in it. I'm also learning that this feeling can be shared and trusted."

Delight in Me

There are two kinds of delight on the bottom of the Circle. The first has to do with the moments your little one will turn to you or run to you, not because she is distressed, but because she's feeling the need to fill her emotional cup, a kind of refueling. She may rush in for a quick smile and then, 2 seconds later, be back out on the top of the Circle, ready to take on the world.

> **Delight → Positive Relationships → Love**
>
> "Delight in me" is the only need found on both the top and the bottom of the Circle. Parents who truly delight in their child, whether the child is exploring or needing to be close, promote such a positive relationship that their children tend to be more secure. They also plant the seeds for the capacity to develop intimacy with a romantic partner. Moments of gazing into Mom's or Dad's eyes while experiencing happiness, curiosity, and glee is the start of understanding that very positive feelings can be shared with beloved others and thereby sustained. Some people call it "falling in love."

The second kind of delight on the bottom of the Circle has to do with our subtle ease when our child is feeling upset or overwhelmed. It's not easy to delight in a baby who is screaming in anguish because he's exhausted and doesn't know how to relax himself enough to sleep or a 3-year-old who is writhing in frustration at not having the motor skills to operate a toy or ride a bike. But our children need us to delight in them even when they're in distress—maybe *especially* when they're in distress. This isn't over-the-top delight (which would feel like mocking), but "I sure love you, even when things don't feel so great" delight. You can probably think of times when you've been upset and your go-to person (spouse, best friend, sibling?) not only matches your feeling-shape but also briefly smiles and makes it clear that, even in distress, you are cherished. In that moment your entire body suddenly relaxes. It sometimes requires great equanimity, but being able to experience delight and affection in the face of our child's distress and what might seem like demands for help (even when it's not shown directly) is a great gift we can give to our children. The hidden message: "I know you're upset, I know I love you, and I know this too shall pass." Such affectionate confidence is very reassuring to children.

The Challenge: Again, going too far. The delight we show in a fussy baby or an acting-out child has to be mixed with an accepting understanding of what the child is feeling. To coo at a distressed baby with a big grin on our face or try to jolly a toddler out of frustration could easily send the message that we don't get or want to feel what the child is feeling; we just want it to stop. It can be experienced as our being either clueless or uncaring. Sadly, given the clinical experiences the three of us have had, it is all too common for a parent to push a baby or child away from feelings that seem too intense or difficult. Our need to have a "happy baby" may temporarily pull an infant from her distress, but it will also teach her that some feelings can't be shared.

Organize My Feelings

As described in Chapter 1, emotional regulation is a critical skill for us humans to learn, and it develops in the cradle of secure attachment—within the Circle. Our emotions are hugely valuable as signals to us about what we need, value, and desire, and therefore it's important that we be able to experience them, understand them, trust them, and share them. But it's also essential that we be able to manage them. If we get overwhelmed by them, we won't be able to function very well. If we express them inappropriately, we might block our own goals, impose on others, demonstrate lack of understanding of others' feelings, and have trouble sustaining relationships. Learning to manage feelings and experience empathy from another in our earliest relationships clearly impacts our capacity to experience healthy relationships later in life.

> "Acting out" is distress expressed outwardly through behavior in a way that we can see it—screaming, hitting, throwing a tantrum. "Acting in" is turning distress inward—withdrawal, depression, and, in adolescence, taking distress out on ourselves in ways that are less noticeable to the outside world yet clearly problematic (negativity toward the self and issues of self-harm).

Children enter the world with a rich repertoire of emotions but with little ability to understand what they mean or how to calm them. That's why they need us to help regulate their emotions for them, then with them, and gradually teach them to—some of the time—regulate them on their own. It's important to start this early. Imagine a frightened baby whose parent thinks her "fussiness" can be eased with a little entertainment and who therefore starts to toss her up in the air and catch her, making loud "woo" noises to signal that the baby is supposed to find this fun and exciting. Internally the baby will be saying, "Hey, what's wrong with you? Why don't you get it? Why are you scaring me even more?" and will, with repeat performances of this parental response, begin to think it must be because her feelings are "wrong" or "ugly" and her needs can't be met. How will she respond? Over time she may learn to numb her sadness or fear and lose touch with all the information and guidance those rich emotions offer. Or she may shove them down, where they could fester into the seeds of chronic anxiety or hidden loneliness. She won't have any conscious memory of learning to respond to her feelings in these ways; this learning becomes part of what is called "procedural memory" (see the box on page 78).

By the way, you don't have to "like" your baby's or child's emotions. You don't have to enjoy the expression of them. But you need to demonstrate overall that you can accept your child's feelings and that it's safe for your baby or toddler to share feelings with others who care about them. It also helps to start building your child's vocabulary for emotion. It's important to all of us to be able to name our emotions so we can figure out how to respond to them as well as how to express them. Children (and adults) who aren't taught to distinguish one emotion from another through language often confuse vulnerable feelings like sadness for anger and express all discomfort as anger. You can imagine where that gets them.

The Challenge: Guessing versus stating. Earlier we mentioned the importance of trying to see what our child needs instead of guessing. The same is true with emotions, but when we talk about them with our child, it can be really important to express that we actually are guessing what the child is experiencing. Yet again, clarifying

> We humans are gloriously complex machines, and to operate according to design many systems and functions in the body and mind need to be regulated (e.g., body temperature staying around "normal," hormones being released to do a particular job and then receding, hunger telling us when it's time to eat). Emotions are supposed to be regulated too, which means they're supposed to signal us to take certain types of action and then subside. Dysregulation of emotion (or behavior) is deviation from what's typical in how, when, and how much we experience emotions.

Building Your Child's Procedural Memory

When you meet your children's earliest, fundamental needs around the Circle of Security, you're installing memories that become like an operating system that will hum along in the background of everything they do as they grow up. This particular kind of learning is called "procedural memory," and it's not unlike how we learn to ride a bike. We may not remember the details of being taught to ride a bike, and we don't have to run through a list of steps every time we want to cycle down the road. We just get on and know how to pedal and balance, and off we go. When your toddler has countless experiences of your soothing early on and then, gradually, soothes her own fears or stops crying on her own, it's because she has a positive foundation of procedural memory: "Your soothing is built into my self-soothing." When you say to your red-faced, weeping 9-month-old, "You're angry, and that must feel terrible . . . let me hold you and walk around with you right now, because you're really upset," your baby is learning procedurally that somebody is there with her in her distress. As she grows, you will still be with her, hidden in plain sight, as she manages her own emotions without your physical presence.

Learning through procedural memory is basically like compiling a book. If the pages of the book created by your first relationships are filled with empathy and concern, you know what to do and can proceed with confidence in many situations for which you look up an explanation or a solution. But what if a lot of the pages in your "book" are burned or torn? Then when you need to take out that book to remind yourself what to do in a certain situation or how something works, that flawed or incomplete page is all you have to go on. Now you have to fill in the blanks on your own. It turns out we don't do that very well. We flail around and often take out our confusion and discomfort on ourselves or others. This is how inability to manage emotions turns into acting out or acting in.

that we have separate minds that can be shared has profound implications for a developing child. If you say, "I know you're angry at me" (instead of saying, "I'm wondering if you're angry or upset with me") to your toddler, your child doesn't learn how important it is to try to organize his own feelings by also wondering and then discussing what he feels rather than agreeing to your interpretation of what he's feeling. It's the combination of having his own experience while you scaffold his understanding that develops a child's ability to put himself in someone else's shoes.

The goal is to teach your child that we all have our own internal experience and that, while we share the same general repertoire of emotions, and can get support for our own personal experience from others, what we feel in any given moment is uniquely ours—and ours to use and manage.

How important is it to learn to regulate emotion? What psychologists call "acting out" or "acting in" is an attempt to manage emotions with a limited skill set of healthy options learned in a healthy relationship.

Dysregulated emotion → dysregulated behavior.

The Circle of Adult Security

Self-regulation and self-soothing are essential for intimacy. But contrary to popular understanding, these aren't capacities we possess innately. They are learned in relationships with caring others. So if we want our children to grow up to be skilled in intimate relationships, it's up to us to teach them how to regulate their emotions and self-soothe. Psychologist and relationship expert John Gottman says that what makes relationships work is negotiation. Our ability to be intimate or work well together suffers when we can't negotiate. Negotiation, as it turns out, requires the capacity to recognize and name feelings and to regulate and soothe ourselves (the ability to experience and contain complex emotions) while empathically holding concern for the feelings of another. As we teach our children how to understand feelings, self-regulate, and self-soothe when young, their path through life becomes much smoother since they'll be able to negotiate. That's the gift of meeting our children's needs around the Circle.

Our diagram of the Circle of Security depicts a young child, but in reality we all travel a circle of security throughout life. It gets more complicated, but it's in our nature to seek both autonomy and relatedness. We often seek support from others to undertake new adventures in our lives and also need a haven from exploration where we can just fill our own emotional cup in the "and" of a close relationship. Some-times we switch back and forth distinctly. Maybe you call your spouse or a family member from the office for a pep talk before meeting with your boss to propose a new business plan or ask for a promotion and raise. And when your proposal is rejected, nothing feels better than finding a sympathetic ear and open arms. Other times, because we've learned how important both a secure base and a safe haven are, we can seek to have both needs met at once. Perhaps you have to attend the funeral of a loved one, and you recognize that your partner's or a close friend's quiet presence gives you the courage to explore difficult feelings of grief as well as comfort over your loss. The beauty of being capable of making secure attachments is that our journey from top to bottom of the Circle can, at times, be seamless. As we get what we need most from relationships, we can be more of who we are as individuals.

When you're under stress, try asking yourself
"Where am I on the Circle?"

Accepting Children's Needs

Let's be clear about one thing: It's important to try to interpret what our children are asking for and to respond sensitively. We firmly believe it's the best (possibly only) route to raising happy, healthy children who will become happy, healthy adults. But, as we keep saying, no one does it perfectly. None of us is entirely comfortable with all needs on the top and bottom of the Circle, mainly because we all learned that some needs are more acceptable than others from our own parents—who meant just as well for us as we do for our children. Some of us are more at ease with our children's explorations and achievements. Some are more at ease with closeness and comfort. Some of us may be better able to enjoy with our children on the top of the Circle than we are to just watch over them. Some of us are highly attuned to protecting but have difficulty soothing a distressed child. There are countless variations. You may already have an idea of where you fit in this scheme, and if you want to learn more, you'll find a lot of assistance with self-exploration in Part II.

For now, let's just say it goes without saying that none of us can meet all of our children's needs all the time. Cultural norms come into play too. In cultures that stress independence (if it's possible to generalize in that way at all), parents may be less adept at helping their sons and daughters on the bottom of the Circle. In more insular societies (again, we're not sure any whole societies can be categorized this way, but maybe certain communities, clans, villages, ethnic groups, etc., have certain tendencies), parents may struggle when their children are on the top of the Circle.

> *"There have been times when it felt strange to use the Circle of Security language and share it with families, and it took a lot of practice, but we became so sold on the Circle because it actually works. It now seems strange to hear it said any other way. I am now using the language with the children (as I would mostly only use it when I was talking with other educators). Now I name what I am seeing with the children, and I especially love the words 'I am so glad that you have come back in to see me.'*
>
> *"I continued to practice but still felt like something was missing until I discovered what would be one of my biggest challenges (but also most rewarding) was to work out where I sit on the Circle myself."*
> —Tina Murray, Australia

Think about where you might struggle. Are there situations you don't look forward to experiencing with your child? Circumstances in which you feel awkward or "at a loss for words"? If you viewed those situations as occurring somewhere around the Circle of Security, would you have a better understanding of your own attachment inclinations? We've found, for instance, that parents often have trouble seeing their child looking back for permission to explore, seeking autonomy. It's a microsecond where the initial support for the child's need to explore is requested, and we can easily let it pass. When we do, the child may hesitate just long enough to decide not to explore after all. On the bottom of the Circle one of the most common themes is discomfort with a child's being afraid in social settings. Have you ever seen a parent enter a birthday party for 3-year-olds and act mortified when her child clings to her leg instead of diving in? In this case, parents might be inclined to push their child out quickly instead of recognizing the need for protection and comfort and organization of feelings for another minute or two. When the latter is provided, the child eventually joins in; when our comfort is withheld he may have a hard time throughout the party. Recognizing a child's needs can also acquaint you with your child's unique temperament and help you anticipate certain needs. For example, the slow-to-warm-up child needs a different kind of caregiving than the resilient, go-for-it child. But if we happen to be outgoing and socially adept, we may find the reticent temperament so alien that we don't know what to do. Or, if we're more quiet and inward, having a child with a robust personality may leave us feeling either lost or overwhelmed. The Circle can ground us in a way that we can understand our unique child's needs, as well as our own, and respond appropriately.

> *Children who can use their parents all around the Circle*
> *are more securely attached and more resilient in the face*
> *of life's challenges.*

As you probably recognized through our description of children's needs on the top and bottom of the Circle, and the challenges we all face in meeting those needs, always getting it right is never a goal. What we're looking for is balance. How to aim for that is the subject of the next chapter.

BEING THE HANDS
ON THE CIRCLE

Nine-month-old Max is sitting in his high chair in front of his mother, happily scattering Cheerios around the tray, occasionally grasping a couple in his little fist and slapping his hand against his mouth, with some Cheerios hitting the goal and some ending up back on the playing field. Dana smiles at him with delight whether the Cheerios make it to their destination or not, matching her son's expression of wide-eyed glee whenever he succeeds. For the most part Dana just watches, murmuring "Oh, that tastes good, I bet" and "Yummy" or "Crunch!"

Sometimes the baby wriggles and pounds the tray and kicks so hard that the tray threatens to crash to the floor. Then he seems startled and looks away from his mother. The first time he did this, Dana tried to coax him back, saying, "Hey, Maxie, what's wrong? There's a lot of Cheerios here to finish!" Max would squirm and turn the other way, still avoiding eye contact with his mother. Dana paused, lowered her voice, and said "OK, OK, it's all right. Got a little too excited, huh?" Then she waited.

Within seconds Max had turned back to her and was greeted by her soft gaze and slight smile. He smiled back and returned to his Cheerios. Dana had the luxury of time today, so she sat with her son for about half an hour while he worked on the cereal, looked around the room, explored his fingers, and played with some toys she added to the tray. Sometimes she enjoyed his activity with him; sometimes she offered a little help, nudging a Cheerio closer to his hand when he seemed poised to grasp it but couldn't quite reach. Eventually he seemed bored with the Cheerios and started dropping the toys off the tray. Dana played along, saying, "Uh-oh!" and reaching down to retrieve them. Soon the game got more frantic, and Max started to fuss and whimper. Dana stepped up the entertainment, throwing a toy up in the air before putting it back on the tray. Max started to cry. Finally Mom said, "OK, I'm sorry, buddy. I got carried away, didn't I? I think you've had enough activity for the moment." She picked him up and cradled him, looked deeply into his eyes, and whispered, "Sleepy, baby? Sleepy, sleepy baby?" as she rocked him slowly. Max relaxed into her arms as his eyelids began to droop.

Dana doesn't seem to be doing much in this typical scene involving a mother and a baby, but in reality she is paying close attention to her son, noticing when he needs to explore his Cheerios prowess and when he needs to settle down and relax in Mom's comforting presence. She's tuning in to her son's experiences, following his needs, but whenever necessary, she's also taking charge. *She is showing what it means to be the hands on the Circle of Security.*

Being the hands on the Circle starts with responding sensitively, extending to her son a deep, empathic form of connection we call "Being-With." *Being-With is one of the most important aspects of building a secure attachment and one of the most powerful gifts we can give our children.* When we're trying to meet a child's attachment needs, Being-With is the compass that allows us clear direction almost every moment of the day. Knowing that our primary goal is the Be-With need on the Circle takes the guesswork out of what our child is asking from us. It guides our path to offering acceptance and comfort on the bottom and support and encouragement on the top. It also lets us know when we need to take charge.

We've all heard terms that offer direction for parents who are committed to being sensitive caregivers: "quality time," "attunement," "focused attention"—each valuable in its own way. Over the years we've discovered, however, that the simple term "Being-With" offers parents a single theme they can focus on as they seek to attend to their child's needs on the Circle. Being-With is the way we actually know another person and a direct route to secure love—the kind that says, "I care about your needs. I want to honor each one of them on the Circle. In addition, I want to understand what you're experiencing. I care about what you feel. And I know it's my being here with you with each need at least some of the time and with each feeling that matters most."

In her everyday interaction with her little boy, Dana matches his emotional tone and energy level with what she says and does in response. It's just an ordinary half hour in a typical day, but the connection Dana formed with her son by attuning to his needs and feelings creates a sense of exuberance and supports his emotional growth. Being-With, that one-on-one connection, is a baby's first taste of belonging—not just to this loving mother or father but to a wide-open, welcoming universe. For a child who starts life feeling like a part of something benevolent the potential for success and happiness grows with each personal interaction.

It's All About Quality of Relationship

Attachment in general, our depiction of it via the Circle of Security, and, we believe, healthy child development are all about quality of relationship. There are many aspects to quality of relationship. As we've already stressed, **emotional regulation** is central. Dana demonstrates the progression by which parents help their children build emotional regulation skills. When Max gets fussy, she soothes him in a way that tells him it's perfectly OK to feel that way and with a little help from Mom the distress will pass. Even though he's only 9 months old, Dana is already helping her son regulate his own emotions when she lets him turn away from her for a moment and calm himself when he gets overaroused by the Cheerios game. Parents promote emotional regulation skills by Being-With their children in their experience at each point on the Circle. Being-With is at the very core of our role as the hands on the Circle and makes all other aspects of that role possible. It's the core subject of this chapter.

> *Knowing that a devoted parent or other caregiver is emotionally available to Be-With the child whenever needed is at the heart of secure attachment.*

Another aspect of quality of relationship is **taking charge**. The Circle of Security motto that accompanies a parent's understanding of hands is "Whenever possible, follow your child's needs. Whenever necessary, take charge." Being the hands on the Circle is certainly about being available and sensitive to needs. Yet underlying this availability and sensitivity is our commitment to being someone our child can count on to be in charge. Sensitivity toward your child is essential, but Being-With the child does not preclude stepping in when he is just too little to deal with whatever is happening. A baby whose cries are getting louder and more strident is not suddenly going to shake himself out of his distress because his caregiver is sitting there cooing in sympathy. We need to step in and use our adult skills and experience to take charge of a baby who is spinning out of control. We also need to recognize when a child is crossing a boundary (or testing one) and wants us to show that we can keep him safe by taking charge. Dana does this when she decides that play-and-snack time is over and Max needs a nap. Being-With her baby has told her how he is feeling; through Being-With him she conveys that his feelings are perfectly normal and there is someone on hand who is willing and able to help. We tell parents that their role as hands on the Circle is to be *bigger, stronger, wiser, and kind.* Every moment with your child gives you an opportunity to make the delicate shift between following the child's need and taking charge. Being-With and having a secure attachment doesn't mean being overly nice all the time. It means offering the no-nonsense tenderness that says "I am here for what you need and here to take charge and keep you safe. You can count on me." Being-With and taking charge are equally important in being the hands on the Circle for your child. More on bigger, stronger, wiser, and kind later in this chapter.

A third important aspect of quality of relationship involves **reflection.** We're human. Translation: We make mistakes. The way to lasting, fulfilling relationships throughout life is being able to recognize

ALWAYS BE: BIGGER, STRONGER, WISER, AND KIND.
WHENEVER POSSIBLE: FOLLOW MY CHILD'S NEED.
WHENEVER NECESSARY: TAKE CHARGE.

Parent as the hands on the Circle.

those mistakes, acknowledge them, and repair any hurts or misunderstandings. Perfection is not only impossible but can stand in the way of forming a close connection with those we love. Think about it: Two individuals aspiring to perfection will probably never come fully together because at close range their human flaws would inevitably be revealed. People who can't admit their errors and work to repair misunderstandings and hurt feelings leave their partner feeling misunderstood—and alone. Children need to see those who raise them as simply human and simply flawed, with a willingness to reflect on their part in what goes wrong. Parents who accept their imperfections impart one of the most important lessons a child can learn. Therefore, a large part of being the hands on the Circle is modeling your ability to reflect on your mistakes and make amends.

As parents we often step off the Circle, either intentionally (letting the baby cry longer than we'd like because we really have to take an important call) or inadvertently (we're tired or stressed and just become insensitive—it happens). This is called **rupture**, and as long as it's followed by **repair**, it's not only OK, it's hugely beneficial to your child. When you snap at or ignore your child when she's seeking connection, and then realize you've stepped off the Circle and say "Oh, I'm sorry, baby, I'm a little crabby today" as you pick her up and kiss her, you're showing that people make mistakes and it's not the end of the world—the world being, for your very young child, the relationship with you. When you model rupture and repair, you're promoting your child's development of a reflective self and paving her way for good relationships throughout life.

> *"The great way to think about the Circle is once you have been on it you can always find your way back if you fall off it. It doesn't matter where you get back on, you just have to find an opening somewhere and jump straight back on, and if you have 'the hands for support' waiting, you can go right back to the beginning and start again."*
> —Tina Murray, Australia

Being-With your child doesn't mean being infallibly attuned. Taking charge doesn't mean never having to say you're sorry. Acknowledging that even parents make mistakes and then making the necessary efforts to repair them is as integral to keeping your hands on the Circle as Being-With and taking charge and is the third topic of this chapter.

If we could delete one word from the parenting lexicon, it would be "perfection."

Being-With Your Child

Being-With your child is utterly simple yet deeply profound. It's both the easiest thing in the world and at times the most difficult. Being-With your child is something that you're likely already doing much of the time, because it comes as naturally as your choice to feed your child when she's hungry. Dana demonstrated what Being-With looks like when she was fully there with Max throughout their high-chair play. She didn't direct what he did (most of the time). She didn't constantly check her phone while sitting there. She didn't ignore Max when he started to shift moods. Perhaps most notably, she didn't try to deny how Max felt, talk him out of it, or chastise him for it in any way (which can be as simple as a rolling of the eyes or an exasperated sigh—babies clearly notice because they are that astute).

Remember the scene in Chapter 2 in which Hannah and Sophie grinned at each other as Sophie careened around in her walker? That's Being-With. Hannah was meeting her baby's "delight in me" need as the little girl explored movement and different perspectives in her environment. The two were simply attuned, their feeling of mutual delight resonating almost palpably. You've seen this kind of shared delight—this effortless way parents can feel some of their child's wonder and joy and reflect it back—many times, in many settings, and if you're already a parent, you've felt it.

> Don't hold back on feeling joy with your baby. Research shows that babies who get lots of delight become more cooperative 2-year-olds. Neuropsychologist Allan Schore has noted that shared delight also speeds up brain growth in infants and is a key component in the foundation of self-esteem.

But here's where Being-With becomes more difficult: How do we react when the child is angry, frustrated, or sad? Can we avoid talking her out of these feelings so that *we* don't feel upset and helpless? Can we hold on to the knowledge that this feeling won't harm our child—or us—and that experiencing this emotion has a lot to teach her? And what about when we're tired, stressed, busy, completely out of patience? Can we stay tuned in?

Of course not. No one can Be-With, on cue, all the time, and no one should try. **Welcome to the club.**

All we can do is do our best to Be-With our child during many of our moments together. Although it's tough at times, knowing how much the child stands to gain is quite an incentive. Being-With is the route to meeting your child's needs all around the Circle. Children travel from the top to the bottom of the Circle and back again so rapidly and so many times throughout the day that you can miss a lot of shifts if you're not tuned in. Being-With your child when he's upset tells him that someone is there with him *in* this feeling so he has a way out of feeling bad. It allows him to hang in with the feeling for long enough to learn something about it—what emotion it is, what triggered it, and even how it's an important aspect of being alive. Most of all, he learns that whenever this feeling arises, he's not alone in it: "I may not like this feeling, but it is something I've known before and I've known it with someone I trust and love." In this way difficult feelings aren't overwhelming, nor are they something that must be avoided at all costs. Every feeling, even the ones that can bring distress, can also include memories of shared companionship and trust.

Being able to regulate emotions helps children regulate their behavior.

A pattern of Being-With your child that starts at birth and continues through childhood builds a solid emotional foundation that will serve your child for life (see the box on page 90). In Being-With your child, you are modeling empathy and thereby helping your child develop this capacity that is so critical to all relationships. Children with well-developed empathy grow up to be adults whom others seem drawn to because they quickly respond with understanding that comes from sharing the same human experiences. Being known in this way forges a powerful connection. The influence of our Being-With clearly echoes into future generations.

Everyone has met someone like Paul. He's the guy who can wend his way through a crowd full of strangers and leave in his wake a bunch of new friends. If you asked them what they had found so appealing about Paul upon such a brief encounter, most people would say something like "He just seemed like he was genuinely interested in me"

You Cannot Spoil an Infant

Sometimes parents fear that focusing too much on their child's emotions will make the child weak or demanding or self-centered. It is possible to spoil a child, by teaching him that the whole world stops whenever he has a feeling. But *infants* need precisely this message. In their first year of life they need countless repetitions of soothing and delight throughout each day, offering the unspoken message that they matter and matter absolutely to someone. In this way they learn to know at their core that every feeling they have can be shared. It is here that they learn that there is no feeling they have to experience all alone. Once established, the second year of life and beyond offers the message that every feeling still counts and will be met soon enough, when the time is right. As long as they know this important truth, it can be OK for us to redirect and distract them when the realities of daily life demand that we keep moving to get something done. You'll find that when you instill this trust in your child, you'll get more cooperation anyway. Researchers have found that the more synchrony of emotion between a baby and caregiver during the first year of life, the more the child complied with parental demands and delayed acts upon request at age 2.

or "He wasn't looking over my shoulder at the next conquest when we were introducing ourselves—as if he didn't need to remember my name or my face because we were never going to meet again" or "He seemed honestly modest about his accomplishments—which just made me want to hear more about him, unlike those guys who greet you as if they have their résumé printed on one side of their face and their net worth on the other." To Paul this ability to connect just seems to come naturally. He says, "I don't know—I'm not really thinking about it at all. It just feels like the way to be with people."

Paul's ability to connect was a seed planted when he was an infant being raised by his grandmother. It was in the first few years of his life that Grandma created the holding environment that Paul can now create in all of his relationships. In fact, it comes as no surprise to those who have a chance to meet his 3-year-old son that the little boy seems generally content and friendly, even when his dad's attention is split between him and another adult.

When Paul claimed not to be aware of doing anything in particular to connect with people, he wasn't being modest or holding back some secret way to make friends and influence people that he'd learned from a self-improvement book. The power of Being-With lies in the fact that it teaches babies about emotions and relationships long before they have acquired language (see the box on page 92).

The Mechanics of Being-With

British pediatrician and psychoanalyst Donald Winnicott described what he called a holding environment as any caregiving relationship that provides a genuine and safe experience of belonging. In other words, a holding environment is one in which a parent or other caregiver is able to Be-With the child in all of the child's internal experiences (at least some of the time) and make the child feel safe and connected as she learns about emotions. Our Circle of Security is essentially a holding environment, and we find the concept so powerful that an important aspect of the Circle of Security intervention involves the therapist creating a holding environment for the parent who is trying to learn how to form a secure attachment with his or her child. Being in a holding environment helps make difficult change possible.

Said simply: Being-With your child means following his needs. As Dana demonstrated, this looks like a pretty smooth process. She watches and senses what her child feels, responds accordingly, and then keeps watching for a change so that she can make an almost seamless shift toward his next need. There's no "Step 1, Step 2" sort of herky-jerky procedure. Nevertheless, if we look closely, we can see that Being-With is made up of several components:

- Attunement
- Resonance
- Acceptance
- Holding
- Contingent response to needs

Being-With isn't a technique but a state of mind.

Attunement is one of those easier-said-than-done achievements. Can you tune in to your child's specific feeling(s) when she's too young to name them herself? Despite your immediate connection with your

How Does an Infant Learn the Lessons of Being-With?

It's hard to believe that a baby who has been on this planet for mere months or even weeks can develop an understanding of something as intangible as emotions just from the way Mom or Dad reacts to her when she's sad, angry, frightened, joyful, or experiencing other feelings. How can she start to learn a vocabulary for emotion and the way even the most intense feelings can be managed when she may not even understand the meaning of the words when Mom murmurs "Oh, so sad, so sad . . . poor little girl" or Dad whispers "Awww, did that scare you? Too big and scary"? Children can only learn how to manage emotions in the context of a relationship. They simply cannot do it on their own. Being-With is our nonverbal way of teaching them this valuable skill.

Have you ever performed some action or responded instinctively and had someone ask "How did you know how to do that"? If your answer was "I don't know—I just do," you know how babies learn about emotion through Being-With. Karlen Lyons-Ruth and the Boston Change Process Study Group coined the term "implicit relational knowing" to represent how babies code information without using symbols like language about how to do things with others. In their earliest interactions with caregivers, they learn how to negotiate attachment needs and how to depend on another person to help them regulate emotion (as described in Chapter 3). This implicit relational knowing, also called *procedural memory,* is developed before babies have language and then feels intuitive once they do become verbal. As we said in Chapter 3, it's like riding a bike: it feels like "just how things work." Psychoanalyst Christopher Bollas said 30 years ago, "We learn the grammar of our being before we have the words." Bollas used the term "unthought known" to describe implicit relational knowing or procedural memory. Being-With is the way we achieve the necessary quality of relationship to teach our babies about emotion— which ones are which, what they mean, and how to manage them.

Not all implicit relational knowing is helpful, of course. Babies who learn that certain feelings are not considered acceptable, or that emotions can in fact overwhelm them and there's no help to be found, will grow up believing that that, too, is "just how things work." Do you know any adults who stay away from emotions and do their best never to rely on anyone but themselves? Or any who are continually swamped by intense emotions and always rely on others and never on themselves? What kind of close relationships do they have? Does it begin to make sense that these were lessons learned early, quite possibly before they had language?

child, you'll probably have to get used to her one-of-a-kind signals to determine whether she's sad or angry, happy or curious, and so forth. Some guessing will be involved, but with practice your ability to see what your child is feeling will improve. We've seen first-time mothers take one look at their fussy 3-month-old and know that the child is frustrated or irritated rather than frightened. We've seen new fathers say "Oh, she just wants to cuddle right now—if I put her to bed right away, she'll be upset," because they've been so attuned to the child's needs that they can see what completely escapes others looking on. Of course the opposite happens as well. The same parent who so astutely reads her child's feelings most of the time may project her own irritability on her baby when she herself feels overwhelmed, saying, "Why are you so upset? What do you want from me?" to a baby who's just trying to get the face he usually finds so reassuring to turn toward him.

When Yolanda took her baby to the pediatrician at 9 months and the little boy started crying after getting a shot, she felt so distressed that she instantly said, "Oh, that doesn't hurt! That didn't hurt!" The nurse, who had apparently seen this before, said loudly and sternly, "Yes, it does!" as she slammed out of the room. Yolanda said she stood there feeling mortified but also stunned: Why in the world, she asked herself over and over—for years afterward—would I have thought that shot didn't hurt?*

> Professor of psychiatry Daniel Siegel put it this way: "The observed takes in the observer having taken her in, and the two become joined." Sounds pretty abstract, but it's the most intimate of interpersonal events. Siegel also describes this as "feeling felt."

Resonance is a kind of meeting of the minds in which we feel known by another person, and it may be the most powerful aspect of Being-With. It's where we experience the "and" we've been talking about since the beginning of this book. Have you ever found yourself in a situation with another person where your eyes met and it seemed as if you instantly understood each other's feelings at that moment?

---

*While we welcome Yolanda's self-reflection here, it's unfortunate that she was prompted to ask herself that question in such a harsh manner. Parents, as you may already know, are often their own harshest critics; they don't need outsiders to make them feel they're not good enough as mothers and fathers.

At age 16, Kayla lost her grandfather. It was the first wake she'd ever attended, and suddenly the small groups of relatives laughing and talking near the open casket seemed so surreal that she found herself about to burst into laughter. Appalled at the prospect of being so insensitive, she fidgeted nervously in her chair as far away from the casket as she could get, feeling closer and closer to hysterics. Then she happened to glance over to the side of the room, where she saw her father gazing at her with a mixture of sadness and amusement that instantly told her he knew exactly what was going on in her mind. She smiled at her dad and immediately felt calm. Never in her life, she says today at the age of 40, had she felt so understood.

Which brings us to acceptance.

Acceptance comes through attunement and resonance, but the addition of an understanding, sympathetic smile or a facial expression that mirrors a child's feeling says even more explicitly that Mom or Dad gets it and it's OK. Without words, even a very young child recognizes that a parent has been willing to join temporarily in her feelings. Acceptance means knowing what the child is feeling, resonating with that feeling, and allowing it to be "OK" because we genuinely believe it is. Again, even a very young child will sense when we really mean this feeling is OK and not that we want the child to quickly become OK or that *we* want to feel OK by getting the child's feelings to stop.

Being-With means feeling some of what the child is feeling *but not all of it*. It doesn't mean taking on our child's feelings but helping the child understand that we share a lot of human experience and still remain separate individuals. That "some" is really important. A parent who's Being-With her child may mirror the baby's sad face and narrate what the parent is guessing about what it means: "Ohhh, that's not a happy face. No, no, I think you're feeling sad? Are you sad? You've been sitting here for too long? Maybe you want to get out. Do you want me to hold you? I know, I know." Compare this with the parent who is trying too hard, mimicking the baby's sad face to an almost caricaturish extreme, as if she's trying to surpass the baby's upset. How do you think a tiny baby would react to that? We've seen babies confronted with this adult response react with extreme distress, even terror. Instantly the baby realizes, "This adult is even more worried than I am. There must be something really, really wrong with me! I'm all alone here—even this huge person can't help me!" Now contrast this with the parent who reacts to his baby's distress by being what we attachment researchers call "overbright." Rather than matching the baby's feeling tone at all, he acts as if the distress isn't happening: he effectively tells the baby, "Your feelings are all wrong. See? I'm smiling! It's time to be happy! The only feelings that work with me are happy feelings." In this case the baby may initially scream louder, hoping to get through to the clueless parent, or increasingly shut down, withdrawing into herself because she feels so misunderstood. Eventually she may learn to smile in order to experience at least some sense of connection, but it will be a pretend smile. Sadly, over the years, she may forget that she's pretending.

Which brings us to holding.

Holding is exactly what it says: keeping the child safe and protected while experiencing feelings that might be overwhelmingly distressing. Holding can be expressed physically, but it is fundamentally an emotional event. It's the sum total of attunement, resonance, and acceptance. In this way, Being-With means having someone with you in a difficult feeling so you can find a way out of feeling bad. The baby who hears, sees, and feels this kind of understanding and empathy knows there is at least one person in her life who cares and accepts each and every feeling; a person who will take charge and help her find her way through every discomfort.

A baby who feels held is one who may be able to look calmly at a looming stranger who is trying to get her to laugh at the rattle he's shaking in her face. A toddler who feels held by Dad at his checkup knows it's OK to yell when he feels the needle prick but is also likely to calm quickly when the physical pain ends. An older child might be able to overcome stage fright and sing his part in the school play if he sees Mom out in the audience empathizing with his fear and nodding in that way she has that he knows means "I'm here, and you'll be OK no matter what happens." Here's an example you might be able to identify with:

Alyssa told us that her most memorable interaction with the medical staff in attendance at her daughter's birth was how differently she was treated by different residents at the university hospital. In the middle of active labor, she recalled, residents would enter the room, pulling on gloves, and after a quick announcement of their name and their intent to check her progress, perform an internal exam. Then there was one doctor (whose name she also never forgot) who came in, looked directly into her eyes with a warm expression, and laid a gentle hand on her thigh. Alyssa remembers her breathing calming and this young doctor waiting until he sensed she was a little more at ease before proceeding. Someone who had always chosen female doctors on the supposition that they'd understand what it's like to be a woman, Alyssa was amazed that the doctor she had found so comforting was the only male among the ones she saw. Clearly this demonstration of empathy was not something the residents had learned in medical school. It just seemed to come naturally to the young male doctor.

There's plenty of data to show that a mother's stress during labor can complicate childbirth and adversely affect her baby. This young doctor's ability to Be-With his patients boded well for those he was helping to usher into the world. Our gratitude to his mother, father, or whichever caregiver passed on to him the implicit relational knowing of Being-With.

Contingent responding to needs means reacting in kind to the child's signals—matching the "quality, intensity, and timing" of the child's signals with your own, in the words of Dan Siegel. The obstetrician just described was modeling a contingent response to Alyssa's nonverbally delivered needs. Truly Being-With your child allows you to figure out not only where he is on the Circle and what he needs from you but how urgent and strong the need is. Does your baby want comfort or encouragement? Does he want you to watch over him as he turns to new sights, sounds, and touches? Delight in him as he falls in love with your face? Whatever your child needs on the top or bottom of the Circle, how urgently does she need it? How quickly? By Being-With her, you can match her emotions with your own voice, face, and touch. You can help her learn what her emotions mean by accepting, sharing, and also naming them. Particularly for babies, it's important to verbalize your interpretation of their signals so they learn that crying softly, for example, tells others that they may be feeling sad and lonely or that a screwed-up face says "I'm really, really angry about what just happened and I need you to help me!" (See the box on the facing page.) In Chapter 1 we talked about how secure attachment promotes a strong sense of a coherent self. Contingent responses to your child's needs through Being-With are the path along which that happens.

Verbal Parent, Fluent Child

The implicit relational knowing of how to Be-With others and thereby have trusting, fulfilling relationships does not rely on language. But that doesn't mean we shouldn't talk to babies about their experiences. Not only will talking give them a vocabulary for their emotions and other internal experience, it will also promote the development of language and boost intelligence overall. In 1995, after a decade-long study, researchers from the University of Kansas reported that how many words their parents had spoken to children by age 3 was related directly to their academic success at age 9. More recent studies showed this difference started to appear as early as 18 months, and scientists believe that talking to our children might matter starting right at birth. Interestingly, it's not just how many words the child hears—say, on TV or while listening to older children or adults talking among themselves. What matters is how many words are spoken *to the child*. In other words, *it's in the context of relationships that language and intelligence thrive.*

So, when your child is "out" exploring his world, talk and talk and talk with him about the world: "That sand feels soft and cool, doesn't it?" "Wow, it's such a bright, sunny day. Isn't that blue sky beautiful?" "You threw that ball really hard—look how far it rolled!" "A lot of kids are out playing today. Maybe we'll make some new friends!" Even if you feel silly babbling away at your infant, who can't respond verbally, or your toddler, who may be too busy with other things, or your older child, who just doesn't want to, know that you're setting your child on the road to learning (or perfecting) language. As long as you're not intruding on the child's activity by talking, narrate away. Hint: If your narration suddenly becomes quizzing and looking for "right answers," you've likely stepped toward intrusion. Rule of thumb: Keep the focus on your child's moment-to-moment experience, not your goals regarding his future capacity to "shine."

Also talk to your baby about whether she's going out (on the top of the Circle: "Going to check out that grass?") or coming in (on the bottom: "Want to come up and snuggle?") and whether she's feeling OK ("That feels good, doesn't it?") or not OK ("That was a little scary, huh?"). A very young child might be able to stay out, exploring, for only a couple of seconds before coming back in to fill her emotional cup. Narrating these shifts will not only hone your ability to see and respond to your child's needs sensitively and accurately but also help your child understand her own experience and her own needs. Children who understand their own needs can negotiate their attachment needs in all relationships.

The Challenge

Being-With your child is, as we've already said, the most natural thing in the world and can also be the most difficult. Whether your child is a day old or a decade, here is this being you cherish, someone you would move the earth to protect. Can you "just sit there" while your child is in pain? Of course you can't. That's fine: Being-With is *not* just sitting there. We hope that's clear from the explanation and description you've just read. But that doesn't mean it's easy to Be-With your child and not try to do more: make the child's discomfort go away by denying it exists or minimizing it . . . distract the child so that he doesn't think about what he's feeling . . . manage the situation or activity to "improve" the outcome for your child . . . simply apply your superior intellect and wisdom because, after all, you are the adult. Oddly enough, within the

---

The Danger of Misunderstanding Being-With

There's an old adage among psychologists that the unconscious doesn't have a digestive tract—what we push down will eventually come back up. Which is to say that if we deny feelings they won't disappear, they'll just reappear later (hours, weeks, or years) in ways that can often wreak havoc on our lives. But there's an opposite problem, and it can show up precisely as some of us are learning about the importance of Being-With. We can shift 180 degrees and now give ourselves permission to become overly focused on our child's feelings. The danger here is that a child learns that her feelings are all-important and that the world needs to stop every time she has a feeling. The danger is that a child now thinks her feelings deserve focus 100% of the time.

Being-With is about balance, one in which each child learns that his feelings are profound and essential and deserve full availability . . . some of the time. If a child has a caregiver who suddenly stops and commits to being fully available every time the child starts to feel, emotions would begin to rule the household in a very unhealthy way.

All children need to know that their feelings are central to someone some of the time, and they also need to know that other people have feelings that are just as central to them. We do get to feel, but we live in a world with others and lead a life that includes getting things done.

Balance. Balance. Balance.

---

context of Being-With, our tendency to "do more" is often experienced as *not* Being-With. (And doing more can occur in the form of overprivileging a child's every emotion; see the box on the facing page.)

There are a million things we can improve for our children, and with a pattern of Being-With in place, we can even redirect or distract our children from a difficult feeling when practical necessity demands it. But these improvements we can make have little to do with the child's attachment needs. They likely have nothing to do with the child's experiencing emotions. We can make life easier and better for our children in many ways, but we can't engineer or control how they will eventually figure out how to be themselves and also in relationships. We can't halt or detour the drive to explore the world and also seek personal connection. We are their sponsors, their protectors, their guides on this unalterable path.

Modern life also makes Being-With our children a challenge. We're so busy. There's so much we have to get done. We're so worried we won't be up to the task(s). The need to champion our child's healthy development in this very quiet, very still way can sometimes fall by the wayside. But sometimes devoting our attention to something that seems to involve doing so little is the best way we can take charge.

"Imagine [that] you don't have to perform or smile. . . . You don't have to be tickled or otherwise provoked to laughter for daddy or mommy to find ecstasy in your company. You don't have to do anything. You are enough. Just being near you and watching what you might choose to do fills your parents with pleasure and gratitude. Just imagine the level of self-confidence this instills, the comfort with every aspect of self."

—Janet Lansbury, Elevating Childcare*

"Whenever I go away, I know when I get home you will be there to greet me with open arms."

—Part of a Mother's Day message from a 15-year-old boy

*Lansbury teaches parents in the Resources for Infant Education (RIE) method of child raising founded by Magda Gerber. RIE helps parents treat each child as a person from the start, allowing the child to be just who that child is. Behind the RIE philosophy is a state of mind very much like Being-With. This brief excerpt is from a longer post on her website, *janetlansbury.com*, on June 8, 2010.

Taking Charge:
Bigger, Stronger, Wiser, and Kind

Being-With can help us know what our children need around the Circle from moment to moment, and that certainly includes their needing us to take charge. To be hands on the Circle is to "be bigger, stronger, wiser, and kind" for our children. Fortunately, we humans are hard-wired to offer this balanced, in-charge, compassionate stance. Through the years we've noticed that parents who balance all four aspects of this motto create the kind of security we all hope to provide for our children. As might be imagined, many of us struggle here to a certain degree. We've found that most parents either get overzealous about taking charge in general or overemphasize one aspect of being bigger, stronger, wiser, and kind while simultaneously underemphasizing another aspect.

Overzealous Hands

We all struggle at times to enter into our children's emotional experience without adopting it as our own. We make lots of sacrifices for our children, and sometimes we'd happily take a child's pain on ourselves if doing so would relieve the child of it. Unfortunately, that would leave the child feeling like he shouldn't have had that feeling to begin with. It would also prevent him from learning how to manage it. He'd wrestle with emotion for the rest of his life.

Our instinct to rush in and rescue comes from the bigger, stronger, wiser, and kind aspect of being the hands on the Circle. Whenever possible, we should follow our child's need. But when necessary we should take charge. For many of us, taking charge seems like what parenting is all about. Dad thinks, "I'm the adult here. I can handle this for Joey. If I don't, I'm abdicating my responsibility to protect him." Nana says, "You don't have to cry about those mean kids, honey. Let's go get some cookies." Mom tells herself, "I'll know when he's ready to deal with this kind of disappointment. At 3, no one should feel deprived." All three of these caregivers might be right, depending on the circumstances and whether they've already established a pattern of Being-With the child in question. But have they tried to follow the child's need first? Could Joey just need Dad's quiet support to handle his discomfort on his own? Is it possible that the little girl who was rejected by the children at the playground should be allowed to cry over her hurt while Nana holds her and tells her she knows how tough it is to feel that way? Should Mom have let her son take the lead, Being-With him as he tries to handle his disappointment, stepping in only when he shows he really can't handle it? These are all tough calls. It's not always easy to see when it's time to take charge rather than follow a child's need. When it comes to painful emotion, many of us opt for taking charge because of our protective instincts or because these emotions make *us* too uncomfortable.

You'll find as you follow your child's needs around the Circle that you are more comfortable Being-With the child on certain parts of the Circle. Welcome to the club. As we discuss in Chapter 5, all of us carry the legacy of our own upbringing into our parenting, and we may very well be slightly uneasy in the same places on the Circle as our own parents were with us. So the first aspect of being hands is taking charge of ourselves and being willing to notice where we're uncomfortable while accepting and holding that discomfort long enough to support a need on the Circle that isn't so easy for us. Maybe you look on with pride and joy when your little girl fearlessly launches herself down the slide at age 2, but you feel a little restless when she wants to sit on your lap and cuddle for 20 minutes. Perhaps you're really in your element, as if this is what you were born to do, when your child wants to be held, but you cringe with anxiety when he turns his back to you and runs off to be with a new friend on the playground. These inclinations aren't harmful to your child unless they're so extreme that your child is completely blocked from either getting comfort or exploring the world.

It is, however, instructive and helpful to know where we feel uncomfortable, because (1) our children are (surprisingly) so attuned to us that they notice even our mild anxiety about certain needs on the Circle, and (2) our awareness of where we are somewhat anxious will diminish their anxiety about ours while giving us new choices about how to respond that will in turn promote our child's healthy development.

"When we do our COS group, we take the children from the parents and do a concurrent theraplay group with them. One evening 3-year-old Janaya got 'loose' from the theraplay group and came running into our group and began asking Mom and Dad a million questions. 'Where are we going for dinner?' 'Who will I sit with?' 'What will we do after that?' Mom and Dad sat politely and calmly answered each and

every question until I got Janaya out of the room. I asked them, 'What was that like for you?' and they responded, 'If there was one thing we could change about Janaya, it would be that she asks so many questions!'

"*Janaya loves to ask questions with that bright happy face, but underneath it is how she is managing her arousal. She really is on the bottom of the Circle, looking for Mom and Dad to take charge, but they keep backing off the Circle somewhat by not seeing her distress and let her drive the interaction. One of the phrases we use to describe attachment is 'I've got you' or 'I've got this,' and Dad really liked that. When they got home that night, Janaya began her bedtime ritual, which was to ask a million questions about sleep, getting up, monsters, etc. Dad started taking charge every time she asked questions by saying, 'Don't worry, I've got you.' Both parents kept that up all week whenever the questions started coming. Almost a whole week later, Dad was tucking Janaya in one night and she was about to start the litany of questions when she looked up at Dad with those adorable huge eyes and smiled and said, 'You've got me,' and went to sleep.*"

—Joanne Brown, Winnipeg, Canada

Overdoing One Part of Bigger, Stronger, Wiser, and Kind

We tell parents, especially those who are having difficulty concerning discipline and problematic behavior, that functioning as the hands on the Circle always means being bigger, stronger, wiser, *and* kind. But just as parents are typically more comfortable on either the top or the bottom of the Circle, or with certain specific needs than others, many of us favor either bigger-and-stronger parenting or wiser-and-kind parenting. Of course we'll swing back and forth on this pendulum as our child's shifting needs demand. But it's always best to try to picture ourselves perched on the fulcrum.

> *Being the hands on the Circle means remembering to be bigger, stronger, wiser, and kind—or bigger, stronger, and kind, while being wise enough to step back and notice the difference.*

Rosa is pushing her cart through the crowded supermarket aisles with 2-year-old Carmen buckled into the seat. Carmen's nap has been postponed by the errand, and it shows. She keeps whining and yelping and pulling at the seat belt in her attempts to stand up in the cart to signal that she's had enough of shopping. Rosa murmurs, "I know, I know" as she tries to keep her daughter seated and simultaneously read her grocery list, pluck items from the shelves, and get them into the cart out of Carmen's reach. As Carmen's protests crescendo and the little girl starts tossing anything she can reach in the cart to the floor, Rosa nervously glances around at the other shoppers and says, "Honey, sweetie, could you help Mommy, please? Can you be good for Mommy for just a little longer?" Three more aisles to go, and Carmen has wriggled out of the belt while her mother reads a package label. Rosa turns toward her in alarm and pleads, "Carmen, would it be OK if you sat down for just a little minute longer? Please, honey?" Rosa turns back to her reading and Carmen leans out of the cart to grab a box of cookies from the shelf. Rosa turns back just in time to keep her daughter from rocketing to the floor onto her head. Carmen screams, her face turning beet red, grabs a box of tea bags, and hurls it forward, where it hits an elderly gentleman in the back of the head. "Oh, I'm so sorry," says Rosa to the startled shopper and then "Carmen, can you say you're sorry? Carmen? Aren't you sorry, honey?" The targeted shopper shakes his head in disgust and heads for the next aisle as Carmen is tearing open a bag of grapes, scattering them all over the cart and floor.

If you have a toddler at home, you'll either groan or laugh at this story. We've all been there. But for Rosa this isn't an isolated incident. In her desire to be "nicer" than her own mother was to her, she asks her little girl's permission to take charge and rarely acts as if she believes she is bigger and stronger. She's only kind. As a result, in cases like the grocery store scene, Rosa doesn't follow Carmen's need to have her mother manage her cranky overarousal. She's quite uncomfortable with taking charge. And, sadly, Rosa's discomfort leaves her daughter with a perception of her parent as someone who is weak.

Our children need us to be bigger and stronger so they can feel safe, knowing that someone is willing and able to protect them. But it's not just for safety. It's important for them to know they can rely on us—that we're not going to let something happen to them, that we're going to do our best to be there. Like their steady rock. And in the real world where things need to get done and time is often short, it's simply not always possible to follow your child's needs. For example, a child's desire to explore a new toy can sometimes clash with our need to get to an appointment. Or fulfilling a child's need to be comforted may mean passing him over to the sitter if we have to get to work. Although they may protest, our children appreciate the sense of safety that comes from knowing we are in charge.

Taking charge does not, of course, imply being an authoritarian tyrant. It never requires stepping into being mean. Taking charge in a kind way is a way of saying, explicitly and implicitly, "I'm always going to be there for you, but that doesn't mean that I always have to be overly nice, because sometimes it is about really letting you know that that is a boundary, you've crossed it, and we need to step back." Carmen had reached that boundary long before bopping the shopper on the back of the head, but since Rosa didn't insist that they step back at the appropriate time, Carmen was going to keep trying to figure out where that line was.

Children who want their parents to take charge often push limits.

Being bigger, stronger, wiser, and kind gives our children access to a kind of no-nonsense tenderness that leads to security. This is a balance between firmness and affection. It's not that there are bigger and stronger moments and kind moments. It's that every moment requires us to find a way to blend the two. That's where wisdom comes in. It's where Being-With helps, because our quiet, attuned awareness enables us to fine-tune our response to strike just the right balance of firmness and affection.

> The opposite of bigger, stronger, wiser, and kind is mean, weak, or gone. Every parent may occasionally snap at a child, cave, or check out. Recognizing that we've taken our hands off the Circle, we can repair the rupture.

John Bowlby used the term "bigger, stronger, and wiser" to describe the role of parents as early as 1988. We added "kind" in acknowledgment that sometimes, again often depending on how they were raised, caregivers forget that parenting isn't just a matter of acting as the authority. Sadly, some parents grew up believing that children have to be afraid of their caregiver if they're to obey. Being kind means recognizing, for instance, that a toddler having a tantrum might be having a really hard time with something and needs to fill his emotional cup. So instead of imposing a time-out or other punishment, the parent slows everything down, lifts him onto her lap, and finds a way to help organize his feelings (more on this "time-in" alternative in Chapter 8). Once established as a "go-to" option, Being-With often works wonders.

When you are bigger, stronger, wiser, and kind, your child will get a sense of your confident presence. Whether 1 year old or 21, your child will understand that you are confident in your ability to take charge in a kind

> It's not uncommon for parents to differ in which part of bigger, stronger, wiser, and kind they favor, and obviously these differences can cause conflict. See Part II for a bit more on this tricky issue.

way and that you are as present as you can be. Your child will then be endowed with a sense of trust in you and in your relationship that yelling, demanding, fear, pleading, or pampering can never provide.

Jay is sitting on the floor with 3-year-old Abby. They are playing house. Abby has decided that Jay should be the baby while she is the mommy. Jay goes along with the story line with gentle good humor, letting his daughter direct him that it's time to go to bed for a nap or eat his dinner while she tucks him in or prepares the meal. Abby is sure of Jay. She knows he's really Daddy and that he's always there to keep her safe. She also knows that he likes to play with her and gets a certain twinkle in his eye when she lets her imagination run wild. If Jay had suggested that Abby be Mommy and Jay be Baby, and Jay did not exude a confident presence most of the time they were together, Abby might have gotten easily overwhelmed with the responsibility of playing at being in charge. Instead, Jay's confident presence tells her, "I am organizing this experience, you are safe, and I am still in charge." She is being held by this father, who is keeping her safe even in this exploration of imaginary roles.

The Challenge

To put it simply, the challenge is just to stay aware of what aspect of bigger, stronger, wiser, and kind you favor and keep trying to achieve balance. We all falter here. It's a challenge to fully recognize what kind of hands we usually are. We pick up our parents' habits so automatically, through implicit relational knowing, that they can feel like "just the way things are." To help you see clearly, consider asking yourself whether your own parent(s) tended to be bigger and stronger or wiser and kind when you were growing up. More help exploring this area is in Part II of this book. For now, ask yourself: When things seem to be spinning out of control for your child, are you more likely to step in and exercise your authority or to acquiesce, or to support and comfort? Once you know, you can ask yourself in individual interactions with your child whether that's what your child needs at that moment.

Consider using "bigger, stronger, wiser, and kind" as a mantra. Or pick the part you know you don't usually lean toward and use that to remind you to be the hands on the Circle.

One day Tina was riding the city bus with her young son and daughter, and the children were running up and down the aisle, getting in the way of other passengers and generally wreaking havoc. Tina looked on helplessly until this thought suddenly popped into her head: "Wait. I'm bigger and stronger!" She took her children by the hand, firmly sat them down on either side of her, and didn't let go until they got off the bus.

Helping Your Child Develop a Reflective Self: Rupture and Repair

> The world breaks every one and afterward many are strong at the broken places.
> —ERNEST HEMINGWAY, *A Farewell to Arms*

If it hasn't been said often enough, know that we're meant to make mistakes. Our children's healthy development depends on our making mistakes and then offering the appropriate repair. This doesn't mean saying penance, asking forgiveness, doing a mitzvah, punishing ourselves, or "paying off" the offended child with gifts or privileges. Rupturing the Circle of Security simply means stepping off the Circle, not Being-With our children in a way that repeats a common struggle, leaving a need unmet. Repair simply means acknowledging that we made a mistake and then returning to good-enough parenting once more (see the box on the facing page).

A rupture can be yelling at a cranky child and sending her to her room instead of finding out what's bothering her because we're so stressed out from a tough day at work that we don't have the energy or the patience. It can be leaving a child to figure out alone why he feels

When It Comes to Attachment, What's Really "Good Enough"?

This is a question that parents often ask. We usually say we mean Being-With their child and responding to their needs much of the time. We used to say "most of the time," but for all the overachievers out there that single word begged questions about percentages (what was "most"—51%? 75%? 99%?).

With the huge diversity of circumstances, family needs, and cultures, it would be foolish for us to try to suggest that being good-enough parents requires everyone to respond to situation A with reaction B. All we can really advise with confidence is that keeping your intention to be a bigger, stronger, wiser, and kind parent front and center is key. Children who know we consistently do our best to follow their needs and also to take charge in a kind way feel secure (enough). They come to trust in "the possibility of goodness," which includes knowing that good things follow bad things; repair tends to follow ruptures.

The trouble with focusing on what it means to be "good enough" as a parent is that it removes the focus from the *intention* to be bigger, stronger, wiser, and kind and transfers it to some achievement of our own. As we said in Chapter 2, children will intuitively ask, "Is this about your need to be a good parent or about my need in this particular moment?"

Where "good enough" is concerned,
our intentions are central.

scared because some procedural memory tells us if we "coddle" him he'll end up weak and so it's better to ignore little fears. We (unintentionally) rupture the Circle when we have to leave for the day and our child is really going to miss us. We even step off the Circle when we're talking with a friend and our preschooler comes running to us with his latest artistic creation and we laugh with embarrassment (because, really, how many dogs are purple and have ears four times longer than their legs?).

We make reparations when we go to our child's room and sincerely apologize for being harsh, sitting down on the bed with her and cuddling while taking a few minutes to read a book. We repair a rupture when we tell our son that we're sorry we were insensitive and ask him to tell us what scared him—and then choose to Be-With him as he explains, showing our understanding instead of trying to "correct" or explain away his fright. We repair a very necessary departure for work by acknowledging that it's hard to be apart, that we don't like it either, and promising to spend time together at the end of the day—and keeping that promise. We repair the pain caused by our insensitive laugh by saying that we know that must have hurt and sometimes parents' imagination isn't as good as a child's. In moments like this it also helps when we take the time to ask our child to describe the drawing (and listening closely).

These exchanges happen in every household every day, often numerous times. Ruptures happen. Repairs can also happen. This is a very positive thing, because *children end up being more secure when they find that good things can follow bad things.* We're not perfect, and if we were, we'd be setting our children up for severe disappointment in a world that is anything but perfect. Plus, we'd be preventing them from developing a resilient sense of self that trusts mistakes are a normal—even healthy—part of genuine relationships.

As we mentioned in the last chapter, when babies are born, one of the main goals of their psychological development is to figure out that they are unique, separate from other people. During their first few years of life, object relations theorists believe, the baby first has to go through a process called *splitting.* Newborn babies don't understand that other people are made up of a complex amalgam of characteristics, motives, behaviors, and abilities. It's almost as though, each time they are exposed to a person, it's a separate individual. Mom comes running to feed and cuddle the baby when she cries, and that's Good Mom. When the same woman responds to the baby's cries in the middle of the night, exhausted and fuzzy minded, and stone-facedly offers what's needed, the baby sees her as a new person. Let's call her Bad Mom. Because the baby is equipped with a strong sense of self-preservation and an intuitive sense that she's not up to the task of taking care of herself, she instinctively knows that it would be beneficial to keep Good Mom nearby and avoid Bad Mom.

Meanwhile, it's important that the baby figure out that Mom is actually multidimensional.

If interactions with Mom feel positive, then the baby begins to see both the caregiver and herself in a positive light. If the interactions are negative, that quality will be transferred to her perspective on herself and Mom. Rupture and repair are ways for the baby to begin to accumulate enough interactions to recognize that something good (repair) can in fact follow from something bad (rupture) *from the same person.* The baby has a critical revelation: Good Mom and Bad Mom are the same person who can be both "good" and "bad"! This must mean that *everyone* can be both good and bad. *This is why it's so critical that most ruptures get repaired.* If they aren't repaired, the baby will continue to view Mom (or Dad) as a good being and a bad one. This baby may well carry this split into the rest of his life, especially when under stress, which will make it really tough to form intimate relationships. How can you have a relationship with someone over the long term if you always view people in black-and-white terms? How can you understand that being human means being flawed and forgive the ruptures that occur in all relationships? How can you see yourself as capable of good and bad and make reparations after your own mistakes? How can you negotiate being married, being an employee, having a boss, getting along with neighbors, or raising children if you can't recognize that we're all capable of making mistakes and then working them through?

> *It's not avoiding ruptures that promotes healthy psychological development but being sure to make repairs.*

Recognizing that he sometimes feels good while interacting with Mom and sometimes not so good cements the baby's awareness that Mom really is a separate person: she has her own emotions, thoughts, drives, beliefs, behaviors. Have you ever met anyone who expresses outrage when anyone disagrees with him about anything? Or who thinks that whatever she's feeling, everyone else is feeling the same way at exactly the same time? You can't have a conversation with someone who thinks we all think alike, and you certainly can't have a healthy relationship with someone who is incapable of acknowledging and sharing someone else's feelings.

A child who thinks everyone is either bad or good will develop all kinds of defenses to avoid the bad people he imagines others to be and will also decide that he himself is all good or all bad. Upholding a self-image of all good or deflecting attention to his badness is an exhausting effort and distracts the growing child (and later adult) from developing the capacities that an integrated bad/good self has. These are capacities like the ability to:

- Experience a wide range of emotions, as well as mastery and pleasure
- Be alone without feeling abandoned and to be close with others without feeling overwhelmed
- Maintain a consistent sense of who you are over time
- Soothe yourself
- Be creative
- Solve problems

When a baby develops an understanding of the fact that we are all separate beings and that we can perceive and understand ourselves and one another in terms of psychological states like feelings, beliefs, intentions, and desires, he has the capacity for what developmental psychologists call *reflective functioning*. When you as a parent can truly Be-With your child, conveying that you understand relatively accurately what the child may be experiencing but also maintain and communicate your separateness, you are helping your child develop a reflective self. It's your capacity for reflective functioning that allows you to recognize a rupture as a rupture—to know how it made your child feel—and therefore recognize the need for a repair and what type of response on your part really will repair the rupture in a particular case.

In Chapter 1 we mentioned a research instrument called the Strange Situation Procedure (SSP), which is meant to help scientists observe the attachment style between a particular caregiver and child. Essentially, the way it works is that the adult and child are in a room equipped with seating and age-appropriate toys. The set-up involves having the caregiver briefly leave the room, once leaving the child alone and once with a stranger present. The researchers observe what happens when the caregiver exits, but particularly what happens when the caregiver returns and is reunited with the child. How does the child react? In broad strokes, a securely attached 1-year-old will be upset when the caregiver leaves and then relieved (while initially distressed) when the caregiver returns, seeking comfort upon being reunited.

The SSP is essentially a contrived rupture and repair. What we learn from how the child reacts when the caregiver returns is what kind of repair the child expects from the caregiver, based on past experiences. Part of what we learn from the caregiver's behavior is the caregiver's capacity for reflective functioning. A parent who gets defensive at the child's distress ("They made me leave you here alone!") or dismissing of distress ("You're fine; I was only gone for a few minutes") likely does not have a well-developed capacity for reflection, is not adept at repair, and has not formed a secure attachment with the child. Secure parents aren't focused on making themselves feel better; they're focused on making their child feel better. As in other effective repairs, the secure returning caregiver acknowledges the child's distress, apologizes for leaving, and offers a safe haven of comfort until the child is once again ready to go out and explore.

For some parents, more ruptures and fewer repairs occur on either the top or the bottom of the Circle.

Melissa tries to lure her 4-year-old son back to her side when they're at a family gathering, with food or a new little toy or a tickle, rupturing the Circle at the top. When she can let go of her defenses for long enough to see that her son really wants to go play with his cousins, she stops and says, "Hey, go play with everybody! I'll still be here" and then grits her teeth to resist the temptation to follow him.

Ming stiffens visibly when her 6-month-old cries. Instead of looking in her eyes to see if she can discern what's wrong, she says, "I'm busy right now!" and then makes sure she is. Or she pulls out a toy and sets it in front of the baby as she turns away. But lately, she's begun working on repair in these situations, trying to stay close and talk with her daughter until her own distress at the baby's crying subsides a little and then picking her up.

We talk more about why we're all at least a little more comfortable on one part of the Circle than the other and how our children respond to these sensitivities in Chapter 5.

The Challenge

Actually, making effective repairs is such a tricky balancing act for many of us that there's not just one main challenge; there are several:

• *Being able to say you're sorry and mean it is a big issue in rupture and repair.* If you yield to a desire to be right all the time, your child won't build trust in his own perspective. Nor will he learn to trust his own perspective if you leap to conclusions (such as that your child is feeling the way you might feel in a given situation) and misinterpret your child's feelings over and over. Your child starts out turning to you for guidance—you are, after all, bigger, stronger, wiser, and kind—aren't you? It's a double-edged sword that must be used wisely. Ultimately, unless you model healthy reflection, your child will believe there's no difference between himself and others and therefore won't be able to put himself in anyone else's shoes. He'll have trouble developing empathy, and he'll have a hard time understanding his own internal experience as well.

● *Blame erects another roadblock to effective repair.* Many ruptures occur when we blame our children for being the problem instead of seeing that they need help with a problem. It's hard to repair a blame-driven rupture if you feel the whole thing is your child's fault. We hear many parents say "He just wants attention!" when all a little boy or girl really wants is connection. As it turns out, most of us learned these attitudes at our own parents' feet.

● *Then there's self-blame.* If you are convinced that you *are* in fact bad, and therefore you're incapable of being a good parent, you're going to abdicate responsibility and just give up on any possible repair. Or you're going to feel the need to apologize so many times a day that your child will begin to assume you feel incompetent as a parent.

● *If you are primarily a bigger-and-stronger kind of parent by inclination, you also might have trouble with almost any repair because it feels like you're giving up your authority, admitting some kind of inferiority, if you apologize.* After all, you're the adult, you tell yourself. If you start apologizing, your children won't think that you know better than they do about *anything.* Even from a behavioral point of view, we know now that there's a big difference between being authoritarian and being authoritative. Being authoritative flows from the confident presence of being bigger, stronger, wiser, and kind and from prioritizing helping our children feel better over making ourselves feel better.

● *Another challenge with making effective repairs comes from overdoing it.* Some parents believe their child's every feeling and need is at the center of the world. If you feel this way, you might find yourself apologizing for everything all the time. If you've been around someone who gushes apologies, you know how empty they become. If you're overly focused on sensitivity to your child's feelings, you might also have a hard time taking charge.

• *Keep in mind that reflection won't get you very far unless it leads to resolution.* Reflection is critical—we can't repair our ruptures without it. But we need to make sure it doesn't end up being mere intellectualizing. Sometimes we try to "explain away" what just happened. Saying "You know I never like it when you treat your sister that way, so that's why I yelled at you" isn't repair, it's just another way to shift blame. Saying something like this, in contrast, leads to a resolution: "I know it hurts a lot when I yell like I just did. I'm sorry about yelling, and first of all I want you to tell me how you feel. Second, we've got to come up with a way for you to stop pushing her when you get upset." Repair includes honoring feelings and also looking to find another approach, *together.*

If you're wondering how we can fall into so many traps that prevent us from making repairs, keep in mind that we're vulnerable because so many of these challenges are ingrained within our procedural memory. We're not doing these things "on purpose." We're often doing what we learned in our day-to-day interactions growing up. This is learning that went on without words, when we were young and figuring out how life works. As was just stated, sometimes we know we're supposed to repair a rupture, but under the surface we really want our child to learn a lesson. Were you blamed as a child? If so, your procedural memory of that may drive you to "even the score" by blaming your own child, even if it's the last thing you consciously want to do. As painful as it is to consider, your implicit relational knowing can influence you in such a way that you want your child to feel some of what you felt as a child. In part this allows you to feel a little less alone in that feeling—which is still bubbling along under the surface of your conscious mind. In addition, your unconscious holds the memory of feeling unfairly blamed in that long ago interaction, so (strange though it may seem) blaming your own child feels like you've got some power and you're finally getting back at someone.

It can also be a replay of an unfinished, unrepaired scenario where you've unconsciously shifted roles: you're now the shaming parent, and your child is now living out what you went through many years ago. No parent likes recognizing these things, but it's far more common than most of us would imagine. In our experience it's hard to think of families where these issues don't happen some of the time.

You may find that simply understanding how to be the hands on the Circle is enough to make you take on this role with great success.

Many of us, though, despite a new understanding of *what* to do, still can't quite keep our intention to be bigger, stronger, wiser, and kind front and center—at least not as often or as thoroughly as we'd like. We all want to be good parents. Why do we struggle on one part of the Circle more than others? Why do we find ourselves uncomfortable with some parts of child rearing even though we want to be the best parents we can be? What force is at work that sometimes makes us feel as if we're on a different wavelength from this child we love so much?

We call it "shark music," and you'll learn about it in the next chapter.

SHARK MUSIC

How Our Childhood Echoes
in Our Parenting

It's Henry's third birthday, and all of his preschool classmates have been invited to the party. As the children arrive with a parent or a sitter, Henry's mom, Susan, greets them with a bright smile and points to the game some of the children are playing in a cluster in one corner. The room rapidly gets crowded and noisy as adults and children pile into a space that's not nearly as big as the preschool room.

Will, whose dad has heartily clapped his little boy on the back and proclaimed cheerfully, "You're going to have a *great* time, son!" as he backed out of the door, is sitting by himself with his back to the other children, quietly playing with a Tonka truck. When Susan squats down and gently asks him if he wants to play with Henry, the 3½-year-old looks up with a serious expression, says he has to "finish this job first," and starts pushing the truck vigorously across the carpet. She hesitates, then shrugs and says, "Well, OK, but you come over and join in when you're ready." Will doesn't turn toward the center of the room.

Bella, the tallest girl in the class, is squashed awkwardly on the couch next to her mother, her legs sticking out off the edge. Every time someone brushes against her feet trying to squeeze by, she utters a little whine, squirms, and looks up at her mother. Mom rubs her shoulder and pulls her daughter closer. Making the rounds of her guests,

Susan tells Bella they could really use another player in the game that's now in full swing. Bella's eyes light up and she starts to slide forward as her mother says, "Sure, that would be fun, wouldn't it, honey?" But she still has a grip on her daughter's arm, and when she gives it a squeeze, Bella looks up at her mom and then nestles back in. Her eyes are focused on the lively goings-on across the room.

In the midst of the fray is Callie, who's winning the game and refusing to give the next player a turn as her mother leans in from where she's sitting on the floor, saying, "Good job, Callie! Good *job*! Way to go! You did that just like I taught you! Oh, oh, OK, your turn's over . . . I know, you don't want to . . . hey, kids, you don't mind if Callie takes another turn, do you? It'll just take a minute. Callie's been practicing this really hard. Watch her—she's *really* good at it!" Henry wanders off to see what Will's up to, and a couple of the other children follow.

It's a pretty typical 3-year-old's birthday party. Children play together or alone or alternate between the two. Parents stick close by or keep their distance. There's fun and chaos and the occasional meltdown. Henry's so excited he has a hard time keeping it together and at one point swats a friend who won't give up the toy he wants to play with, who then bursts into tears. After the gift-opening ritual that one parent laughingly calls a "feeding frenzy" and the cake and juice ritual that leaves the entire room sticky, Susan looks a little like the Bride of Frankenstein.

All in all, she says, the party was a rousing success. But why didn't Will ever play with everyone else? How come Bella rarely ventured from the couch? Why wouldn't Callie's mother quit cheering her daughter on?

Maybe shark music was playing in the background.

Sometimes parents feel uncomfortable with certain needs their child expresses around the Circle. They're not always consciously aware of their discomfort, but they react to an urge to avoid that need in some way—to redirect their child from the top of the Circle (a need to explore) to the bottom (a need for comfort) or vice versa . . . to check out emotionally or physically . . . maybe to distract the child until she stops feeling the way she feels. Children get the message loud and clear, even if we parents don't realize we're sending it: Will's "unthought known" involves the idea that it's not OK for him to need the safety and comfort of his dad in a strange environment. Bella's implicit relational knowing says she's supposed to need Mom more than new experiences. Callie's being taught that she is, and needs to be, at the head of every class.

To illustrate how parents can feel like escaping from something as innocuous as a certain type of attachment need from their child, we show them a film of a beautiful beach scene, first with the serene *Pachelbel's Canon in D* by Bach playing in the background and then with a soundtrack evoking the bass line of the movie *Jaws*. The message is unavoidable: Mental associations can make something unthreatening feel dangerous. A parent in our original Circle of Security research study of the 1990s aptly said that feeling an urge to avoid certain needs around the Circle was like hearing "shark music," and we've used this metaphor in our group sessions with parents ever since.

All children have real needs on the top and bottom of the Circle, and their healthy development depends on both types of needs being met much of the time. Yet, as it turns out, almost all parents seem to be more comfortable with one type than the other. *How* uncomfortable we feel with certain needs varies from individual to individual. But we tend to struggle some of the time with certain needs on the Circle. What it comes down to is that those particular needs feel uncomfortable-unto-dangerous, for reasons that rather consistently seem to suggest seeds that were planted in our childhood. Now, when our own children express such needs, an alarm goes off: shark music. We may not hear it consciously. We probably can't put our finger on why we then react the way we do. But we do react, in ways that signal to the child that these particular needs are to be hidden and not acted on or expressed.

When it's only occasionally that we deliver a message that those needs are to be avoided, and especially when we repair the rupture of not meeting our child's need, development proceeds (all other factors being equal) as designed. When, however, this avoidance by a parent becomes a pattern, the same sensitivity can often end up being passed on to the child.

Is this a big deal? Not necessarily. *We all have these sensitivities: The young brain is wired to tune in to the lessons taught by our trusted early protectors, and these lessons commonly include Mom's or Dad's own sensitivities.* Whether this sensitivity ends up being a hindrance to the child who absorbs it is largely a matter of degree. Besides, childhood attachment does not have to be destiny. With the help of happenstance in the form of new secure attachment figures entering our life, and a healthy ability to reflect, we can earn security at any time during the lifespan (more on this under "But change can happen" on page 134).

Of course no one can foresee a child's path through life. If the parents of Will, Bella, and Callie hear their shark music and unconsciously teach their children to believe its warning on a regular basis, Will could *possibly* end up highly independent but lacking intimacy skills in his adult life. Bella might end up afraid to fly (literally as well as figuratively) and also struggle in relationships because she'll have difficulty trusting herself and her own capacities in adult life. Callie may end up lacking an accurate perspective of people's needs, always considering her own the most important. As to her close relationships, many people may begin to realize that her limitations with empathy come with a hypersensitivity to being found less than exceptional or special.

Right now, everything seems generally OK for these children. Will's preschool teacher writes in reports to his parents that he's very mature for his age, very independent—although she'd like to see him be a little more sociable at times. Bella seems very content, says the teacher, likely to kindly hand over a toy she's playing with to anyone who wants a turn with it. Privately, though, she has wondered why Bella then runs to her mom at pickup and clings to her leg as if she's been holding back distress all day. Callie is a high achiever, a "total go-getter," as the teacher puts it to her beaming parents (privately cringing a bit at how much Callie's dad boasts about her to the other parents during events at the school).

Nothing really unusual—or "wrong"—is happening to these children. The echoes of our childhood show up in our adult lives in all kinds of ways, both obvious and subtle, and being "just like Dad" or "the image of Mom" is not necessarily a bad thing. But in our work we've noticed that shark music is remarkably universal, a warning system that implies a genuine need on the Circle is somehow dangerous. Because of this perceived (albeit unconscious) danger, shark music often prevents us from seeing and supporting what our child needs in that moment. Over time, when we believe and then heed those alarms, a defensive pattern sets in.

"Having defenses" in our parenting has become sort of a dirty phrase for many, a marker for failing to do whatever seems so obviously "right" to observers (often then chalked up to the parent's favoring her own needs over her child's). It's as if we believe that being nervous about certain feelings or needs is a conscious decision. It's not. There's a more accurate (and much kinder) way to see this common occurrence of a parent establishing a pattern of staying away from an aspect of a relationship that feels unsafe. If, as a child, every time you felt sad your father seemed upset or your mother got nervous and told you to "Look on the bright side," it's understandable that you would grow up feeling uncomfortable (and lonely) whenever you started to feel upset. Sadness now equals someone important getting uncomfortable or anxious. Sadness equals feeling unmet and alone. The very understandable conclusion would be that it's really smart to stay away from sadness. Shark music would then simply be that early detection system that warns you "Oh no, here it comes again. Keep your distance!" In this way, it can be seen as a sign of caring for your child if you do what you can to pass on the same warning system, hoping to protect her from the same pain you learned to avoid.

Will's father couldn't see that the little boy was worried about being left alone at the party. Bella's mother couldn't see that her daughter really wanted to jump into the game with the other children. Callie's mom didn't grasp that Callie felt agitated during that game, and upset when she noticed the children starting to drop out of it. If they had seen these needs, they might have responded differently. Will's dad might have stayed at the party, at least until Will got settled in, and Will might have ended up playing with the other children. Bella's mother might have recognized Bella's need to play with the others and resisted holding her back. Callie's mother might have seen that her little girl was getting overstimulated (in part by a need to excel) and gently removed her from the center of the game, where she could calm down before diving back in.

These well-meaning, loving parents may not have seen their children's needs because shark music blinded them to those very needs. This is why it's so important to start exploring our own shark music. Understanding why an alarm is repeatedly triggered by something as typically unthreatening as our child's need for a hug or encouragement to go play has a way of soothing the unconscious mind so that a long-held defensive pattern suddenly feels less necessary. That understanding, combined with having the Circle of Security map at hand, can open up a world of possibilities, for us, for our child, and for our relationship.

Getting to know your shark music offers an exciting chance to deepen your relationship with your child—and improve your child's chances of having healthy relationships throughout life.

Let's Not Forget the "And"

In introducing the idea that shark music can obscure your child's needs from you, we barely mentioned one important factor. What's going on in your unconscious mind is not the only thing concealing certain needs your child is experiencing. Attachment behavior is an interpersonal dance; it takes two—that is, you may not just be sidestepping what your child needs. Your child might be colluding, unconsciously, with you in this avoidance of shark music. When our children learn—and they do learn this when really young, well before they have language with which to understand it—that we are uncomfortable with certain needs, they join us (also unconsciously) to avoid expressing them. Children learn all kinds of strategies to hide their needs when they sense a parent's discomfort with them, because their priority is to keep Mom or Dad available and as comfortable as possible . . . anything but anxious. They'll do whatever it takes to keep the parent close, in the best mood possible. If this means no longer heading too far out by playing with that new boy on the playground or no longer crying when her feelings are hurt, then that becomes the child's game plan. These unconscious strategies are the subject of Chapter 6.

Now you may be wondering how you can possibly learn to discern what your child really needs in every moment if your shark music is obscuring it and your child is collaborating in this subconscious ruse. We explain how you can learn to do just that in the next chapter, but for now, remember that children aren't magicians. They really do experience those needs, so they are not going to be able to keep them completely under wraps.

There is, however, a magician at work in the attachment dance. Let's reveal him for the humbug he really is.

Pay Attention to That Man Behind the Curtain

"Oh—You're a very bad man!"

"Oh, no, my dear. I'm a very good man. I'm just a very bad Wizard."

In the film of L. Frank Baum's *The Wonderful Wizard of Oz*, the flim-flam man posing as the wizard exhorts Dorothy and friends to pay no attention to that man behind the curtain when he's suddenly been revealed. This is similar to the way the procedural memory that triggers shark music operates. The mind stores implicit memories so that they're there to serve us as needed, without getting in the way of the conscious thoughts that guide us through the business of our day. These implicit memories guide our behavior too, but more the way the nervous system makes sure we keep breathing. We don't have to think about inhaling and exhaling, and we don't think about our childhood attachment experiences when faced with our child's bid for comfort or encouragement. We just act in ways to discourage those needs in our own children when ours went unanswered by our parents, in the same way that our nervous system makes sure we gasp for air after being deprived of oxygen. Both types of unconscious guidance are protective. Like the little old fortune-teller from Kansas, implicit relational knowing is not ill intentioned (quite the opposite, in fact), but sometimes it gets overblown and oversteps its bounds. So does the nervous system, sometimes pushing us into hyperventilating when it detects fear and decides we need to be flooded with oxygen to prepare for fight or flight.

Here's a brief summary of how procedural memory of our earliest attachment experiences gives rise to shark music:

1. A child cries and reaches for comfort from a parent *or* tries to venture away from the parent to explore the world.
2. Some deep-seated memory of what typically happened when that child, now a parent, asked for comfort or encouragement is cued during adulthood, and shark music is triggered.
3. Whether or not the parent is aware of feeling any discomfort, the parent tries to divert the child from that need; or conveys displeasure, even subtly; or offers the child the opposite of what the child is asking for; or becomes physically, emotionally, and/or mentally distant.
4. This pattern occurs over and over between this child and this parent.
5. The child gets the message: That need on the top or bottom of the Circle makes Mom or Dad uncomfortable enough to become less available.
6. The child concludes: *This is somehow dangerous—it's making her anxious, or making him distant, or causing her to seem embarrassed or displeased. This feels unsafe. I'll do whatever it takes to bring Mom or Dad back to feeling less upset.*

7. The child learns to stifle the need and/or act like he needs the opposite (a secure base instead of a safe haven or vice versa).
8. Presto! Mom or Dad calms, which means this particular need on the Circle really must be unacceptable. "This must be the fundamental truth about relationships."
9. The child takes this procedural memory, firmly implanted in his unconscious, with him into adult life as an ingrained state of mind, where . . .
10. It pulls his strings when his own child expresses that very same "unacceptable" need.

The key point in this sequence is that it unfolds without any conscious awareness on our part. This is a tough concept to accept. We all want the best for our children, so it's hard to believe we're not in total control of how we react to their needs or that we're not just making rational decisions in the child's best interest. When Will's father leaves him at the party, he firmly believes he's helping his little boy become self-sufficient. Bella's mother would say she didn't think her daughter was feeling entirely well and didn't want her to "overdo it." Callie's parents, like many of us, just want her to succeed so she'll be competent in a competitive world.

Referring to the unconscious may also call up images of Freud, or lying on a couch trying to uncover buried memories of childhood harm to explain current unhappiness. Many people don't want to go down that path, and we assure you that's not what we're talking about. This is all simply the stuff of everyday struggles in parenting, without any implication of major harm to you or your children. **A compelling reason to look at these unconscious processes is that we are among the first generations to have access to attachment research that allows us to fine-tune our parenting—*without blame*—in a way that supports an increased sense of security in our children.** Knowing we don't want our children to deal with some of the nagging difficulties we've encountered in our close relationships, many of us welcome having this simple road map to offer our children an even more secure foundation than the one we knew growing up.

Here are some examples of precisely the kind of behavior that baffles us and that we likely don't want to continue. Let's say your 2-year-old son gets startled by a shadow in the dark and starts to cry, and you find yourself snapping at him (or maybe just looking sternly), letting him know that he's "being a baby." Why would you do that when you know rationally that he's just being 2? Or your 3-year-old daughter is quietly occupying herself with a new toy—something you wished for out loud just yesterday so you could have a break from being her constant playmate—and suddenly you're interrupting with questions about what she's doing, whether she's hungry, and the next thing you know you're down on the floor asking if you can play too. These incidents can be explained away as the product of unusual stress, boredom, or just a bad day. But they may happen with some regularity even when we're feeling just fine.

Patterns like these are incredibly hard to discern if you don't even know they're there, and they can maintain a strong grip on our behavior. This is why it's so important to pull back the curtain. When you understand what's pulling your strings, you give yourself a chance to make different choices in how you respond to your child. You can turn down the volume on your shark music to meet your child's attachment needs more consistently, conferring all the benefits of secure attachment on the child, yourself, and the relationship:

- Less parent–child conflict
- A stronger sense of being able to have an impact on how your child feels and acts
- More comfort and ease in parenting
- A closer connection to your child
- More insight into how all kinds of relationships work

One good reason to understand your shark music is that, like the humbug "wizard," its warnings are, while well-intentioned, deceptive. The amygdala, where shark music is likely born, is not the brain's best thinker. (It thinks fast, but without access to a larger sense of wisdom.)

How Shark Music Is Born

Children are born seeking at least one person they can attach to, who will be there for them while they figure out how to deal with the world and the feelings it evokes. As incredible as it seems, a newborn baby already knows that attachment is paramount. Your son or daughter will do anything to keep you accessible, because her physical and emotional survival depends on it. As we've explained, your child learns how to regulate emotions with you and from you. In the shared regulatory system described in Chapter 1, a parent who reacts to shark music instead of to his child's need is not going to help the child learn to regulate that particular emotion or feel safe with that particular need on the Circle on her own because there's no coregulation going on.

Your baby also begins to form mental representations of caregivers—images held in the mind of what a caregiver is—based on interactions with you. As he grows, he'll take these internal models of relationship along with him, applying what he knows about you to new relationships: If holding out his arms to be held by you is typically met with a welcoming smile and a hug, he might be inclined to be affectionate and trusting with Aunt Beth when she starts to babysit for him. If you love to talk and sing with him, he might coo and babble when other adults enter his sphere. Even without language, babies form fairly complex images of caregivers via their internal models learned with us.

Of course these models of relationships aren't set in stone—or at least they shouldn't be. Fortunately, the mind boasts a robust capacity for new learning as well as for maintaining the status quo (see the description of homeostasis below). So we revise, modify, and even replace our internal working models given enough new information (and trust in those who offer it) to justify the shift. John Bowlby said that in attachment terms health can be defined as the ability to do just this. Flexibility and growth are always helpful to surviving and even thriving.

Nevertheless, flexibility can be hard to come by regarding internal working models. That's because they're stored in the amygdala. This

Many organisms, including the human being, have a self-regulating capacity called "homeostasis," a process by which the organism maintains stability or equilibrium. For us humans, homeostasis maintains both physiological and psychological stability. Think of body temperature. The hypothalamus in the brain controls a complex system involving breathing, metabolism, circulation, and so on to keep our body temperature steady at about 98.6 degrees. In attachment theory, homeostasis essentially ensures that any new information we store in our procedural memory about relationships largely confirms our earliest internal working models. (The fact that many of us are raised for roughly 18 years by the same parent, who cares for us in the same way over time, also reinforces our earliest picture of caregivers.) The resulting stable—even stubborn—internal working model of parenting serves children pretty well: it enables them to broach new relationships somewhat informed instead of as if they had been dropped to Earth from another planet and are meeting their first human—over and over.

brain structure, part of the larger limbic system, is heavily involved in memory and emotions, social processing, and also decision making. Procedural memory related to attachment is likely stored mainly in the amygdala, which is connected to other brain structures, as a sort of reference library of "facts" that add up to our internal working models. Here's the problem: Fear is one of our fundamental emotions, and the amygdala is there to store memories of what is dangerous, scan the environment for signs of it, and then evoke fear so we'll fight our "attacker," flee, or freeze in the name of self-preservation. This is where shark music is born.

If Will got the impression early on that his dad greeted needs for safety and comfort with aversion, his amygdala library filed that tidbit away, and whenever he was scared and needed to be offered gentle presence, his amygdala fired off a "Danger!" alert—"If Dad sees that you feel this way, he might pull away!"—so Will learned to shut down his need for comfort. Bella's shark music started screaming at her when she felt like leaving Mom's side to play or explore her surroundings, because Mom seemed fearful. So Bella largely acted like she needed to stay with Mom, which in turn seemed to make Mom relax. Callie sensed that both of her parents were a little embarrassed when she wasn't number one at everything she did, so she aggressively pursued excellence.

If it sounds like we're exaggerating the vehemence of shark music, that's because its warning can feel as urgent as the instinct to dive out of the way of a speeding bus—even though there is no bus.

If you asked these children why they did these things, they wouldn't be able to tell you (although they might get uncomfortable just thinking about these types of situations). When they grow up, though, the amygdala will set off a shark music alarm when their own children exhibit the same needs, telling them there is danger where there actually is none. As we often say to parents, shark music triggers fear of a necessary and healthy need. They'll listen to this signal and respond accordingly if their experience in the interim years has not revised their internal working model.

When we use a video of a scene along the Oregon coast to help explain shark music to parents, our intent is to show that something as apparently unintrusive as background music can completely transform our perceptions. As the camera follows the path down to the beach with *Pachelbel's Canon in D* playing, viewers naturally feel good about what's to come—maybe a refreshing swim or a picnic on the sand. When we play the same video but with the shark music soundtrack, instantly the viewers feel a sense of dread: *What's at the end of that path?* That background music is procedural memory—it's what tells us whether a need expressed by our child is "safe" to see and to meet or "dangerous."

The trouble is, of course, that none of the needs on the Circle are actually dangerous. Whatever distress we felt when we were so very young and pained by our parent's distress and resulting distance— "Being-Without" (see the box on the facing page)—it's not what is happening right now. That parent isn't before us, we're not the ones feeling the need for comfort or encouragement, and there really is nothing to be afraid of. The amygdala peddles truth and humbug as if they're both the real thing, issuing the same alarms for both. It's up to us to figure out what's authentic and what's just an impostor, and that's not easy.*

How to Lower the Volume

> Fear is the cheapest room in the house.
> I would like to see you living in better conditions.
> —HAFEZ, 14th-century Persian poet

The amygdala doesn't just send us a preliminary memo. In the words of psychologist and emotional intelligence champion Daniel Goleman, the amygdala simply hijacks us. Unfortunately, adults who have an amygdala library packed with shelves of painful attachment memories are particularly vulnerable and tend to be on high alert much of the time. A groundbreaking assessment tool called the Adult Attachment Interview (AAI), developed by Carol George, Nancy Kaplan, and Mary Main in 1985, helps therapists and researchers identify whether adults have a secure attachment style without having been able to observe them as young children. In one study, adults found to be insecurely attached on the AAI showed more activation in the amygdala and felt more irritation when they heard a baby crying than securely attached adults. Neuropsychologist Allan Schore notes that severe, traumatic ruptures that occur without repair over and over substantially alter the

---

*On our website, *www.circleofsecurity.com*, you can view a 4-minute video titled "Circle of Security Animation."

The Echo of Being-Without

The 10-month-old boy lies quietly, the warm crease of the sheet beneath him feeling damp and familiar. The time since his last cry for help seems to expand into an untouchable distance far beyond his ability to watch it. The feeling increases—dark, then darker, then falling into blackness. Finally, there is a sound that rushes toward his almost rigid mouth and he lets the full force of his need begin to release. Just as quickly, the blackness he swims in stops the expression and he quickly backs away from his spasm of urgency. All that remains is a whimper, a sober whispering of sound that says little of what he would really want to reach for.

When she is suddenly there at the door, their eyes meet for but a brief glance, and each looks away. Yet even in that momentary touching of eyes, her exasperation reaches him and scolds his need of her. She does not want to be reminded of lack and yearning, not his and most certainly not her own. And once again the decision developing in his tiny brain tightens its grip on this thing of togetherness: "Stop the wanting, at all costs stash it away. Banish it to the farthest reaches of experience. Whenever it returns, hate it with the same intensity you now see in her eyes. There is no place for longing. Swallow it now and swallow it always."

Being-Without is a devastating feeling for anyone, and most certainly for an infant. Unfortunately, these feelings of loneliness, fear, anger, mistrust, and shame learned early also burn late. Indeed, they seem to radiate from one generation into the next. When, for a child, the context of relationship is one of insensitivity and a lack of availability, when the wick of the developing self is dipped repeatedly in the wax of missed cues, neglect, disregard, hostility, and abandonment, that child's subsequent experiences will inevitably reflect this context of pain. This 10-month-old boy is already afraid to ask for the closeness and nurturing he needs. He has, even at this young age, begun to replicate a pattern that was probably familiar to his mother when she was at a similar stage of development. The sad truth is that, without intervention, this child will very likely grow up and pass the same pattern of distance and loneliness on to his own children.

biochemistry of the right brain—which is developing so fast during the first 3 years of life—and a child's attachment history can become part of the child's personality. In very extreme cases of neglect or abuse, more serious psychological problems can develop. Amazingly, though, we've found that the Circle of Security intervention can help even parents with the most tragic attachment backgrounds.

Make It Verbal

The Circle of Security addresses the dilemma of a stubborn amygdala by making procedural memory verbal—by making the implicit explicit. Just putting a name to the phenomenon—shark music—has a powerful effect on many parents, giving them a little space in which to stop and consider whether the alarm is accurate. But putting into words what their specific shark music is and when it is cued takes them even further and can help them turn down the volume preemptively.

Making it verbal includes being able to name your emotions, thoughts, and behaviors. How can you begin to know when you're in distress and why if you don't know what you're feeling and thinking? We all have varying abilities to identify what's in our minds and hearts, and some people grow up with a limited vocabulary for emotion in particular. Shark music is a highly emotional phenomenon (that's how the amygdala gets our attention), so it's good to start asking yourself, whenever you're responding to your child, *exactly what you're feeling.*

> **Wisdom is not found in the feeling brain (limbic system)
> or the thinking brain (prefrontal cortex) but in the
> dialogue between the two.**

There's really no way to erase the shark music recordings in your limbic system, but that's OK. Remember that your shark music is a natural defense intended to protect you. Writer G. K. Chesterton wisely advised us never to tear down a fence until we know why it was put up in the first place. Understanding your shark music's origins has a way of easing your stress and boosting your self-compassion along with compassion for your child. You can definitely turn the volume down. One father who had a very tough childhood put it perfectly: "I still hear my shark music. I just don't believe there are any sharks in the water anymore."

Get Some Distance

Another way that the Circle of Security intervention helps parents override their shark music is through the use of video. We film parents using the SSP introduced in Chapter 4 and then judiciously show them clips of their interactions with their child. This allows them to see their attachment behaviors at a safe distance from the pressure to meet the child's needs in the moment. Filming yourself with your child is probably neither practical nor necessary for you, but you can learn about attachment struggles on the top and bottom of the Circle, and with the hands on the Circle, through the descriptions later in this chapter. There are other ways you can explore your shark music as well; see Chapter 7.

Everyone who has learned about these struggles around the Circle of Security seems to naturally start to see examples of shark music–triggered responses everywhere. At risk of becoming one of those people who "diagnoses" everyone else, you might see if you notice shark music at work or on the playground when you're in naturalistic settings. But don't expect to have 20–20 vision. It takes expert knowledge and hundreds of hours of practice to begin to identify where parents and children struggle around the Circle with real accuracy. That is in part because researchers have found there's not that strong an association between caregiving *behavior* and attachment bond. That is, a parent can assiduously comfort a crying baby, help a toddler investigate a garden, sit close enough to a group of children to signal availability if there's a problem without interfering, and do so consistently, and that behavior will not predict what type of attachment the parent has with the child. So just watching the way a parent takes care of her child won't definitively tell you enough without much more experience with interpreting subtle behaviors that signify state of mind.

Apparently it is *state of mind* that influences secure attachment (or the lack thereof). In fact, researchers have found that the state of mind of women assessed while pregnant predicted what type of attachment they would form with their baby more accurately than any measurable ways they took care of the baby after it was born. Somehow, the youngest babies can sense ease versus impatience, delight versus resentment or irritation, comfort versus restlessness, genuine versus pretending, or other positive versus negative responses in a parent when these reactions aren't evident to a casual observer. Little babies may pick up on the smallest sigh, the subtlest shift in tone of voice, a certain glance, or some type of body language and know the parent is genuinely comfortable or definitely not pleased. So it might take a lot of observation to start to make even a good guess about anyone other than yourself.

Your best "subject," therefore, will be yourself with your own family. The bond that forms naturally between you and your child makes it much easier to get to know what's really going on in an up-close, personal, and accurate way. The goal isn't to find problems. Rather, it's to discover those places, somewhere on the Circle, where you find yourself anxious or on-the-way-to-anxious: Places that we researchers call "micro-interactions" that aren't about pathology but rather about struggles that go unnoticed from parent to child and generation to generation. Using what you've just been reading, you'll likely be able to quiet the interference of shark music and use the Circle of Security map to help you make an empathic shift toward your child's needs despite any (even minor) discomfort you may feel. You may also find that attachment/shark music moments from your own history spontaneously come to mind.

It's essential to understand that this is not a route to blaming yourself or one of your caregivers for whatever you struggle with today. Again, the Circle of Security repeatedly brings forth empathy and compassion in those who view their present and past relationships through its lens. One man described being speechless when his mother related how the man at age 2 had started crying when he was leaving the house of a friend and his mother proudly reported that she just turned her back on the little boy . . . who never did *that* again. Years later when he was introduced to the Circle of Security, he found himself moved to tears when he thought about how his mother had lost his older sister at age 6 months, just a year before he was born. Could his mother have been distant sometimes because of the memory of that specific grief or, he surmised, more likely because she had grown up in a family that had taught her to stay far away from all grief?

If you already have children and you find that you're struggling somewhere on the Circle, it can be painful to explore your procedural memory when shark music is blaring relentlessly at you. Some parents approach the task with a heavy burden of shame as well, maybe because they entered parenthood determined not to repeat the "mistakes" of their own parents and impose the same pain on their own children—and here they are doing exactly that. We've seen parents watch COS video clips of themselves with their young child and point to the child saying, "That's me when I was little, and there I am, doing just what my mother did."

Reflect

When a child expresses a need that triggers shark music, it's as if the parent is suddenly watching an old movie of the same kind of scene from her own childhood. She ends up reenacting her own childhood role, her parent's role, or—by overcompensating—a fantasy of what she wishes had happened. Because the movie never changes, she ends up trapped in reruns. The primary and best way to make new choices is to use her powers of reflection. In this book, *reflective functioning* means the psychological ability to stand back and recognize what we're doing and not doing to meet the needs of our children. It also includes the capacity to see how our children are already approaching needs on the Circle in the same ways we do. With reflection, your defenses just might start to soften—or at least feel tolerable while you reflect on whether you're really seeing what your child needs right now and can respond the way you want.

Any parent who can stand back and make sense of how she was parented and then see similar patterns in how she parents illustrates how valuable the insights are that can emerge through the reflection process. But please keep in mind that seeing clearly doesn't always translate to immediately *doing* things differently. Procedural memory and shark music exert a powerful grip on us, and it can take a while to loosen their hold. One father who had learned in the COS intervention that his shark music tended to keep him from showing his child affection started saying as he was about to enter the room where his little boy was waiting "Kiss my baby, kiss my baby, kiss my baby" and then walked into the room, stepped over the baby sitting on the rug, and stood looking out the window. A failure to reflect? Hardly. His little boy called out and Dad turned around, said under his breath, "There's that shark music," and gave the child a kiss as he picked him up.

Remember That You're Doing It All Out of Love

Comfort and courage can come from understanding that we actually heed our shark music as a way of protecting our child. Imagine that when you were little, you were locked in your room every time you raised your voice. You'd probably become pretty quiet so you wouldn't get sent away. Now, faced with your own rambunctious son, you might try to keep him quiet too. Being loud represents shark-infested waters to you, and your amygdala is there to help you keep your child safe from the inevitable (yet no longer present) predators. The same is true for all the needs on the Circle. You may have learned that exploration or comfort seeking was unacceptable to your parents, and so you stopped asking for it. Believe it or not, your unconscious desire to keep your child from asking for these same needs is a loving gesture.

Remember this as you explore your shark music. And trust your ability to reflect. It will help you shift from focusing on what your child is doing and how it makes you feel to what you are doing and how that makes your child feel. *That's* the best protection you can possibly provide.

> ***Reflection means stopping to ask yourself questions,***
> ***not only about where you are on the Circle but also***
> ***about what your shark music is.***

The Invisible Family Heirloom

> The past is always present in the moment.
> —SALVADOR MINUCHIN, family therapist

One reason we became so fascinated by attachment theory as family therapists was that in getting to know parents who were struggling in their relationship with their child, we almost always found their particular problems were connected to related problems in their own upbringing. That might seem like a cliché as timeworn as "the apple doesn't fall far from the tree." But in attachment terms, it's much more complex and, we believe, potent. Sociologists and public policymakers are constantly seeking broad measures that will break the cycle of poverty, abuse, undereducation and underemployment, family instability, and more. We humbly suggest that everyone addressing these problems needs to learn about attachment research as an essential component in finding solutions. It's our belief that this learning needs to be offered in a way that makes immediate and intuitive sense. This, of course, is why we created the Circle of Security.

There's little doubt today that relationships are essential to success and happiness in all domains of life. But it's attachment theory that helps us understand why some people seem to form connections so much more easily than others, how some of us can trust a relationship wholeheartedly without losing ourselves while others have to choose between being consumed and being isolated, and why certain individuals genuinely feel comfortable and at ease with friends while others can appear this way but internally are always second-guessing themselves and feeling self-critical. Naturally, many different factors affect our personality and temperament, social and emotional skills, and potential and how much we fulfill it. But attachment style is passed down from generation to generation at an amazing rate of about 75%. Picture this:

Bianca loves her mother, Rosetta, a single parent who continues to struggle after a messy divorce. At 4 years old, Bianca already knows that her mom is overwhelmed. Depressed and unsure of their future, Bianca's mother does her best to stay upbeat and supportive. But with a new job, bills, and a joint custody agreement that isn't to her liking, she often feels "down and overwhelmed," as she tells her daughter.

Rosetta describes her little girl as "an exceptionally anxious child," one who cannot sleep through the night without demanding that her mother sleep with her. "I just have no choice but to meet her need for me."

Night after night, Bianca tries to go to bed on her own and Rosetta pleads with her to go to sleep. And night after night, Bianca begins to cry until her mother stops whatever she is doing and climbs into bed with her. Only then can Bianca fall asleep, a sleep so light that any attempt by her mother to get up to attend to the rest of her life leads to wails and demands that pull her mother back into bed.

When Rosetta tries to tell her own mother how difficult this routine is for her, her mother replies with an exasperated "Well, she's just like you, Rosetta. I couldn't do one thing without you insisting that I pick you up first. I hardly ever got anything done around the house at all!" Funny, what Rosetta remembers is that her mother wouldn't let her go on playdates or sleepovers, saying she'd catch whatever bug the other children had, and that you never know what other families thought was a proper dinner for a child, and that a girl belongs with her own mother. But then when Rosetta did stay home with her mother and tried to play with her or go to her for comfort, Rosetta's mom would act distracted and a little irritable. Rosetta remembers always being put down while she was still crying when she was really young.

If we could work with Rosetta's mother, we'd find out that her father had been raised to believe that "You can't depend on anyone but family" and had been discouraged from going away to college. He'd married a woman who was happy to depend on him as the head of the household, although he had a habit of complaining that he had to make all the decisions and even do the grocery shopping because his wife was so helpless.

Without the insights of attachment theory, we might easily conclude that this family had passed down a lot of explicit self-protective ideas about life to each generation. But what was so much more powerful—and so hard to change—was the fact that at least one of the parents in each generation was hypervigilant and nervous about needs on the top of the Circle, afraid to allow children to get much distance or experience much autonomy but also a little ill at ease with offering comfort. And all of this information was passed down outside of conscious awareness—what pioneering child psychologist Selma Fraiberg called "ghosts in the nursery." This is why Rosetta doesn't even recognize that it's not only Bianca that's pulling her to stay close at all times but, more centrally, something inside herself. Ghosts are invisible.

But change can happen. The apple can roll away from the tree. Reflective functioning is the main key to making this shift. If parents recognize how their shark music is guiding their state of mind, they can make efforts to change that state of mind and thereby avoid transmitting it unwittingly to their child. A lot of different biological and environmental factors shape the development of a child, and with reflection we all have the opportunity at any point in our lives to earn security and develop a more coherent approach to relationship.

We've found in our Circle of Security work that high-risk parents (homeless teen mothers, parents who were abused as children, and others) who are strong in reflective functioning are already more likely to have a secure attachment with their children. They have been able to see the difference between their own experiences as children and what's happening with their own child and act in the here and now. Happily, this doesn't mean those with lower reflective functioning can't earn security for themselves and their children. We've found that those who come to the COS intervention with the weakest capacity for reflection have a real chance of developing a secure attachment with their children with this help. They reflect as well; it's just that they make the greatest gains in reflective functioning while learning about the Circle of Security. This says a lot about the positive intentionality that everyone brings to parenting—what John Bowlby called a fortuitous type of "preprogramming."

> *The past is never dead. It's not even past.*
> —WILLIAM FAULKNER, *Requiem for a Nun*

Where Do You Struggle on the Circle: Top, Bottom, or Hands?

Parenting demands that we make a lot of decisions about various aspects of child rearing: discipline, diet, breast-feeding versus bottle feeding, cosleeping versus separate sleeping, time-ins versus time-outs, free play versus the use of flash cards or classical music to enhance IQ, child care or stay-at-home parent, and so on. You can subscribe to one or another approach to all of these issues for very good reasons, but if your state of mind doesn't flow from a secure attachment, it might not matter which choices you make about feeding, teaching, or managing behavior. This is why it's worth knowing where your Circle struggles lie.

The Circle of Security map was designed to reflect the attachment classifications identified by Mary Ainsworth starting in the late 1960s and revised by many others since then. The terminology attached to these classifications has evolved too, but we view them simply as struggles with the top, the bottom, or the hands on the Circle. See if you identify with any of the following descriptions.

Shark Music at the Bottom of the Circle

Adults who hear shark music when their child is on the bottom of the Circle tend to feel uncomfortable with emotional and/or physical closeness. They may be dismissive of the importance of these attachment needs and downplay the essential nature of relationships in life. Their shark music may stem from a sense of having no one to "catch" or soothe them when feeling emotionally distressed and therefore experiencing a kind of free fall and emptiness where warmth and support were needed from their caregiver as little children. As a defense against his own childhood pain, and to spare his child the same pain, a parent who is uncomfortable on the bottom of the Circle might focus mainly on the child's achievements, intelligence, or interest in activities (focusing on the top-half exploratory aspects of care*taking* and ignoring emotional care*giving* opportunities).

Parents who have difficulty on the bottom of the Circle often expect their children to be able to do things that they may not be developmentally ready for. Will's dad dropped his 3-year-old off at the party without a glance back because, as he said to Susan on the phone when accepting the invitation, "The little guy is totally fine without me! It's amazing—he's been like that since he was 2!"

Others stress performance and success in their children. Callie's parents pushed her to be a relentless competitor, because, after all, "She needs to learn to swim with the sharks." Ironic metaphor, no? Sometimes Callie's mom didn't seem entirely comfortable with this, however. At preschool family events, another parent could often be seen backed into a corner by her, where she would describe the "awesomeness" of Callie's skill under discussion, ending in "If my dad had not insisted that I work hard at these things, I'd never be where I am today." The other parent often looked like she'd rather be anywhere else, and Callie's mother usually looked like she was trying to convince herself that she was raising Callie "totally right."

Interestingly, bottom-half-struggling parents don't necessarily want their children to be truly independent. They may seem like they don't want their child to need them, but they often want to be nearby, particularly if there's an achievement they can witness. Often concerned that their child's self-esteem is on the line, they may feel a need to cheerlead their child with a series of "Good job!" and "Awesome!" exclamations and hand clapping. These parents may think of and describe their children as gifted (even if they're not) and revel in the esteem their children get for their accomplishments (which can also feel like esteem for the parents).

Of course many struggles on the bottom of the Circle are manifested much more subtly. After learning about the Circle of Security, one mother started to recall minor incidents that she took as bottom-oriented struggles. In a group, she remembered, she tended to hold her son at age 5 months out on her knee, facing the other people in the room. She told herself that that was because the baby was so outgoing and so interested in what was going on around him that he'd be happier if he could see everyone and interact. And he did seem to be. But one day she was in a long line at the post office and saw a 1-year-old baby being held by his mother in front of her, with his head resting on her

> **Reflecting about Bottom-Half Struggles**
>
> 1. Do I worry that my child's sense of self-esteem is in need of continual (often moment-to-moment) maintenance?
> 2. Do I look for ways to keep my child focused on ever-increasing achievement (either physical or intellectual) in a way that limits closeness (cuddling, touch, lap time, etc.)?
> 3. Am I happier when my child is out exploring the world and somewhat ill at ease when it's time to help make sense of emotions or offer comfort when he or she is upset?

shoulder, a contented look on his face, and wondered, "Why doesn't my son like to be held like that?"

Shark Music at the Top of the Circle

Parents who hear shark music when their child is on the top of the Circle aren't dismissive of the importance of emotional attachment—they're actually somewhat preoccupied with it. Uncomfortable with emotional and/or physical separation from their child, they're inclined to come up with diversionary tactics to keep their child close and away from what they may view as "danger"—too much distance, which could be anything that doesn't involve them personally. They come up with a lot of reasons to keep their child close, or at least returning to them often when the child may be perfectly happy exploring some safe corner of his world. Sometimes parents who struggle on the top of the Circle treat their children as if they're much younger than they are or encourage the child to *always* look to them for help, because that keeps the child developmentally dependent on the parent.

Bella's mother not only stayed at the party with her but practically clamped her daughter to her side throughout. She knew on some level that Bella wanted to go out and play, and rationally she could probably have agreed that playing a game with the other children in a friend's living room where she'd be only 10 feet away was certainly safe. But her shark music said otherwise. So she gave her daughter mixed signals, telling her she should go play but then somehow sending a nonverbal signal through her body language or facial expression or tone of voice—something only Bella would pick up on—that it really wasn't OK.

Where Callie's parents treat her as if she's a star in her own right (while getting a lot of satisfaction out of her achievements for themselves), there are other parents who maintain closeness by overidentifying or staying "one-minded" with their child. Such a relationship can, at times, feel "too precious" to an outside observer. This parent treats the child as uniquely special (the focus is on specialness rather than achievement) and can seem totally preoccupied with her perfect little boy or girl. Behind the scenes this parent feels anything but special, but uses the perceived "perfection and specialness" of the child she is identified with to cover over this deeper level of self-doubt. Such a child is encouraged to stay close and like-minded, remaining within the orbit of the parent, never venturing into real autonomy.

Unfortunately, parents who are uncomfortable navigating the top of the Circle also often struggle with providing true comfort. They tend to be focused on satisfying their own need to be needed or be of one mind with their child and don't offer actual or attuned comfort. At first glance, this can be confusing because they can appear to be remarkably involved with their child. The issue is that it's an overly involved stance, at times pushing closeness when the child may not be asking for it. So wrapped up in their own very loud shark music, they may explicitly proclaim that they are staying close to meet the needs of their child. While truly worried about what might happen to their child upon separation, they are also significantly worried about what will happen to *them*.

Reflecting about Top-Half Struggles

1. Do I worry that my child will quit being so available to me?
2. Do I look for ways to draw my child's focus back to our relationship?
3. Am I happier when my child is nearby and stays focused on us?

Shark Music While Being the Hands on the Circle

Let's make one thing very clear: All parents struggle to be the hands on the Circle. At some times, in some places, under certain circumstances, we're going to want to abdicate the parental role, at least to a degree. We're going to feel like just ignoring a tantrum or sending the screaming child to bed. We're going to give in to pleading and begging and let the child have something we don't want him to have. We're going to snap at our children, saying something we wish we could take back (and then ask ourselves incredulously, "Who was *that?*").

This doesn't make us monsters, and it might not even mean we're hearing our shark music at the time. Excess stress can easily make any of us take our hands off the Circle momentarily. The key is to make a repair when these ruptures occur—and make it as quickly as possible (see the boxes on pages 140–141 and 142). There's nothing more threatening to a child than having his beloved caregiver act mean, weak, or gone. Without adequate repair, "mean, weak, or gone" can be damaging to a young child.

Adults who had a parent who was often absent or abusive, emotionally and/or in other significant ways, often have a very hard time taking charge of their own child. They may completely lack a model of caregiving that is authoritative and comforting, of a parent who can keep them safe rather than be the main danger in their lives. Often these adults struggle mightily around issues of discipline and can unconsciously replay the mean or gone caregiver while also often falling into being weak in an attempt not to repeat the harshness they knew growing up. The good news is that we've found they can form a secure attachment with their children, especially as they double down on honoring their reflective functioning, with a healthy vigilance regarding lapses into mean, weak, or gone.

Callie's father struggles to be the hands on the Circle as well as struggling on the bottom. His own father meted out harsh "discipline" when Ben didn't measure up to his expectations on the high school basketball court, and he had been doing the same regarding Ben's academic performance since the little boy could barely read. So Ben is sometimes mean when Callie doesn't "measure up" either, and then feels horrible about it and showers her with gifts. As described above, Callie's mother, Lisa, is less convinced that she should be pushing her daughter to excel, despite the fact that she corrals every parent she can to tell him or her of her daughter's achievements.

Lisa's father made it very clear to Lisa's mother that if Lisa didn't bring home straight As and get elected to the student council, it was because Lisa's mother wasn't taking charge of Lisa's upbringing—after all, he was busy working to provide for both of them. Now all these years later Lisa's shark music has a bass line that sounds a lot like her father's yelling at her mother night after night. In spite of her knowing

How Do We Repair "Mean, Weak, or Gone"?

Anytime we can't respond to our child's attachment needs we are, to some degree, rupturing the Circle. The key in all cases is to make the repair quickly, honestly, and sincerely as often as we can. This, of course, requires (1) our positive intentionality and (2) reflective functioning (knowing where our shark music just triggered taking ourselves off the Circle)—that is, we need to show our child that we feel bad about not meeting his needs because it's our ongoing desire to be there for him and that we understand what need we failed to meet. We can also offer a brief explanation of why we couldn't meet it in that moment.

Sometimes we take our top hand off the Circle: "I'm sorry, I think I may have just caused you to think I didn't want you to think for yourself." Sometimes we take our bottom hand off the Circle: "I'm sorry, I think I might have made it seem that you couldn't come to me for some comfort." Sometimes we take both hands off the Circle by being mean, weak, or gone. To repair these "hands moments" is very important, because being bigger, stronger, wiser, and kind is at the heart of the parental role: "I'm sorry, I know what I just did must have felt mean to you [or weak or gone]. I want you to know I'm back and we'll find a way to make things better."

The way to judge whether our repairs have been adequate is to figure out whether the relationship is better following the repairs. This can be a simple matter when we create a rupture on the bottom of the Circle, ignoring a child's need for soothing because we're under a lot of stress, or on the top, getting testy with a child who wants to dress himself because we can't tolerate unmatched or messy outfits or the time it takes. A simple apology (nothing too emotional or drawn out) and quickly offering what was missing can produce a smiling child who comes to us confident in our welcome and support for the rest of the day. Struggles with being the hands on the Circle often occur as more of a regular pattern, however, because often they evolve out of lacking a model of bigger, stronger, wiser, and kind when we were young.

If we're inclined to reverse roles with our child and abdicate the responsibility of taking charge, or if we discipline harshly because that's all we ever experienced as children, the earlier we can build in the experience (and memory) of rupture and repair, the better for our child. If we've had difficulty taking charge kindly and wisely, our efforts at repair with an 11-year-old will take longer to build trust than if we start early. Even so, dozens, hundreds, and ultimately countless experiences of "I'm truly sorry" combined with an acknowledgment of what went wrong and the intention to return to being a strong and kind parent can be of huge value no matter what the child's age when we start. Even with a 14-year-old, getting in the habit of saying something like this can improve your relationship and build security for a young teen: "I'm sorry, I just got all cranky and did something I don't like doing and I'm sure you don't want it coming from me. The issue is I'm tired, it's been a long day, but I have no right to yell at you, and the answer is still no, you can't go out on a school night to hang out with your friends. We can talk this through if you want to because I really care about you. I am also clear that I'm not changing my mind on your request." Firm, no-nonsense caring is always a remarkable antidote to our periodic ventures into mean, weak, or gone. In Chapter 9 we show you what it looks like to respond with your hands on the Circle at different stages of your child's development.

---

better, achievement has become the way Lisa keeps the sharks (still perceived to be close by) at a distance.

It's clear that at least one of Callie's parents needs to recognize the shark music that's running their lives. Ideally, both would see that their past is still impacting their view of the present. But even one parent recognizing the themes of where the struggles in the family are can begin to make a difference. A sense of clarity, and the resulting choice to make a difference in new ways, can bring change.

Reflecting about Hands Struggles

1. Do I have the capacity to say no with firmness and kindness in a way that my child knows I'm in charge?
2. Do I get angry in a way that causes my child to shrink back, always agree, or hide thoughts and feelings?
3. Do I ask my child to be in charge (by either taking care of me/focusing on my needs or being overcompliant/running scared of my anger)?
4. Do I expect my child to deal with difficult circumstances and strong emotions without my support?

If You Can't Help Being "Gone"

Sometimes we can't help being "gone" as parents. Severe stresses, such as those caused by the loss of a family member or financial stability, divorce, mental health problems, or serious illness can deplete our resources so that we simply don't have the strength to keep our hands on the Circle. In these cases, the most important thing we can do for our child is to continue to express our desire to be there and to make the same kinds of verbal repairs we would for minor, temporary ruptures, while doing what we can to provide another caregiver who can serve as a stand-in as needed. As we said in Chapter 3, when it comes to attached caregivers, it's always helpful to have some spares, and a relative or other close adult who can help with keeping hands on a child's Circle of Security will be of great benefit. At the same time, sometimes we all need help for ourselves. If you feel you can't remain bigger, stronger, wiser, and kind for your child right now, please seek whatever personal or professional help you might need. It's been our experience that such a choice is often the lifeline that parents need during times of confusion or significant stress.

As you read the descriptions of struggles around the Circle, did anything make you uncomfortable? If so, was it the depiction of the bottom, top, or hands struggles? If you found yourself squirming or feeling defensive or sad or had any other uneasy feeling, it might be a clue to where you struggle around the Circle in your own relationships. Even if you're not yet a parent, you might find that with family or friends or coworkers you wrestle with closeness and expressions of feeling or with interactions and activities that require independence and adventure. The closer and more important a relationship is to you, the more it can be a helpful crucible for your attachment struggles.

How you felt while reading these descriptions might be worth exploring even though you know you're unlikely to match these profiles. They were drawn in broad strokes to give you an idea of what the differences are, but many readers will likely recognize only a minor struggle at one or several points on the Circle. Why, then, does it matter? Because the psychological immunity of secure attachment (the ongoing emotional health that buffers our children through so much that is difficult in life) is remarkably valuable to your growing child.

And because when times are tough—when life throws you its inevitable crises and challenges—you're likely to struggle even more with those exact needs on a particular part of the Circle, and you're going to want to be alert for ruptures and attentive to making repairs. You can, of course, continue to follow your hardwiring to be the best parent possible—which will serve you well on its own—and you can explicitly reflect on where you tend to struggle and intentionally choose security for your child. You'll find a lot more help with exploring this direction in Part II of this book. Choosing security is always an essential step with huge rewards.

CHOOSING SECURITY

Your Child's Need:

When your child's *need* requires a response that is not comfortable for you . . .

Shark Music:

You suddenly *feel* uncomfortable (e.g., lonely, unsafe, rejected, abandoned, angry, controlled).

Choice Point:

You can *respond* to your child's need (in spite of the discomfort it causes you).

Or:

You can *protect* yourself from further pain by overriding your child's need (limiting or avoiding a response). If you protect yourself from uncomfortable feelings, your child's need will go unmet. Over time he or she will begin to express that need indirectly, causing both of you difficulty.

All parents hear shark music with some of their child's needs. The parents of secure children *recognize* their shark music. Often (not always) they *choose* to find a way to meet their child's need, in spite of the temporary pain it causes them.

Steps to Security:

1. Recognize the discomfort ("Here's my shark music again").

2. Honor the discomfort ("I hurt now because this particular need triggers my shark music").

3. Respond to your child's need.

What Does the Being-With Circle Tell You?

Another clue to where you might struggle around the Circle can be found in discovering which specific emotions were allowed into the Circle with your parents . . . and which weren't. We've chosen to focus on six key emotions: joy, sadness, anger, curiosity, fear, and shame. (Curiosity isn't actually a feeling, but it has a lot to do with the feelings associated with autonomy.) For some of us, some of these feelings were allowed all the way into what we call the "Being-With Circle." For example, maybe our parent or parents felt fine about letting us bring our fear to them when we felt anxious as a child. In this way, our fear was sponsored and supported and coregulated. This was a feeling that we learned was normal and acceptable, an emotion that could be accepted and shared, a feeling that would not devour us. But there may be another feeling that wasn't so fully accepted. For example, our sadness, which was only allowed partway in, was a feeling that could be accepted as long as we downplayed it enough not to make our parents shut down and try to divert it with explanations or laughter or quickly changing the subject. Possibly the most telling information comes from any emotions that were completely banished: ones that our parent (or parents) conveyed an unwillingness to deal with at all.

If you're interested in what you might learn from this exercise, draw a circle like the one shown on the facing page to write in the

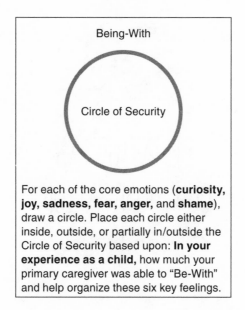

Being-With

Circle of Security

For each of the core emotions (**curiosity, joy, sadness, fear, anger,** and **shame**), draw a circle. Place each circle either inside, outside, or partially in/outside the Circle of Security based upon: **In your experience as a child,** how much your primary caregiver was able to "Be-With" and help organize these six key feelings.

emotions where you believe they fit (fully in, partway in, or completely outside the Being-With Circle) during your childhood.

If you learned as a child that you weren't supposed to have certain emotions, what do you think you did about it? In some way or another, without ever planning or scheming or analyzing consciously, you pretended not to feel that way. You developed what we call miscues—strategies to keep a caregiver on hand because you were definitely in distress but knew that expressing your full emotion or a real need on the Circle was likely to drive the parent away. As an adult, you may act as your coolest, most self-contained self when you're actually feeling sad and lonely. If you're a parent, you might be your cheeriest and most upbeat when you sense your child needs to crawl up into your lap and be held. Somewhere deep inside you know that, no matter how desperately in need of comfort and connection you feel, if you express it you'll end up feeling worse. You learned this in childhood, and you're now trying to protect your child by passing on the lesson.

Children are quick learners. Their miscues, modeled by you, will fast become part of the attachment dance between the two of you. The next chapter shows you what they look like and the messages children are really trying to send.

BEHAVIOR AS COMMUNICATION

Cues and Miscues

Three-year-old Tariq is "happy and resilient," says the preschool aide. His new best friend, Carson, holds back more with the other children, is quieter, and likes to take on little projects of his own, but Tariq manages to draw him into the group. Lily seems to be in a transitional stage socially, running back and forth to stick close to the teacher and then out to choose a toy, and then back again to the teacher. The teacher is beginning to think this in-between stage is lasting a long time. Andre pronounces himself king of the world on a regular basis but has trouble pulling himself together when he's knocked off that mountain by another child. Amelia is the class clown, and the teacher has never seen a tear on her cheek, even when she's been pretty upset. Marisol and Oliver are the "behavior problems" in the room—more likely to hit than talk when there's a conflict, inclined to pout and refuse to budge or speak when named as the instigators. Jordan is the class's "little professor," often sitting at a table surrounded by books or "experiments." The children run up to him to get answers to all kinds of factual questions. The teacher thinks he needs a bit more exercise.

Is Lily just a butterfly, flighty and fickle? Is Andre a natural bully? Will Amelia grow up to be a joker, dismissed as impossible to take seri-

146

ously? Are Oliver and Marisol troublemakers? Will Jordan be labeled full of himself because he seems to know more than his peers? Of course not. Children are not their behaviors. Labeling them that way can be tempting when we see a pattern develop ("He *always* acts that way"), but yielding to that temptation robs us of a valuable opportunity. We don't need to characterize children by their behavior, as if it's simply a reflection of personality traits. We need to try to understand that behavior. *Behavior is communication.* So the question we need to ask ourselves is "What are these children trying to tell us?" The answers we get to that question can tell us what these children need, whether they're getting it, and if not, what we can do about it. This information is important, because we all want our children's horizons to be as wide as possible. We want security for them, because that trust in the possibility of goodness can keep the doorway to their potential for health, happiness, and success unobstructed.

> *"One of the most essential things I learned from the Circle of Security was to think about why things were happening rather than what was happening."*
> —Sue Brown, Cootamundra, New South Wales, Australia

If we had our choice, we'd probably all want our children to be like Tariq—happy and resilient, able to get along with and even help others. And if we have a Carson, and he's just shy, don't we hope we can keep that characteristic from becoming an obstacle to whatever he wants to do with his life?

We *do* have choices. We can understand that children's behavior, particularly in relationships, is very often connected to their attachment needs and how they try to get them met. Preschoolers like Andre and Marisol might just be having a bad day, although even the way they handle a bad day can tell us something about their attachment style. Jordan might run around more with the others if he weren't already, at the age of 3, afraid of not being good at things—and he knows he's good at facts; his parents tell him so every day. Andre might let someone take the throne once in a while if he didn't worry that he'll be ignored if he gets off. Oliver feels angry a lot, although he doesn't really know why. Lily thinks big girls don't cry.

Children absorb the messages they've gotten from the way their parents respond to hearing shark music, and these messages often take shape in their behavior. When it comes to attachment, children's behavior comes in the form of cues (direct, clear bids for a need to be answered) and miscues (indirect, contradictory messages, or misdirection away from the child's true need), and the trick is to know which you're seeing.

Jordan might need support and encouragement to engage in physical play but doesn't think he'll get it, so he pretends he's not interested—that's a miscue of a need on the top of the Circle. Oliver's parents have been distant a lot—his mother is very ill and his dad is busy taking care of her—so he acts angry, a miscue of his need to connect on the bottom of the Circle. Amelia gets big, encouraging smiles from Mom when she sucks up her tears, and lots of applause for entertaining the adults in the family with her wit, so she entertains, using these miscues when she's feeling hurt and vulnerable. Lily's mother constantly warns her about the dangers of the world, so Lily miscues her need to go out and explore by running back to Mom's or the teacher's side. (Because Mom then acts uneasy with Lily's apparent bid for comfort, Lily runs out again, but soon she returns because she knows Mom doesn't like it when she strays too far. It's complicated, which is why we've devoted a whole chapter to miscues.)

These children don't miscue all the time with their parents. When an emotion or a need has been received with acceptance and help, they feel safe in cuing it directly. Carson can tell his parents when he's afraid the other boys and girls won't like him, and his mom and dad tell him they get that it's a little scary to meet new children and that they'll come with him the first time. Carson knows it's OK to be shy and that he'll get help from his parents to go out on the top of the Circle anyway. Tariq gives his parents fairly direct cues about what he needs, whether it's "delight in me" or "help me," "protect me" or "enjoy with me," and whether he's on the top or bottom of the Circle.

But we all tend to struggle more on one part of the Circle than the other, and that's where our child's miscues are bound to crop up. (On the other hand, it's important to know when you're observing your child that when we struggle mainly on one part of the Circle, we also struggle somewhat on the other; see the box on the facing page.) Tariq has a secure attachment with both of his parents, but his mother is more comfortable with needs on the top of the Circle and his father is more comfortable with needs on the bottom. When Mom is stressed by work, she sometimes brushes Tariq off when he tries to snuggle next to her on the couch while she's reading a report she couldn't get to at

Insecurity Peeks through All Around the Circle

A secure attachment is formed when a child's primary caregiver is generally comfortable all around the Circle, willing and able much of the time to meet a child's needs for a safe haven and for a secure base as the child travels between the two types of needs throughout the day. The parent's overall comfort with the child's needs translates to the child's comfort with asking for those needs to be met. In the cradle of the "and," parent and child relax in the knowledge that they'll work through those needs together. This doesn't mean there are no stumbles or wrong turns. It means that even when the child is struggling to deal with a confusing and uncomfortable emotion and the parent isn't quite sure what type of help to offer, the parent offers the reassuring sense of being there to take charge, to remain bigger and stronger, to be kind, and to apply whatever wisdom the parent has managed to amass over the years. Instead of seizing up and panicking about what she doesn't know, the parent reaches out for the child and exudes a feeling that "We're in this together and we'll get through it together." The parent is secure in her knowledge that she's bigger and stronger than her child and, perhaps more significantly, that *the relationship is bigger and stronger than both of them.* Her trust in the relationship—in the power of the "and"—can carry her child not only through this moment's distress but also through the child's relationship negotiations throughout life.

With security holding this type of power, it's no surprise that insecurity has tendrils too. It's important to understand that, although we all inevitably struggle more on one side of the Circle, we also aren't fully comfortable on the other. Where we struggle most may be born of shark music on the bottom or top of the Circle, but the insecurity that results isn't completely limited to that domain. A parent who can't support exploration is also going to be less than at ease with comfort (either underdoing it or overdoing it). *Insecurity is insecurity is insecurity.* If we feel at a loss with one type of needs around the Circle, our insecurity is likely to permeate the entire realm of parenting to some degree. This is not a bad thing—it's just something to be aware of, and perhaps a further incentive to understand our shark music and make a commitment to making conscious choices of how to respond to our child's needs wherever we can.

the office. When Dad is stressed by work, he sometimes ignores Tariq's requests for Dad to teach him a new game they've bought together and tries to get Tariq to sit quietly and watch TV next to him. If these patterns become entrenched, by the time Tariq is in elementary school he might feel like he can't go to Mom to talk to her about his fears; he might hesitate to ask Dad to help coach his soccer team. So what happens when Tariq is on the bottom of the Circle and only Mom is around or he's on the top and only Dad is there? His needs might tend to go unanswered.

But if Tariq's parents become aware of their shark music, they can use their reflective functioning to notice when it starts blaring at them (or to anticipate it), and when they find themselves denying a need of their son's, they can repair the rupture. They can also be alert for any miscues from their child.

That's what Oliver's dad did when the preschool teacher reported that Oliver seemed to have changed and was acting quite angry at the other children and the teachers. The teacher asked if anything was going on at home that she should know about so she could help support Oliver at school. Oliver's dad told her about his wife's illness, and the teacher speculated that Oliver might be acting particularly aggressive when he was actually feeling the saddest. He missed the connection with both of his parents. The teacher promised to give Oliver space to calm himself and an increased sense of connection with her, whenever he seemed to be "acting out" in the classroom. At the same time Oliver's dad started changing the way he responded to Oliver's boisterous behavior at home. When his son started throwing toys or trying to hit the family's cat, his dad got down on the floor next to him, softly held his arms, and looked into his eyes with a gentle smile. "Feeling lonely, buddy?" he asked. Oliver paused but only briefly and then went back to slamming around the room. But his father remained focused and kept responding in this way, and over the next few weeks the teacher was happy to report that Oliver seemed more at ease during the day. Based on her suggestion, he even began coming to her for a hug whenever he started to feel agitated.

"Behavior problems" are not a demand for attention.

They are a sign that the child finds the cost of revealing his true need higher than living with the painful consequences of the misbehavior.

When children have started miscuing as an attachment strategy, even when we do change the way we respond to our shark music, it can take time to convince the child's mind that the rules have changed. But making this effort—intentionally choosing security for your child—can pay off in keeping your child's horizons as wide as they were meant to be. Children who know at their core that all of their emotions are acceptable and all of their needs are normal—and that there are trusted others in the world to help them manage them—have a good chance of ending up like Tariq: open, interested, joyful, friendly. They'll be better able to deal with life's challenges because they're not wasting energy on diversionary tactics designed to steer them away from emotions and needs they think they shouldn't have.

You may find that choosing security doesn't demand that big an effort after all. Now that you know something about your shark music, you'll probably find you already have started to recognize one or two of your child's miscues. (If you don't have any idea where your shark music might arise, you can explore it further in Chapter 7.) Most parents introduced to the phenomenon of shark music immediately begin to recognize where their own struggles are around the Circle. That alone can sharpen their vision enough to see where their children may be struggling.

Lester went through the Circle of Security group sessions and started to look back at how he'd raised his older son, Kevin. Now he could see that he was a lot more comfortable with sending Kevin out to learn and explore and discover on his own than he was holding him on his lap or helping him make sense of his tears when he was hurt. Suddenly Lester thought of the first time his son had gone on a sleepover at a friend's house at the age of 4 and how confused he'd been when the little boy looked at him impassively when picked up the next day, almost as if his son was bored by his dad's appearance. On the drive home, Lester kept trying to talk to Kevin about whether he'd had fun, what he and his friend had done, what the parents had given him for dinner, and was surprised (and maybe a bit hurt) when Kevin just stared out the passenger-side window and gave one-syllable answers. Now, Lester announced with sadness, he realized this had been a miscue: his son had learned from him that he was supposed to be independent and brave. And so he gave Lester the reaction he thought Lester wanted, when he had probably been homesick and would have rather run up to hug his father to reestablish the connection with him that he needed.

Lester has decided to try to make different choices with his younger son, now age 3. At first he thought the way to fight his shark music was to show Tyler more affection than he ordinarily would feel moved to give. He started hugging and kissing Tyler on a kind of "schedule" to be sure he created a safe haven for his little boy. Tyler responded by often wriggling away from Dad or scowling at him. "I still wasn't following his need," Lester later said with an embarrassed laugh. "It was all about me being 'good at' attachment." Lester found ways to shut off what he calls his "self-esteem police" and just Be-With Tyler. Pretty soon he found he could spot when Tyler needed a hug, whether Tyler issued a cue or a miscue. And he could turn down the volume of his shark music for long enough to offer one (how he learned to do that is described in Part II). He was also glad to see how his new learning translated into a new sense of connection with his first son, Kevin. Like many parents, Lester was learning that it's never too late.

Attuning to your child's needs starts with reminding yourself at all times that behavior is communication. Make no mistake about it: Much of what our very young children do—the way they act, how they express emotions, even their energy level—is intended to tell us what they need from us. What they need is not just our attention. Sure, they need us to pay attention, but what they really need is our sensitive attunement to how they're feeling, how we can help them understand and accept their feelings, and how they can learn to manage them.

This is so important that we'll say it again:
Adults often make the mistake of believing that babies and
children only want our attention when what they really
want is connection.

Attachment Strategies: A Universal Defense

In Chapter 5 we described how shark music becomes part of the soundtrack of our lives and how its themes can set the tone for our relationships. But why do we need it? Why does everyone seem to have shark music?

Shark music is part of the defensive strategy we all use to protect us from the agony of feeling alone and adrift. We need that protection, because the reality is that no one can be perfectly attuned, 100% of the time, to anyone else's needs. When the inevitable ruptures occur, we need to have a way to deal with them without giving up completely on trust and connection. Defenses are a way for our children (and the adults they will become) to handle the awareness that, even when they can't have a need genuinely attended to, they can rely on a defensive strategy to block the pain of an unmet need.

The sequence of events that includes shark music is part of what we call the "defensive triad"*:

Need ➡ *Pain* ➡ *Defense*

During attachment interactions, your child will feel the **need** for something on either the top or bottom of the Circle or for hands on the Circle. If that need isn't met, the child feels **pain**, which will set off a **defense**. Miscues are those defenses. (Shark music is actually the warning signal telling us, "Pain is about to happen! Miscue immediately to avoid the pain.") Over time, depending on how intense the pain caused by unmet need and how frequently it's felt, the child's defenses may evolve into certain behavioral patterns or strategies. With a parent who struggles on the bottom of the Circle, as described in Chapter 5, the child will likely develop defenses similar to the parent's: a parent who overemphasizes achievement (like Callie's parents in Chapter 5) may end up with a child who not only acts self-sufficient (miscuing) as a toddler (like Will in Chapter 5) but grows up to feel superior and entitled, who can't admit to flaws, who is highly sensitive to criticism, who avoids vulnerability, and/or who may have no close relationships where he shares his private pain. We often inaccurately attribute this legacy to personality passed on through genes.

But it's all a matter of degree. The bigger the pain, the bigger the defense:

Need ➡ **PAIN** ➡ **DEFENSE**

For the average adult, the defensive triad may result in strategies like comforting yourself with food or drink when you feel sad and alone or distracting yourself with shopping or binge TV watching when you feel anxious about making a job change or you're worried that your partner is losing interest in you.

---

*Our gratitude to psychiatrists James Masterson and Ralph Klein for their introduction of the basic theme of this triad.

Children who learn to miscue on a regular basis are sadly being denied the full spectrum of emotional experience and of life. If we want our children to lead the fullest lives possible, they need to feel that they can, much of the time, cue their attachment needs—express them directly, with confidence that the person they're entrusting with their deepest emotional experience will try to be there for and with them. (See Chapter 4 for the dangers of a parent working too hard to Be-With every emotion all of the time.) To be denied the full experience and appropriate expression of attachment needs and still be expected to live a satisfying life would be like asking an artist to paint with only part of the spectrum available or an author to write with only part of the alphabet.

Imagine what it would be like to live without blue or red or yellow in your life—or without access to the letters a, c, f, g, j, k, n, p, r, t, u, and y. That's the kind of limitation imposed by having to miscue certain attachment needs.

A Dance of Procedural Certainty

In Chapter 5, we mentioned that attachment style—where we struggle and miscue—is passed down from generation to generation at the whopping rate of about 75%. It's an enduring legacy for two reasons: (1) the entire dance to shark music is based on procedural certainty—it just feels right, it's unconscious, and so we tend not to question it; and (2) it's perpetuated through an implicit covenant between parent and child that's hard to separate into two roles. We've done that artificially in this book, by talking first about shark music, the parent's part (which of course originated when that parent was a child), and now about the child's part (which, in the absence of the kind of reflection we're encouraging in this book, will become the parent's part in the next generation). Let's look more closely at the child's part.

Zoe, age 18 months, is sitting on the carpet staring at the door her mother has just closed behind her. Her bottom lip starts to quiver and she takes a few gaspy breaths and then bursts into tears. She turns briefly toward the woman sitting nearby on a couch and gives her a look of deep distress, as if to say, "Help me—my mom is gone!" but then quickly turns back toward the door and continues to cry. The not-Mom utters a few consoling words, and within a couple minutes

Zoe's prayers are answered: Mom opens the door and walks in, saying, "I'm sorry, sweetie, I had to go talk to someone." Darla steps over
her baby and picks up a stuffed animal from the toys scattered on the
floor, takes it over to her daughter, and starts pointing out the animal's
features: "Ooo, look, Teddy has such big eyes! And what a cute little
mouth, just like yours!" She's petting Teddy and holding the toy out to
Zoe, who has quickly stifled her crying and is looking at the toy with a
blank expression, reaching out a chubby little hand to each feature that
Mom describes enthusiastically.

This is a description of one segment of the Strange Situation Procedure (SSP) used in attachment research and described in Chapter 4.
In the SSP, a parent or other caregiver and a young child are in a room
with toys and a stranger. A hidden camera films what happens when
the parent exits the room, leaving the child with the stranger for a
few short minutes, and then returns. Naturally, babies and toddlers
become distressed when Mom or Dad exits, leaving them with someone they don't know, and they show it, as Zoe does. (The parent is
absent for a very brief time, to avoid overly stressing the little boy or
girl.) What tells researchers the most about the attachment between
parent and child, however, is the reunion.

In a securely attached relationship, a 1-year-old child will typically
show the parent that he felt bad when Mom or Dad left and will seek
comfort when the parent returns. The parent will sensitively respond
to this need, picking the child up and holding him until he shows signs
of wanting to get down and do something else. This child and parent
have made a circuit from bottom to top of the Circle of Security in just
a few brief moments—as children and parents do over and over across
the globe, all day long, in natural settings.

So what was going on with Zoe and Darla? Darla didn't pick Zoe
up when she re-entered the room, even though the tiny girl was wailing with distress. Instead, she picked up a stuffed animal and started
playing with it and trying to get her daughter involved in that activity. Zoe shut off her tears—within seconds of Darla's return—as her
mother stepped over her and dutifully started paying attention to the
toy as her mother wanted.

Scientists highly trained in interpreting video of the SSP would
say that Zoe's abrupt shift from upset to OK was a miscue. It's not that
Zoe was instantly fine when her mother returned or that she didn't feel
the need to be comforted. How do we know this? It's only common

sense that defenseless babies and toddlers are distressed when their caregiver leaves, but this has also been confirmed by research showing that their heart rate and cortisol levels go up at these times—hallmark symptoms of stress. Zoe was all but guaranteed to have been upset. (The understanding is that all children in the SSP during separation from their primary caregiver experience significant distress.) So why didn't she show it when her mother came back? Our research supports the conclusion that Zoe absorbed a message, through countless interactions in her young life, that Darla is uncomfortable with answering the need for comfort—that is, Darla hears shark music when Zoe is upset and needs to be soothed. Over the short span of her life so far, Zoe has developed an unconscious strategy to do two things: (1) protect herself from the pain of having her need denied, and (2) ensure that she doesn't upset Mom so much that Mom backs away even more.

As described in Chapter 5, Darla isn't purposely denying her daughter the comfort she needs. She's trying to protect the baby from whatever disappointment or pain she herself felt when she expressed the same need as a child. *Again, all of these "intentions" and behaviors by mother and daughter are going on largely, if not completely, outside their conscious awareness.*

When stressed, Zoe's limited security on the bottom of the Circle comes out more strongly (see the box on page 157). On ordinary good days, all you might notice about her in preschool is that she rarely cries and doesn't ask for the teacher's help even when the task she's trying to perform is clearly beyond her developmental capabilities. It would be very easy to admire Zoe for being so "independent" and "mature." There's nothing wrong with either of those characteristics, except that being described that way just reinforces the messages Zoe's shark music is sending and encourages her to miscue further. It's not that Zoe will end up having a miserable life. But in some ways, primarily around issues of shared vulnerability, it will be limited. In oversimplified terms, she could get so adept at acting like she's just fine when she's actually not that she could miss out on developing emotional regulation of her sadness. When a deeply painful event occurs—the loss of a loved one, for example—she might not be able to turn to others for help and might not feel like it's OK for her to fully experience her grief. Shutting down in this way, her physical and psychological health might suffer as a result.

Here's another example of how tightly choreographed the dance of defensive attachment strategies can be:

Stress Reveals Insecurity

While it's hypothetically possible that a 1-year-old who miscues on the bottom of the Circle has a largely secure attachment to her parent, it's not that likely. The research evidence is fairly robust that what you see is what is actually going on. If a child's behavior is avoidant under stress one day, it's usually avoidant the next. It's the nature of a stress test and one reason the SSP is such a reliable indicator of attachment. The intensity of need under such stress only brings out the inherent avoidance all the more clearly. So if you think your child is acting in a certain way only because she's "having a bad day," it might be instead that a "bad day" (for either of you) can provide a lot of information about your child's shark music and your own.

Nomi likes her toys. Especially those she has come to know well. She particularly likes her "best friend" Carrie, a sock doll given to her by her older brother. Nomi's mom, Allison, smiles with affectionate understanding when her 3-year-old daughter won't leave the house without Carrie. In fact, she is so eager to show Nomi that it's OK to need the comfort of a "security" toy that whenever Nomi starts to reach for her doll, Allison comments on how "our Carrie" is such a good friend. Nomi keeps talking to her doll, but her smile fades a bit. She's gotten into the habit lately of finding an excuse to take Carrie into another room, where she can talk to her doll in private. Allison follows, wondering what "the three of us" will do together. Sometimes these playtimes disintegrate quickly. Nomi throws Carrie across the room in anger and starts to fuss and frown. Allison then pulls her daughter onto her lap and squeezes her, saying, "Oh, you probably need a little rest time. Maybe you need a break from Carrie. Here, Mommy will rock you." Nomi seems to force out a little cry and settles into Mom's lap as Allison says (with about the same tone of discomfort), "There, there." Nomi then pushes off her mother's lap, rushes over to pick up Carrie, and starts playing with her back to Allison. Allison says, in a slightly dejected tone, "OK, OK, that's fine," and Nomi seems to sigh as she turns toward her mother and climbs back onto her lap with her doll. Allison says, "Yes, Carrie and I can make you feel all better."

Allison doesn't recognize that her daughter was having a perfectly good time playing with her doll by herself. All she remembers is that her daughter got "all fussy and really needed a nap." Why couldn't she see that Nomi was on the top of the Circle and wanted to be left alone in her room with her doll, at least for a little while? Because shark music told her that Nomi's drive for autonomy in this normal way was threatening. She couldn't see that Nomi's climbing back on her mother's lap was not a cue for comfort but a miscue. Nomi was attending to her mother's bid for closeness rather than cuing her own.

When attachment is secure, children divide their attention between the relationship with the parent and the environment. A child who miscues on the bottom of the Circle typically pays more attention to the environment while finding ways not to make bids for soothing, whereas a child who miscues on the top of the Circle pays more attention to the relationship while limiting bids for being on his or her own.

Allison wants Nomi to know that she loves being with her. She can't see that she's not giving Nomi the autonomy she needs at that moment because the two are entwined in a tightly choreographed defensive dance. Nomi is doing what she thinks her mother needs to stay happy and therefore available. Nomi's miscue tells Allison what she wants to hear, and Allison is honestly trying to do what's best for her little girl. Mother and daughter are in step in all of this. But Allison is not attuned to what her daughter really needs. Her shark music is drowning that out.

Unfortunately, the parent and child in this defensive dance can't see it for what it is—and does. But from the outside it becomes clear as the child gets older that something is wrong. For example, the interactions between parent and child can begin to look troubled (increasingly dramatic and filled with upset) or "too smooth/too perfect" as if parent and child are simply reading a script. In each case children will comply with their parent's defensive strategies, until the compliance begins to wear thin. Then an innate and healthy need for autonomy might start showing up with upset and even fury about needing to have a separate sense of self. Whether asked to go along with a parent's shark music on the top or bottom of the Circle, as children move toward their teenage years a much needed request for what's been missing will likely begin to arise. (This does not mean it's too late to strengthen the attachment bond, however. See Chapter 9 for illustrations of how we can respond with security to typical problems our children present us with at different ages.)

It's hard not to see what we want to believe, especially when those "wants" are humming along in procedural memory rather than in conscious thoughts and feelings. That's why it's helpful to bring some understanding of your shark music to your efforts to attune to your child's needs. It's a two-person dance, and when you know which foot you're leading with, you can see more clearly how your child might have to follow if he is not to stumble and get hurt. We'll give you some ways to look more closely at your own children and your attachment bond with them in Part II of this book, but meanwhile, here's an overview of what children's messages typically look like depending on whether their attachment with a parent is secure or insecure.

Secure Attachment: In Step *and* Attuned

Children with a secure attachment to their parent tend to cue their needs directly. When in a new place and suddenly without the parent 1-year-olds cry and hold up their arms to be picked up when Mom or Dad returns to rescue them from the hurt and pain of being left without the beloved parent. Parents with a secure attachment to their child respond empathically—they recognize the cue for comfort and give their child the comfort the child needs. If Zoe and Darla had a secure attachment, their SSP video might have shown Zoe continuing to cry for a while after her mother returned. Her heart rate probably would have stayed elevated for a minute or so. Darla's warm consolation would have been welcomed by Zoe and would have succeeded in calming the little girl relatively quickly.

When attachment is generally secure, the child's cues are largely direct and clear:

- When distressed in a new setting and suddenly feeling alone, a 1-year-old boy's eyes widen and he reaches for his dad (cuing fear and a need for safety).
- Unstressed, an infant grins with sparkling eyes at her mother as she spins around in her walker (cuing a need for "delight in me"

on the top of the Circle—remember Hannah and Sophie from Chapter 2?).

The child will continue to share cues with Mom or Dad:

- Juan is crawling around in the grass while his mother talks over the fence with a neighbor. He starts yelling for her attention. As she continues her conversation, looking over her shoulder occasionally to make sure Juan isn't eating a rock or doing something else dangerous, his shouts get louder. He knows she can be counted on, so he keeps trying until Mom finally comes over and carries him back to the fence with her.
- The baby in his high chair (remember Max and Dana from Chapter 4?) happily interacts with Dad over a tray of Cheerios, then looks away when overstimulated, but looks back again after Dad has waited patiently for him to calm down and smiles at him once more.

The child will come to the parent to have a need met:

- A baby crawls over to Mom and reaches up to be picked up when he's feeling left out while she's talking on the phone.
- A 4-year-old about to ascend the steps of a climbing structure looks back at Dad to make eye contact and receive a brief, nonverbal signal that it's OK before proceeding.

The child is willing to be comforted and willing to explore at a distance:

- After a 3-minute separation in the SSP, an 18-month-old visibly settles and calms after her father picks her up and holds her for a minute and then wriggles to get down. (In the research, a secure child of this age will have an elevated heart rate for only about a minute after her parent returns.)
- A 2-year-old boy who wants to explore begins walking away from his mom but stays close enough to check back in with her if he wants to.

The child can begin to regulate his emotions at a distance from Mom or Dad:

- A 3-year-old pulls back his hand after starting to slap at another child in anger while they're in the sandbox together. Remembering what he's learned with his mother in similar circumstances, he does this now on his own.

- A 12-month-old baby who has been calling out to be taken out of her crib doesn't get an immediate response, starts to cry, and then starts to babble softly to herself until Dad arrives, knowing he will.

It's important to note that cues are direct and clear in that the child is expressing a need for whatever is bothering him to be resolved. But that doesn't mean that only one emotion is associated with a particular need. A child who, for instance, is upset about being separated from a parent will not always express the emotion of sadness that we might expect. The child might act angry, or pout briefly, but each emotional expression will say directly that the child is unhappy with the separation and can be resolved within a relationship that is used to working things through to a sense of resolution. When children carry an internal confidence that they are being cared for by someone who is committed to responding to their emotional needs in a bigger, stronger, wiser, and kind way, resolution is never far away.

Miscues: Circles of Limited Security

We call patterns of miscues **Circles of Limited Security** (in the attachment field they are considered different types of insecure attachment). Zoe and Darla repeatedly experience what we call a limited bottom of the Circle. Instead of attending to her own needs and directly asking for comfort, out of the trust that Mom will provide it, Zoe attends to her mother's needs and asks only for the doll that her mother is offering. At this young age Zoe has figured out exactly what her mom can (and can't) tolerate. And if Mom can tolerate it, Mom will stick around, which for a helpless baby or toddler is Priority Number One.

As described in Chapter 5, Darla is miscuing too. She doesn't consciously believe that an 18-month-old child should be "big and strong and brave" and feel just fine with being left alone with a stranger. But deep down inside, she believes (and remembers) that children who openly request comfort often get the opposite of what they ask for. So she pretends—miscuing her daughter—by implying that there's nothing to be upset about and the best thing to do is just "keep calm and carry on." The whole pattern adds up to an implicit, unspoken, unrecognized bargain: "I [child] will pretend I need X because I know you [parent] get uncomfortable when I need Y. You, in turn, will stick around so I'm not left feeling completely alone." Sadly, our children often learn to say, "I'll forgo my need to have a separate self (my genuine need for autonomy) if that will keep you close" or "I'll forgo my need for soothing (my genuine need to be vulnerable with someone) if that will keep you from further distance." No parent sets out to teach these lessons, but through the ages, all around the world, these are precisely the fundamental patterns that children have unconsciously learned and then passed on to the next generation.

Ironically, in these scenarios, no one is actually calm at all. In the SSP research, when children like Zoe are reunited with their parent, they may appear calm when Mom reappears, but their heart rate says otherwise: it remains elevated long after the reunion (not just for a minute) despite Mom's presence. Children and parents who engage in miscues at the top of the Circle are kind of a mix. These children will keep crying long after the reunion while clinging close and then inexplicably asking to be put down. Upset, crying, in Mom's arms, now out of her arms, and all the while their heart rate is still high. They will then reach to be held again (like Lily, described above). In both cases of Circles of Limited Security, the child's stress is prolonged, and genuine resolution to the rupture is never fully reached. Of course, how could it be? The countless experiences of never being fully allowed to explore or fully allowed to find soothing show up now in this momentary crisis because, as explained in Chapter 5, no deeper pattern of real repair has ever been established. The uncomfortable drama or uneasy coolness we see on the surface tells precisely what is happening underground: a painful disconnection where simple connection might have been.

Sadly, this can have various problematic effects down the road. First, there are the health effects of excess stress, described in Chapter 1. Then there's the psychological impact: While children with attachment struggles are not all destined to have later psychological problems, children who learn to miscue on the bottom of the Circle seem to have a higher rate of so-called externalizing problems—hostility, aggression, conduct disorders. Alan Sroufe has remarked that this is no wonder: To varying degrees their caregiver has been emotionally unavailable when they've needed help with painful feelings, and this can make a person angry and, ultimately, alienated (as with Oliver and Marisol). Such children end up attempting to protect themselves in the same way their well-intentioned parents tried to protect them—by hiding their feelings, denying painful emotions, and dismissing painful memories or incidents and even the importance of being attached to anyone. Children who learn to miscue on the top of the Circle seem more likely to have anxiety-related issues when older. Both types of limited security have also been associated with a slightly higher rate of depression than is seen in children who grew up with a secure attachment—they may both have simply lost hope of getting the emotional help and support they need from loved ones.

Persistent struggles with the hands on the Circle can be quite serious and do severe harm to children. We're not talking about parents who cannot take charge quite as much as they should or who tend to be slightly tough disciplinarians. Nor are we talking about parents who end up temporarily absent through no fault of their own, such as due to health problems or other crises. But when parents are mean, weak, or gone to the point of being abusive or negligent or chronically absent due to substance abuse or mental illness, choosing the needs of their partner over the needs of their child, and so on, children are left with a dilemma that feels impossible to resolve: They fear their parent, but that parent is the one person on whom they are supposed to rely. The dilemma goes like this: "The one I most need is now the one I'm most afraid of." A caregiver who is consistently or intermittently significantly mean, weak, or gone establishes this exact dilemma in her or his child.

> Children who are securely attached fear danger.
>
> Children (and parents) who miscue on the bottom of the Circle fear closeness.
>
> Children (and parents) who miscue on the top of the Circle fear separation.
>
> Children without hands on the Circle—a parent who is chronically mean, weak, or gone—fear their caregiver.

In the SSP, an infant or toddler reunited with the parent who is consistently mean, weak, or gone might actually run away from the returning parent, or run toward the parent but then abruptly turn around and run away screaming. To an observer, the child's behavior makes no sense. And there is no sense to it. For this child the Circle of Security isn't just limited; when there are no hands, the Circle all but disappears.

Unfortunately, children's miscues, when they become an entrenched pattern and last into adulthood, become the next genera-

Circle of Limited Security:
Child frightened by not being able to find the parent's hands.

tion's shark music. This is a vicious Circle of Insecurity that gives rise to lives limited by the anticipated emotional unavailability of those they rely on most. It can result in children growing into adults who enter relationships throughout life with the expectation that only half (or less) of their emotional needs will be met. Intimacy is curtailed. Self-confidence is missing. Trust is diminished or unavailable.

Obviously, insecure attachment limits life. Let's look a little more closely at how those limitations show up depending on where on the Circle the miscues occur.

Miscues on the Bottom of the Circle: "Of Course I'm Fine, Mommy!"

When the bottom of the Circle is limited in a parent–child relationship, the child has trouble going to the parent for soothing and safety because the child senses that the parent is uneasy with or rejecting of needs for emotional comfort—in the parent or in the child. Parents who struggle on one part of the Circle often push their children toward the opposite side when their shark music starts. Instead of saying, "Aw, let me kiss and make it better," and hugging a child who's fallen, they might say, "Oh, you're fine!" or "Big boys don't cry" and send the child off to play again at a distance. They might focus on exploring a toy with their child, as Darla did with Zoe. A child who is used to this parental steering will probably go off and play as if it's what she wants to do, but that's a miscue because if you look closely, the play will often be somewhat flat and repetitive instead of expansive and creative. Or a parent struggling on the bottom of the Circle will be all business when comfort is what's called for, finding a tissue or smoothing the child's hair or rubbing off a smudge on the baby's face instead of hugging, cuddling, or cooing. The child goes along with this too, because, after all, at least it keeps Mom nearby and somewhat engaged. Underneath the behavior, the child has registered the message that bids for emotional comfort make the parent uneasy and stops asking. Some children in the SSP don't even act upset when Mom is gone. Others, like Zoe, act upset when Mom is out of the room but instantly buck up and focus on the toys when she returns.

"You're just so cute!" Linda exclaims, on cue every time Sadie begins to cry. "Cute, cute, cute," Linda declares. "I know you know it. That's why you're about to smile right now. Why don't you smile for Mommy?"

Sadie sucks in her breath and smiles wanly. Sadie is 10 months old.

Sadie is already learning to join her mother in smiling and avoiding any semblance of expressed sadness or upset. It's not that Sadie

Circle of Limited Security: Child miscuing on the bottom of the Circle.

doesn't feel it (any more than Zoe felt fine when reunited with Darla), but she's gotten adept at miscuing on the bottom of the Circle.

Trisha knows how to light up a room. At barely 3, she can enter a gathering of adults and smile in a way that is guaranteed to make adults exclaim. "She's just so adorable," they will say, almost on cue.

Trisha knows how to sparkle.

But Trisha has just begun her first week in child care. Sad, confused, not able to make sense of how she is being left in this new place, she begins to cry when her mother once again begins to walk away on her third day in this new place. Her mother first looks to the child care provider, rolls her eyes with no small amount of embarrassment, and then says, "Honey, you know I have to go to work. Be a big girl and show Miss Joni how much you like to smile." So Trisha smiles. Mom smiles. Her child care provider smiles. "There you go—this can be such a happy place. You'll be so happy here."

Trisha knows how to sparkle.

Sparkling on cue is a typical miscue when the Circle is limited on the bottom.

"What's so hard about trying to fix that by yourself?" asks Eric's father. "If you keep coming to me, you'll never figure anything out on your own."

Eric is 3.

Rather than encouraging his son's competence, Eric's father is chiding him for having needs, especially a need for connection while he attempts something new. So when Eric is on the top of the Circle, he has to stay there—by himself—for the sake of his father's comfort. As he grows, Eric begins to take more and more risks where he doesn't really want to, miscuing as though he loves being totally independent and without fear whenever he's nearing the bottom of the Circle. Of course it's possible that Eric's risk taking has little to do with attachment (see the box on page 167).

> *Does your child readily come to you to fix a toy, pull up his socks, help him with homework?*
> *Are you sure that it's your caretaking that your child really wants and not your caregiving?*

Attachment Style versus Temperament

In the field of psychology, temperament is often viewed as a collection of innate characteristics, such as being introverted or extroverted, quick or slow to soothe, and the like. In fact, over the millennia various philosophers and other sages have classified temperament in many different ways. Attachment style seems to be learned, and not all of a child's behavior or inclinations can be traced to secure or insecure attachment. Some children, for example, just seem to love taking risks. So while Eric's risk taking might be a miscue, it also just might be part of the temperament he was born with. Some children are slow to warm up and tend toward shyness no matter what family they are born into.

Some children who miscue on the bottom of the Circle can, at times, seem like their parent's silent shadow. They might sit nearby, playing quietly, knowing that Mom or Dad will let them stay close if they play "appropriately," without asking for help with emotional distress. In this case their quiet playing would likely qualify as a miscue.

The child who lives with a limited bottom of the Circle might be the child in elementary school who brags about being the best at everything and acts like he deserves special treatment. He knows that acceptance is so contingent on approval for what he does on the top of the Circle that he miscues by pretending he's all about his specialness on the top of the Circle, especially when he's afraid he won't get esteem from others. All but certain that the comfort he needs won't be offered and might even be rebuffed, he'll seek accolades as a way to avoid a growing sense of shame at all costs.

Children who miscue on the bottom of the Circle are often so used to having to perform to gain their parent's approval and proximity that they look like high achievers. Ironically, though, they often don't reach the height of their unique potential because they are so used to judging their own accomplishments by someone else's standards. One of the biggest dangers of a limited bottom of the Circle is its impact on learning. Children end up caught up in compliance toward excellence at the expense of their own innate curiosity. This, of course, reaches its zenith in our educational system, where students are consistently and continually asking, "What does my teacher/professor want?" rather

than focusing on the simple exuberance of learning and the joy in seeing where it can take them. When we introduce the concept of "core
sensitivities" in Chapter 7, we talk about the category called "esteem
sensitivity," and these issues will come more fully into focus.

There's another kind of miscuing on the bottom of the Circle. This
is the child who feels that her caregivers are misattuned (either too
disinterested too interested/enthusiastic) to her needs for comfort and
simple presence, especially when distressed. This child may tend to be
somewhat shy and requires a "not too much, but not too little" form of
availability from her parents. When her parent seems to be "too much"
(trying to read her mind or being overly empathetic and claiming to
understand completely) or "too little" (not interested or even hostile
toward her need for comfort), this child simply steps back and decides
to no longer ask for what she needs on the bottom of the Circle. Instead
she feels a hidden sense of futility, like no one actually "gets it" and
that it's better to remain somewhat invisible and outside the notice of
others. Our discussion of the core sensitivity called "safety sensitivity"
in Chapter 7 will center around the implications of this child's state of
mind.

Miscues on the Top of the Circle:
"Of Course I Need You, Daddy!"

"What's this?" Halley says to Brittany, her 27-month-old daughter.
Brittany has just begun yet another journey toward the other children
on the playground. Halley had intentionally taken her daughter to this
park because it's a place where other parents and children gather to
share the warm summer afternoons. "You need to have some fun with
those kids you played with last week," Halley had said to her daughter
as she buckled her into her car seat just before driving to the park.

Brittany smiles at the other children and then looks back to her
mom.

"Look at what I brought for you, Brit—a new toy!"

And so Brittany begins to play with the toy as her mother reaches
down to bring her in closer.

When parents struggle on the top of the Circle, they often give
very mixed messages. First, Halley encourages her daughter to go off
and play with the other children; then she finds a way to pull her back
in with a new toy instead. Brittany gets the message that straying too

Circle of Limited Security: Child miscuing on the top of the Circle.

far from Mom's side is not OK at all. So she pretends she's interested in the toy when she's really yearning to go play with her peers.

Children who miscue on the top of the Circle sometimes act needy and clingy when they're not feeling that way, because they believe Mom or Dad isn't comfortable with autonomy. But when they come to the parent for the comfort they believe Mom wants to give, they often appear hard to console. They'll go back to Mom to be held, then wriggle down while still crying, then reach back up to be held again. These are miscues designed to keep Mom involved—because, after all, that's what Mom seems to want. They might appear timid and shy when they really are not.

Miscues on the top of the Circle can be a response to parents with two kinds of attachment-related behavior: (1) parents who really are afraid that the world is too dangerous for their child, and (2) parents who are inconsistent. In the first case, the child knows the parent disapproves of the child's being exposed to the world's "dangers," and so acts needy to please the parent and keep her from becoming even more anxious. In the second, the child runs back and forth, like Lily and Nomi, because the child senses that the parent needs to be needed but also is not fully at ease providing care. It's as if the child is hearing two messages: "Please need me. You need me too much." Such a parent likely has a history of either being raised by just such a parent or having a central caregiver who was absent early in life in ways that felt overwhelming. So now, as a parent herself, she is concerned about having another central person in her life leave while also overwhelmed by a child who can be continually demanding because she's been taught to be so.

There is yet another version of this struggle on the top of the Circle. As mentioned in Chapter 5, some parents aren't focused as much on "being needed" as on wanting to be "of one mind" with their child. The goal isn't keeping the child close, but rather keeping the child from differentiating and having his own experiences. Such a parent literally assumes he knows his child's mind as well as the child does. He attempts to "mind read" and, in terms of empathy, actually overdoes it. How can it be possible to be too empathetic? See if you can remember being at a party and describing a difficult circumstance only to have your listener assume she knows precisely what you're talking about while also shifting the topic to her experience "of the exact same thing." Children raised in this way get the message that they aren't actually allowed to have their own mind, and as they get older they will either feel the need to comply with the "party line" of the family (religion, politics, worldview) or rebel. Each child needs to have her own thoughts and feelings, shared with another who listens and cares without presuming to be inside the experience.

The Tough Task of Interpreting Miscues

If you're expecting your first child, just understanding that Being-With your child, trying to stay attuned to the best of your ability (realistically and self-compassionately), and knowing that we all struggle with some attachment needs can actually promote secure attachment between you and your baby. As counterintuitive as it may at first seem, choosing to *not* be the "perfect" parent is actually one of the best approaches to becoming a secure parent.

Once you have your little one, simply utilize your innate wisdom to begin spotting potential miscues, especially during times of stress or crisis. That's when your shark music will tend to play, your empathy will be challenged, and your ability to see versus guess will be compromised. Older patterns, the ones you bring from your own history, will bring moments where you stumble, space out, and possibly rupture the Circle. In that case, you can step back, recognize the potential rupture, and make a simple repair. This doesn't have to be hard work; it's just a part of parenting that supports your child in a balanced way. As you might imagine, the effort will be repaid a thousandfold.

There are, however, other, more difficult challenges with recognizing miscues and responding to your child's true need that can arise. Maybe you already have children, and you'd like to improve your relationship with them. It all starts with recognizing your shark music and tuning in to your child's cues and miscues. Being-With is at the heart of this endeavor, and we offer ideas for honing that ability in Part II. Here are a couple of other twists to be aware of:

Shark Music → Child's Miscues: Not Necessarily a Straight Line

Because the defensive dance that can occur in attachment strategies is complex and subtle, we've described children's miscues as if they usually mirror a parent's struggles around the Circle. This is often the case, but not always. You may see this if you already have children. For instance, if you struggle on the bottom of the Circle, you might see that one of your children is an eager achiever who wants to succeed to stay connected to you while another rejects what feels like the imposition of your standards and instead becomes very distant. You could find yourself wondering how you ended up with one offspring who's your natural protégé and one who's a rebel or noticeably private and even distant: One dresses like a mini you and the other wears whatever you consider "outrageous" or highly "unique" to give a simple, superficial example. Or gender will create attachment differences between your children. If you struggle on the top of the Circle, you might find that your daughter is also a "homebody" who depends on you and others while your son, although he accedes to your wishes to stay close to home, has taken to heart the idea that he's quite special and may feel (and act) a little entitled.

As we've stated throughout this book, maintaining the appropriate balance between the top of the Circle and the bottom is critical. Parents who are somewhat intrusive with their children, either because they never want them to leave (shark music on the top of the Circle) or because they want them to achieve at all costs (shark music at the bottom), can end up driving their children away. As adults, these children can be wary of closeness because they fear being smothered. Why? Because they've known the pressure of being taught that approval and acceptance come only through meeting high external standards and/ or "staying on the same page" with their caregivers in ways that feel (profoundly) uncomfortable.

This all becomes even more complicated when two parents are involved.

Conflict between Parents Can Weaken the Parent–Child Bond

Monica is at the top of her game whenever she's going full tilt. For an 11-year-old, Monica pushes the limits of her body about as much as can be imagined. She especially likes climbing: trees, fences, rock formations on the nearby hillside. But she also loves basketball and soccer, playing in every pickup game she can find after school or on weekends.

Devin, Monica's dad, isn't so sure about all of this. He is happy to see his daughter enjoy sports, but he's always afraid that she'll hurt herself. He's not necessarily off base because Monica has—through the years—accumulated a wide assortment of cuts and bruises and several broken bones.

Monica's mom, on the other hand, sees this as "good, clean fun" and "nothing to worry about." Marsha had a similar history and considers the difficulties and the challenges of a risk-taking daughter to be part of healthy parenting.

So it's not uncommon to see Devin and Marsha arguing over their daughter's latest bump or cut. "What if it's something worse next time?"

"Yeah, and what if she's just doing what comes naturally and a few cuts go with the territory of being a kid?" Back and forth the parents go, with Devin's "red flags" getting redder and Marsha's certainty getting more certain.

A couple of unfortunate outcomes can emerge here. One is simply that Monica will develop miscues on the top of the Circle with Devin but not with Marsha, and this may threaten Monica's relationship with her father. She may feel she is required to be more "needy" with her dad to stay connected. In this way top-half struggles might become more central to this family's dynamics in a way that Monica's relationship with her mom might receive less focus. Inadvertently, the potential depth of their mother–daughter bond may suffer.

Differences in attachment styles between parents in two-parent families are complicated and beyond the scope of this book. The complexities of two-parent struggles when one or both parents have a difficult time reflecting on their own shark music are best dealt with by consulting a professional. Finding a way to understand the tension between parents, especially in circumstances of ongoing tension, often requires the clarity of someone trained to offer guidance and support for both parents.

Parental Stress Interferes

Three children, ages 3, 6, and 8, along with being a second-grade teacher all day and a single parent, add up to Ana's sense of being burdened by the needs of her children. All needs. Any needs. Especially the moment she comes through the door at the end of a long day.

For the last few months Ana has come home just hoping her children will be playing happily on their own. Instead, Ana typically walks through the door to find her children yelling at one another. Slinking into her bedroom, Ana tries to pretend there is nothing wrong and that her children don't actually need her.

The moment her door shuts, the shouts and the fighting escalate. Ana counts to 10, then 20, hoping the sound will subside. For a few minutes it does. She turns on her bedroom TV and tries to enjoy her daily dose of talk shows. But it doesn't work. Finally, as if on some kind of timer that goes off each day at the same time, Ana walks out of her bedroom into the front room with all of the commotion and begins to yell at her children for "being so immature."

Stress hurts. It hurts parents, and it certainly damages the attachment bond, in turn hurting children. Single parents often have to deal with more than any one adult can be expected to handle. In this scenario, we see Ana's children in need on the bottom of the Circle as they wait for Mom to come home. Ana is exhausted and, anticipating yet more demands on her waning energy, tries to deny their need for comfort and their need to have someone who is bigger, stronger, wiser, and kind back home. This leads to her becoming weak and gone, which pushes her children to "act out" to get Mom to come back on the Circle, take charge, and offer the comfort that can only come when Ana is available. Ana can't help focusing on the behavior, because it's so in her face, and explosively blames the children for needing comfort. And so the cycle of blame/shame/distance continues, needs on the Circle go unrecognized, and the mother–child relationships deteriorate.

In cases like Ana's, a little professional counseling can go a long way. If Ana can find some ways to reduce her overall stress, she might have a tiny bit of energy left to take advice like allowing even 10 minutes of comfort and connection with her children when she first gets home. This might be enough to fill their emotional cups so that she can get a breather and then venture into a much less stressful evening of Being-With her children as the good-enough mother she knows she can be.

Sometimes Ethan isn't sure if his mother is going to be accepting or angry. She is clearly capable of both responses. In this moment, Ethan's 6-year-old enthusiasm is seen as something she is proud of. An hour later, Ethan's excitement receives a glance that feels as though it would wither everything in sight. He simply can't be sure which response, or which mother, he'll encounter.

So Ethan has become vigilant. He's learned to take the temperature of his mother's moment-to-moment feeling tone, always watching out for just what response she might offer. When she's happy, they laugh in ways that both of them can reference days later. But when she's pulled in and sullen, Ethan retreats to his room. Now even the threat of her harsh stare has begun to cement Ethan's choice to spend ever more time alone in his room.

Ethan's mother may need some professional help too. Sometimes the burdens on parents are just too heavy to allow sufficient opportunity (and internal capacity) for Being-With, for interpreting cues and miscues, for reflecting in order to recognize ruptures, and certainly for making repairs.

Awakening the Sleeping Shark

If, after reading Chapter 5, you started to think about your own shark music, you may find you've awakened your sleeping shark to enlightening effect: Many parents we've worked with told us stories about the insights that began to pop into their minds about their attachment bond with their children or with their own parents. Or they found themselves seeing their attachment style in the way they conduct the other relationships in their life, whether friendships, marriage, at work, or with siblings.

This book is not intended to be an intervention. *There's nothing wrong with you*. It's meant to be a new way of looking at your parenting and the rest of your relationships, and many parents find this awareness enough all by itself to help them make an empathic shift toward increased Being-With their children. Not all the time, not even most of the time in some cases, but enough of the time that their children feel secure (enough) in the knowledge that Mom or Dad can be there for them, accepting, loving, and ready to help them navigate the rough journey through all of their emotional needs.

Maybe what you've read so far is not enough for you. Or maybe you're inspired to explore further. "Where were you when my child was 1?" asked one parent, who felt sad as she considered the choices she could have made if she had been introduced to the Circle of Security when her child was born. Fortunately, it's never too late to choose security. No matter the age of your children, be they toddlers, teens, or well into adulthood, start now to utilize what you're learning.

Hint: As it turns out, it's not helpful to begin saying to your children, no matter their age, that you've suddenly figured everything out and you've decided to try a different approach to being their parent. Such a declaration will, understandably, be met with either cynicism or worse. Rather, allow what you're now considering regarding your own history and theirs in terms of Being-With, Being-Without, shark music, cues and miscues, and so on to quietly influence your regular interactions from this point forward. No stopping on a dime or suddenly seeing the light, just modest yet committed changes in how you are, what you say, what you no longer say, what you emphasize or seem to require . . . on and on. Little yet consistent changes that just might—over time—add up to real and lasting change. Or turn to Part II to find out more about attachments in your own family, how they came about, and what you can do to improve your relationships.

WELCOME TO THE CLUB

Being a parent may just be *the* most difficult job on the planet. Every day, parents—the world over—want the best for their children. And every day, parents—the world over—fail to meet some of the needs of their children. "Help me" moments go unseen. "Watch over me" moments get interrupted. "Comfort me" and "Organize my feelings" moments end up being pushed away or lost in the rush and stress of everyday life.

Welcome to the club.

Of course, it's hard to know that we make mistakes. The good news is that, as parents, we all have an inner wisdom that helps us work with these mistakes. No matter who we are, if we listen to ourselves, there is always something inside us that asks us to keep trying. No matter what our history, if we pay attention, there is a place in our hearts that wants to meet the needs of our children.

All Parents Have Wisdom

The best news is that parenting can be *the* most wonderful job on the planet. And one of the most wonderful parts of being a parent is knowing that we can add to our wisdom. We can recognize our weaknesses, learn from our mistakes, and find new ways to meet the very real needs of our children.

All Parents Struggle

Please know that mistakes in parenting are inevitable. Every parent in the club wishes this weren't so. Each parent in the club is trying very hard to make sure that the needs of her or his child are being met. That's why you have taken the time and energy to read this book. After so much work, to realize that there are things that aren't going right for your child can be upsetting.

Our greatest hope lies in beginning to realize that our weaknesses as a parent tend to be in a particular area on the Circle of Security. Every parent on the planet has an overused side and an underused side on this *Circle*. That isn't the problem. The problem begins when we don't realize that we have a stronger side and a weaker side. The problem gets bigger when we try to overuse our stronger side to make up for underusing our weaker side. The problem continues, one generation after another, when we don't find a way to deal with what it is within us, and in our history, that keeps that side weak.

It's Hard to Give What We Weren't Given

It's hard to give what we weren't given. For example, it gets hard to give as much comfort as our child requires when it wasn't much a part of our own childhood. There will be times when our child cues us, asking for tenderness, and we hurt a little. At those times we may pull back and self-protect without even knowing it. We may get busy or ask our child to focus on a toy—cuing him or her in a subtle way not to make a direct request for comfort—because every time our child asks for the gentle holding we went without, it reminds us of a lack we carry within us, and that causes pain. Understandably, then, we will find ways to avoid those moments. Little ways. Unfortunately, our child will begin to realize this and eventually try to help us out by asking for fewer and fewer of these moments.

Or, maybe our parents weren't so good at letting us go out and explore the world. They kept us close, often too close. Now, as parents ourselves, we tend to feel uneasy when our child steps further away from us into the Circle. We aren't sure, just like our parents weren't sure, that it really is a circle and that our child will soon come running back to our waiting arms.

Sensitive to Pain

If we can know that we are sensitive to pain on one side of the Circle, we can begin to change our behavior. We can step back and watch ourselves ("There I go again"). We can watch ourselves, but not with judgment, and not with criticism. We can learn to stand back and observe our behavior with kindness. Really. We can honor how hard it is to give something to our child that we may have gone without when we were young. ("Of course this is difficult for me.")

And, we can know that while it is hard, it is not impossible. Our wisdom and our genuine desire to meet our child's needs, all the way around the Circle, make it possible for new doors to open. We can come to realize that while it is difficult, if we can just recognize and admit our discomfort for a while (sometimes 15–30 seconds of additional closeness—or distance—is all that our child wants), our child's need will be met. If we can provide that closeness or distance an extra five or six times a day, everyone—child and parent—will be happier and feel more secure.

It just may be that the best part of parenting is being with our child as those real needs are being met . . . all the way around the Circle.

Welcome to the club.

Part II

CREATING AND MAINTAINING THE CIRCLE

How to Be Bigger, Stronger, Wiser, and Kind—and Good Enough

*We don't see things as they are, we see them
as we are.*

—ANAÏS NIN, *The Seduction of the Minotaur*

SHARK BONES

Exploring Our Core Sensitivities

The Mommy and Me class was in full swing. A dozen toddlers gathered around the leader, trying with varying degrees of success to follow a lively singing and clapping game. The mommies (and daddies) were lined up along the back wall, close enough to be accessible if needed, far enough away to give the 2-year-olds their first taste of independence at "school." Most of the adults chatted and laughed quietly among themselves, happy to turn over the supervisory reins to another grown-up for a brief few minutes. Many exhibited the uniquely parental skill of talking to one person (an adult) while looking exclusively at another (their child). Others had pulled out their phones the minute they sat down and never looked up. A couple kept their eyes locked on their child and sat in focused silence.

"Wow," snorted Carla, "if my Jack was this easy to entertain at home, I'd actually get something done!" Most of the parents laughed or nodded in agreement, until interrupted by Sharon, who crowed "Fiona loves singing games at home! I can pay all my bills while she sings along with the stuff I download!" The other parents laughed again and exchanged knowing glances as one said teasingly, "Yeah, Fiona's great, Sharon."

Next to Sharon, Maria wrenched her eyes away from her son and nervously asked "What?" as little Rory glanced timidly over his shoulder at his mother for the tenth time.

At the edge of the group of adults, Ellis hunched over his phone. Occasionally he glanced up, scanning the room as if he was trying to remember what he was doing there.

Suddenly, Rory burst into song and started waving his arms like a miniature conductor. The parents clapped and called out "Go, Rory!" nudging Maria and saying "Look at him!" Maria nodded distractedly; she didn't seem to notice the applause for her son and just edged a little closer to the group of children. By the end of the session she found herself sitting right behind her son, fidgeting restlessly.

Shark-infested waters are everywhere, even in the nurturing environment of Mommy and Me classes. Some of these parents are hearing shark music right now. Others will hear it somewhere else today and in a different place tomorrow. The fact that shark music plays doesn't mean there's something wrong—that the situation is dangerous, that we're terrible parents, or that our children are "in trouble." The important point to take away from this scene is that it's an ordinary setting filled with ordinary people. That's where shark music comes up: in everyday situations. And this is the way we parents react: not by doing "harm" to our children, but by developing our own particular ways of protecting our children and caring for them. Most of the time, those habits of interacting with our children are fairly benign. But there are patterns that we follow, patterns that are evident in the scene just described, that can affect the attachment bond our children take into life with them. Looking a little more deeply into these "shark"-infested waters to understand our own patterns of shark music can help us make the best choices to build security with and for our children.

This chapter will help you explore your own shark music should you wish to do so. We help you start to recognize it in almost all of your relationships, because its recording will tend to play wherever you're attached. But first, try the quiz that starts on the facing page.

Core Sensitivities: The Source of Our Shark Music

We all develop ways of protecting ourselves from pain. Chronically shy Stacey learns to take a friend along to parties to avoid the agony of meeting new people alone. Chang learns not to push through the pangs and twinges but to break up his long run into two short ones to pro-

SHARK MUSIC CHECKLIST

Quickly read through the following items and check off all those that you identify with. Don't agonize over this. If it sounds familiar, check it off. If not, move to the next item.

What Makes Me Feel Particularly Good?

❏ **Sitting next to someone I love who promises to stay close**

❏ <u>Being seen at important events</u>

❏ *Activities I can do alone*

❏ **Pleasing people**

❏ <u>Being recognized for doing an excellent job</u>

❏ *Having breathing room from others*

❏ <u>Associating with successful people</u>

❏ **Feeling needed**

❏ *Long-distance friendships*

❏ **Having someone else take care of a difficult task for me**

❏ <u>Winning</u>

❏ *Being in the audience*

❏ **A cuddly environment**

❏ *Being on my own, doing things I like*

❏ **Taking care of and being taken care of by my closest friends**

❏ <u>Being on top of things</u>

❏ **Having all my important family members and friends nearby**

❏ *Solo vacations*

❏ **Putting other people's needs and feelings ahead of my own**

❏ *Being self-sufficient*

❏ <u>Feeling highly competent</u>

❏ *Being honest, even when it's not popular*

❏ <u>Being with a soul mate who really shares the way I think</u>

What Makes Me Feel Uncomfortable?

❏ **Being alone**

❏ <u>Coming in second place</u>

(continued)

❑ **The silent treatment**

❑ People who seem unmotivated

❑ *People wanting to be very close to me*

❑ Others thinking I've done something wrong

❑ *Feeling obligated to the people I love*

❑ Being around people who whine about their problems when all they have to do is get their act together

❑ **Being with someone who always acts like he or she wants to leave**

❑ Someone who's critical

❑ *Being too isolated*

❑ **Acting confident when I know I'm not**

❑ *Feeling like I'll be too much for people*

❑ Criticism

❑ *Depending on others*

❑ **Being assertive**

❑ **Living alone**

❑ Being considered average

❑ **Saying what I think**

❑ *Being the center of attention*

❑ *Being controlled or manipulated*

❑ Being disappointed by friends

❑ *People wanting to know everything about me*

❑ *Being hugged*

❑ **Being in charge**

❑ Making a mistake

❑ *People feeling like they're on the same page with me*

❑ Failing

❑ Not being understood

❑ The high expectations of others

❑ *People being overly affectionate*

What Do Other People Say about Me or Think of Me?

❑ *I tend to go off on my own when I have a problem to solve.*

❑ **I need to do more on my own.**

(continued)

❏ *I give mixed messages: when I'm alone I sometimes want to be with others, and when I'm with others I often want to be alone.*

❏ **I give in too easily.**

❏ *When I'm upset, I withdraw to figure it out myself.*

❏ **I rely a lot on other people.**

❏ *I "go negative" just to get those closest to me to back away.*

❏ **I need a lot of support from others to get things done.**

❏ <u>I focus on achievement to the detriment of my personal relationships.</u>

❏ *They want more of me than I care to give.*

❏ <u>I boast about my accomplishments.</u>

❏ *I hurt others' feelings by wanting to do things alone.*

❏ *I tend to keep a bit of distance between me and friends.*

❏ <u>I'm a perfectionist.</u>

❏ **I try to get "too close."**

❏ *I show more affection when I miss someone than when the person is right here.*

❏ <u>I can be too critical.</u>

❏ *I tend to "retreat" when someone getting close to me starts to expect additional closeness.*

I Believe:

❏ <u>It's OK to present yourself in a manner that makes others see you in the best light.</u>

❏ **Loving someone means never having him or her feel alone.**

❏ *It's very hard to tell someone you love him or her.*

❏ **It's much more important to have friends than to be considered successful.**

❏ <u>Winning is among the best things in life.</u>

❏ **People who need people are the luckiest people in the world.**

❏ <u>No one likes losers.</u>

❏ **Winning doesn't matter—I just want everyone to get along.**

❏ *Being too close to others is unsafe.*

❏ **Being placed in isolation is the worst punishment possible.**

❏ <u>Even when everyone thinks I'm great, I often think I'm not doing enough.</u>

❏ **The best way to show people you love them is to never want to be away from them.**

(continued)

❑ *If I get too connected, I'll be too much for people.*

❑ **When someone wants you to do things on your own, it means he or she doesn't care about you.**

❑ *People are often trying to control or manipulate me.*

❑ **If I argue with someone, I might lose him or her.**

❑ *A few friends is plenty.*

❑ **My opinions aren't that important.**

❑ <u>I try to have amazingly outstanding friends.</u>

❑ **It's more important to stay connected to someone than to be right.**

❑ <u>I constantly have to prove myself with my work and studies.</u>

❑ **Other people know how to do things better than me.**

❑ *Other people's needs can leave little room for me the closer they get.*

❑ **If I could take care of myself, people wouldn't take care of me.**

❑ <u>I have a very special purpose for my life.</u>

❑ <u>People can be vicious when you make a mistake.</u>

❑ **Independence means nothing if you don't have someone who cares about you.**

❑ <u>Even when I do things right, I'm probably an imposter.</u>

❑ **It's OK to ask for help even when you can figure it out yourself.**

❑ <u>Anything I do that I'm really proud of I worry I won't be able to do again.</u>

❑ *It's important to be really good at what I do even if no one knows it.*

❑ **Having children means you don't have to feel alone.**

❑ <u>When people can see how good I am, everything in life is better.</u>

❑ *When people get close, they can emotionally smother you.*

❑ <u>Even when I am wrong I have a hard time admitting it.</u>

Scoring

Now add up the number of items you checked that are **bold**, <u>underlined</u>, and *italic* and enter each number below.

Bold: _____

<u>Underlined:</u> _____

Italic: _____

tect his worn-out knees. Vince meditates before his weekly call to his mother so he doesn't end up feeling so guilty about her loneliness that he gets off the phone quickly—and then feels even worse. Jan learns to come out swinging in real estate negotiations to disarm her "opponent" and avoid the humiliation of revealing she just hasn't prepared as well.

These are all conscious decisions made to defend against pain. Shark music is, as explained in Chapter 5, an unconscious defense against emotional pain experienced in our earliest attachment relationships—ruptures that went without repair—or memories of the painful aspects of relationships that we don't want to repeat. Conscious defenses don't always have positive outcomes, as Jan eventually figured out when she got tired of losing sales and began to let down her guard, finding that leaving herself vulnerable often turned adversaries into allies and resulted in better deals all around. Shark music doesn't always create positive outcomes either. Our presumed self-protection doesn't work all that well for us, and—as you may well have discovered by this point in the book—though well intentioned, it also isn't helpful for our children. This chapter is an invitation to bring the unconscious defense of shark music into our consciousness so that our shark music doesn't make our parenting decisions for us.

> *It is easier for a patient to remember trauma than to remember nothing happening when it might have happened.*
> —DONALD WINNICOTT, pediatrician and psychoanalyst

Shark music is triggered by painful thoughts and memories, usually focused on a key theme that felt particularly hurtful to us as we were growing up. While there can be a wide variety of painful moments, it's common for us to find one theme around which we focus our defenses against further pain. This specific theme is what we call a "core sensitivity"* in the Circle of Security approach that we

---

*This is a complex topic rooted in psychoanalytic and object relations theory, attachment theory, and the clinical insight of James Masterson, MD, and Ralph Klein, MD. In those fields of study, the ideas formed about attachment during our own childhood become defenses of the self that, at their most extreme, lead to personality disorders. In our lexicon, these core sensitivities exist to some extent in all of us, and while they are defenses, in the huge majority of cases they're simply a part of our personalities, worthy of recognizing and then reconsidering from the position that adulthood now offers.

use with parents. These sensitivities fall into three somewhat distinct categories:

- Separation sensitivity
- Esteem sensitivity
- Safety sensitivity

Each core sensitivity has its own unique shark music—that is, each of us is likely to hear a specific shark music theme when we sense (accurately or inaccurately) threats of either abandonment (separation sensitivity), criticism or rejection (esteem sensitivity), or intrusion (safety sensitivity) in our relationships. The Mommy and Me session illustrates all three sensitivities in broad strokes: Maria doesn't want to be left alone—ever. She pays a lot of attention to what others seem to want from her and gives it to them so they'll stay with her. Sharon is focused on specialness and performance. Sensitive to criticism and judgment, she places a lot of her attention on what others think of her (and her child). Ellis is wary of the intrusion of others, of people asking too much from him, of losing himself in relationships. He's not really cognizant of this wariness despite the fact that it steers him to keep his distance in most interactions, at times from his own child.

You may already recognize yourself in one of these three sensitivities. In a very general way, separation sensitivity predisposes us to struggle around the top of the Circle as described in Chapter 5. If you feel more nervous about your child's attempts at autonomy, but you also have trouble asserting your parental authority (except when you finally get fed up and jump to the other extreme), you might be separation sensitive. Esteem sensitivity leaves us vulnerable to struggles around the bottom of the Circle, particularly concerning issues of, well, vulnerability. If you read all the parenting books to give your child the chance to be the best and the brightest (anything but average), you could be esteem sensitive. Safety sensitivity usually leads us to struggle on the bottom of the Circle as well. If having a child with whom you can share affection but who also welcomes plenty of distance (doesn't seem to need you too much) seems ideal to you, you may be safety sensitive.

If you don't yet have children, with the help of this chapter you can still find clues to your core sensitivity by considering other important relationships in your life. Meanwhile, what did the Shark Music Checklist say about your core sensitivity?

- If you checked more **bold** items than the other two, you may lean toward separation sensitivity.
- If you checked more <u>underlined</u> items, you might be more esteem sensitive.
- If you checked more *italic* items, you might tend toward being safety sensitive.

You likely checked some items in each group.* That's normal. Most of us have aspects of each sensitivity, but it's our dominant core sensitivity that plays the loudest shark music for us—especially when we're under stress. So it's good to know where your main sensitivity lies. It might be where you're most vulnerable to ruptures in your relationships and where you find it hardest to offer repair (see the box on page 190).

As you can see from the box, our core sensitivities can lead us to construct unspoken rules for how to behave in relationships or interact with others. Unconsciously we're trying to give ourselves some emotional stability and protection, but in reality our game plan has unspoken rules that create expectations for others to follow. In adult relationships this often results in our unwittingly violating another person's own unexpressed sensitivity. Alyssa asks Guy for lots of reassurance that he loves her to ease her fear of being left alone, but these requests feel intrusive to Guy, which only makes him try to get more distance from her. A rupture has occurred on both sides, but without an understanding of their own and each other's core sensitivity, repairs are likely to be hit or miss or to simply never happen. When Alyssa keeps their 4-year-old daughter, Lia, near her most of the time, Lia develops miscues designed to maintain her mom's availability while also (barely) maintaining a bit of her need for autonomy: she runs back to Alyssa repeatedly while playing, acting as if she's upset (a miscue), but then, while appearing inconsolable, she wriggles away to play again. Lia is doing what her unconscious mind is telling her will please her mother even though she could never put that into words.

When you do become acquainted with your core sensitivity, you can reflect on how it may be influencing your responses to your child's

---

*Some items in the checklist can also apply to more than one sensitivity. Feeling uncomfortable when faced with the high expectations of others, for example, could come from safety sensitivity in addition to esteem sensitivity. In real people, nothing is absolute or universal. The checklist was designed to give you a general impression.

Core Sensitivities and Ruptures

Shark music can be like one of those supersensitive car alarms—intended to prevent theft but prone to screaming a warning about the slightest vibration caused by a gust of wind or a mild touch. In that sense shark music can be a false signal, leading us to react to the needs of our children in ways we never intended to. One way to get to know your core sensitivity is to reflect on where you often have hair-trigger or automatic responses that you later regret or at least question. If you already have children . . .

- Do you find yourself automatically saying, "I think we should stay home today" or "No, I don't think that's a good idea" when your child wants to go off on his own somewhere—even though later you could honestly say there was no reason to object?

- Do you scold your toddler for refusing to share or insist she behave in certain ways "because the other kids won't like you" or "You're not being kind enough," even though on reflection you could see you were expecting more than a 2-year-old could possibly do?

- Do you automatically get your 3-year-old to "think about a better plan" or quickly get focused on playing with a toy when he comes to you whimpering with a skinned knee or say, "Now isn't the best time" when he seems to want to get on your lap—even though part of you really wants to pick him up to comfort him or just cuddle?

Patterns of these kinds of reflexive responses might tell you what your core sensitivity is. The next time those occasions come up, you can learn more by asking yourself, "Where was my child on the Circle?"

needs around the Circle and decide to override the shark music alarm. During the Mommy and Me session, some of the parents were doing just that. One mother knew she tended to get very nervous when her toddler was out of arm's reach. To avoid standing in the way of his exploring (what we call "going out," or being on the top of the Circle), she repeated to herself silently, "He's fine, he's fine, he's fine" and

tapped her foot in time with the rhythm of the words. No one sus-
pected she was struggling at all. It was different for Maria. She felt
uneasy seeing Rory engaged elsewhere, with his back to her, even
though she had no idea why. She just found herself scooting closer and
closer to the children. It was different for Ellis too. He shifted between
the urge to get closer to his son when the little boy seemed to stop participating and the urge to turn back to his phone when his son started
to whimper. Sharon, too, lacked the self-awareness that would help her
ignore her shark music when she wanted to. A sheepish expression flit-
ted across Sharon's face for a moment when her friend told her Fiona
was a great girl, and then she seemed calm, serenely gazing around
the room over everyone's head. Inside she was telling herself that the
other parents had no idea how great Fiona really was. Besides, she had
read all the books and knew how much affirmation little ones needed.
The fact that Fiona was clearly ahead of her peers in development was
proof. Underneath those thoughts she felt twinges of something else: a
foreboding that simply didn't make sense.

If you already have children, some of these illustrations might
seem familiar. If you're expecting your first, you can explore your other
close relationships for clues to your core sensitivity.

Spouses, Partners, Best Friends: How Our Adult Relationships Reveal Our Core Sensitivities

Do you ever feel like the thought of being close to someone is very
comforting in theory but when your partner presents you with certain
needs the closeness feels too demanding in reality? Or does emotional
distance from a partner start to feel quite threatening? Or maybe you
find yourself caught up in trying to be perfect within your relationship
more than simply being in the relationship? All of these are likely indi-
cations of your core sensitivity. So one effective way to start figuring
out where your core sensitivity might be is by looking at your adult
relationships, particularly those with intimate partners. The following
overview of the core sensitivities includes some questions you can ask
about those relationships, past and current, to start accumulating self-
knowledge. We also offer a "Core Sensitivities within Close Relationships" chart on pages 192–193.

Core Sensitivities within Close Relationships

	Conclusion	Procedural Certainty	Common Procedural Triggers	Others Say	Healthy Goal	Truth Be Told
Separation Sensitive I think I must comply with what others want, need, and feel while not focusing on my own wants, needs, and feelings.	I do what I can to focus on the needs of those close to me. Otherwise, I'm afraid they will be upset and leave me. Alternatively, I can often get upset because those close to me don't seem to be doing their part to take care of me.	In order to feel close, I must remain needy, good, weak, and, if necessary, incompetent/helpless. Then I will be taken care of and not feel alone.	I am vigilant, scanning for signs that something is wrong in the relationship (thus keeping the relationship center stage, often within a state of upset and difficulty); I fear taking a stand with significant others. I tend to be preoccupied with whether or not I am being loved enough.	"You want too much from me." "It feels like you're clinging to me." "It's like you want me to threaten to leave and then dramatically decide to stay."	To give up my perceptions, opinions, and needs is to deny who I actually am and, thus, to deny a deeper level of intimacy.	"Just below the surface, I think you will leave me." "If I don't focus on you, you'll walk out." "I can get helpless so you'll come near and take care of me."
Esteem Sensitive I believe that who I am, just as I am, is not enough to be valued. I continually attempt to prove that I am worthy through performance and achievement.	Perceptions of me feel all-important. I attempt to be in control of perceptions. I am vigilant about any view of me as having failed or being inadequate. Those around me tend to "walk on eggshells." I am often disappointed in others for not "getting it."	In order to be noticed and responded to, I must perform, accomplish, be perfect, and think like the "all-important other" (anyone I admire for their intelligence, beauty, and/or power). When I'm performing well and/or with someone I admire, I feel special and not alone.	I scan for others' positive and negative perceptions. I have a hair-trigger reaction to criticism; I need to be right; I need not to be wrong. I desire to "be on the same page" with others close to me.	"It's not always about you." "It's just criticism, not the end of the world." "I'm not an extension of you." "I feel pressured to always be upbeat or only say nice things about you; if I don't you'll feel criticized, angry, or cold."	Recognizing that mistakes are inevitable. Sharing my needs and vulnerability can be fulfilling.	Just below the surface, I'm fairly certain that I'm not really worthy." "I may get angry if you don't fit my ideal." "I may withdraw if your disagreement upsets my fantasy that we always think alike."

192

Safety Sensitive						
The cost of being connected to significant others requires giving up having choices about who I really am and what I really want.	I attempt to be in control of closeness. When I get close to another my sense of safety is at risk.	To be in a relationship is to be intruded upon and controlled. To be in a relationship is to risk being enslaved. The best I can hope for is closeness from a distance.	Scanning for any sign of someone being dominant, manipulative, intrusive, or being "too close" ("too intimate," "too understanding," "too concerned"). Exposure/being seen can feel excruciating.	"I want more from you." "It's like you disappear on me." "Why do you go into hiding whenever I ask about yourself?" "I don't want to control you; I just want to be close."	Within a context of negotiation, closeness doesn't require being intruded upon, invaded, or controlled; intimacy can be safe.	"Once again, I just got frightened because it felt like we were getting too close." "I think I just retreated into my self-sufficient mode, sure that you'd try to control things."

Based on the original teaching of James Masterson, MD, and Ralph Klein, MD.

Separation Sensitive

People who are separation sensitive are focused on keeping relationships close. Any suggestion of distance, such as the sense that the other person *isn't* so focused on the relationship, might feel threatening. Because of a fear of abandonment, some separation-sensitive people might sacrifice their own individuality—their wants, needs, and feelings—or well-being to make the relationship "work."

Separation-sensitive people are those we described as **struggling on the top of the Circle** in Chapter 5, and **Maria** is an example.

Security camera: Our core sensitivities are a lens through which we scan our relationship environment for "sharks." It's as if we're equipped with a security camera that alerts us to the presence of a perceived threat. To feel at least somewhat secure, the separation-sensitive person scans constantly for signs that something is wrong in the relationship or that someone who is relied on might potentially leave the relationship.

• **In love relationships, have you often agonized over whether your love is returned?** Separation-sensitive people can ask for continual reassurance of their partner's love; some may appear to be "the jealous type," with a theme of "I'm afraid you'll leave me" as central.

• **With intimate partners and even close friends, do you dissect the relationship to make sure nothing is wrong?** Sometimes separation-sensitive people unwittingly stir the pot, highlighting difficulties and creating upset to test the relationship and make sure it's not about to fall apart (which, ironically, can put additional stress on the relationship). They also often use a sense of helplessness as a way to keep others close, by continually soliciting help with emotional pain.

• **Do you avoid taking a stand with your loved ones?** By nature, being assertive can create distance from others. This may feel too risky if you're separation sensitive ("Having my own opinion might mean separating from you and being left alone"). Of interest is that separation-sensitive people might withhold being assertive but often pick fights. While assertion claims competence and might push you away, arguing with you keeps us embroiled in the relationship and therefore close.

Esteem Sensitive

Esteem-sensitive folks feel compelled to be distinguished positively, with an emphasis on their own accomplishments and perceived perfection, because deep down they don't believe their unadorned, naturally flawed human selves will be considered acceptable. Imperfection equals rejection. They try to get emotional "supplies" (admiration and acknowledgment) from an all-important other person but may also act like they don't have emotional needs. To be vulnerable is to risk being found wanting and then shamed or humiliated. Abandonment is a fear here too, but the focus is rejection for imperfection. The goal is to always perform exceedingly well, to be special and always be above average.

Esteem-sensitive people are those we described as **struggling on the bottom of the Circle** in Chapter 5, and Susan is an example.

Security camera: The only way for esteem-sensitive people to be convinced of being "secure" is to be convinced others perceive them in a positive/exceptional light, so they constantly scan others for potential negative and positive perceptions of themselves.

• **Do you find criticism hard to take?** Esteem-sensitive people not only feel the need to be right but even more need *not* to be wrong. This inclination is pervasive, showing up in personal and professional relationships. The esteem-sensitive partner may find apologizing very difficult because it implies being wrong and being wrong brings memories of criticism and humiliation. Or the esteem-sensitive partner may apologize or put himself down almost incessantly. While at first this appears to be almost humble, beneath the surface this habit can be preemptive: "If I criticize myself first, either you won't or, even if you do, it can't hurt as much because I got there first."

• **In love and friendships, are you looking for those who are on the same page with you?** For esteem-sensitive people, the ideal is someone who can "understand perfectly," who "totally gets it," and who shares the same thoughts and feelings and is in full agreement on almost everything. This is called "one-mindedness." ("To the degree that we're of the same mind we won't have the differences that lead to criticism and eventual rejection.")

• **Does your intimate relationship need to be perfect?** Esteem-sensitive people may find vulnerability excruciating, so a relationship with even modest flaws or cracks in it can feel too fragile. ("Perfection means neither of us will ever have to say we're sorry.")

Safety Sensitive

People who are safety sensitive are something of an enigma, especially to those who are in relationships that are typically close—parent/child and intimate partners, maybe even close friends. Those who are safety sensitive believe the cost of making a close connection with another person is the loss of themselves. Get too close and you'll have to yield to the other person, sacrifice what you really want and who you really are, and ultimately end up being manipulated or controlled. On the other hand, not yielding and having a sense of self implies being all alone. Therefore, to be safety sensitive is to always be stuck in a dilemma about being connected versus being oneself, a genuinely difficult struggle.

Another way to think about safety sensitivity is to consider it to be a kind of "intrusion" sensitivity. People who are safety sensitive are conscious of how others are potentially intruding into their sense of self. The paradox is that they want and even long for closeness but often find themselves uneasy when having to interact within an actual relationship. Finding ways to be self-sufficient becomes a central goal.

Safety-sensitive people tend to struggle on the bottom because they fear exposing their need for others and getting too close (which, of course, implies potential intrusion). Ellis shows signs of safety sensitivity—not wanting to get too close or stay too far away, from either his child or the rest of the parents.

Security camera: Security means keeping a distance for safety-sensitive people. So they are constantly scanning for signs of intrusion, dominance, or manipulation. Just below the surface, they are also scanning for any indication that they may be "too much" for others, doing what they can not to be intrusive themselves.

• **Do you act torn about new relationships, getting close and then pulling back over and over?** Safety-sensitive people want relationships and want connection but often feel uncomfortable once they have them. This can be misunderstood as an "unwillingness to commit." While it can appear this way to someone wanting more closeness, the discomfort and pulling away have to do with fear of intrusion, of someone who will inevitably want too much.

● **Do those in close relationships with you accuse you of suddenly withdrawing or going into hiding?** A variety of triggers (too much empathy, too much understanding, too much physical contact) can make the safety-sensitive person feel threatened, which results in backing away or shutting down.

● **Do potential partners view you as aloof or insensitive, more interested in honesty and the truth than people's feelings?** Safety-sensitive people live by the rhetorical question, "If I can't trust myself, who can I trust?" They have plenty of empathy and secretly experience much longing for connection, but sharing either may lead to another coming too close. Hence they often focus where they feel safer: unwavering honesty and a willingness to stay with the facts (even when this may cause distance). This commitment to honesty allows personal integrity and it also tends to push others away, both of which can feel "safe" in the short run. Sadly, this sense of safety often leads to a sense of being alone.

> *"In my own relationship with my partner I sometimes feel like I just want to escape from long hugs, but I can remind myself that he is needing his cup filled and it's actually OK getting a hug even though it makes me want to squirm away sometimes. I think 'There is no real danger here, just my shark music.'"*
> —Alison Bruce, Karratha, Western Australia

You may be wondering how your core sensitivity might affect your ability to function as the hands on the Circle; see the box on pages 198–199.

Although your core sensitivities influence you most in your closest relationships, they can also shape your responses in many other common daily interactions; see the box on pages 199–200.

Now that you've had a look at a lot of descriptions and illustrations of core sensitivities in a variety of relationships, take a look at how they apply to you in the quiz on page 201 if you feel like it. What the quiz indicates may be obvious to you, or you can tally your score.

Core Sensitivities and Our Hands on the Circle

Remember, we have the option of keeping both hands on the Circle or, when we rupture, we can take either one hand or both hands off the Circle.

Separation Sensitive

If you're separation sensitive, you may often find yourself taking your hand off the top of the Circle, just at the moment your child begins to venture farther away from you. Taking that hand off leaves your child feeling less secure, so he runs back to you, giving you the illusion of feeling secure again now that your security camera has revealed a shark and you've found a way to avoid it. Or you may have difficulty taking charge when your child needs firmness from you, because you confuse being authoritative with being authoritarian and fear losing your child's affection and closeness if you act bigger and stronger.

Esteem Sensitive

If you're esteem sensitive, you might find yourself taking your hand off the bottom of the Circle when your child needs comfort or help with organizing any strong emotion—maybe you were expected to "rise above it" or "make lemons from lemonade" when you were small, and you're unconsciously driven to impart the same lesson. If it's time to take charge, you might move toward scolding or shaming (using words or rolling your eyes), a form of being critical that repeats the shame you were familiar with growing up. Or, not wanting to risk being "of two minds," you may allow your child to run the show, afraid to step up and clarify that you do, in fact, have two distinctly separate minds and "It's now time that you listen to the one that is bigger, stronger, wiser, and kind about this particular issue in this particular moment!"

Safety Sensitive

Typically, a safety-sensitive parent will take his or her hand off the bottom of the Circle, wanting to have the child close but not too close. Sometimes the parent will also take his or her hand off the top, wanting the child to remain "close enough" that the parent doesn't feel too lonely. This, of course, can be confusing to the child, who essentially hears, "Please don't go too far away, but also don't get too close."

Mean, Weak, and Gone for Each Core Sensitivity

In the most extreme cases of each core sensitivity, some parents grew up with a parent who was chronically negligent, mentally ill, abusive, or always expected the child to be the designated family caregiver, leaving that child with no model for the hands on the Circle. In this case, regardless of your core sensitivity, in times of distress your hands can't reach the Circle at all, even though you very much want to reach out and meet your child's needs by being bigger, stronger, wiser, and kind. Miraculously, we have seen parents of each core sensitivity who had consistently mean, weak, or gone caregivers leave that negative legacy behind by learning the Circle of Security and using its simple coherence as a road map in difficult situations. They have also often benefited from getting professional help when feeling overwhelmed.

Prompt and Response:
Core Sensitivities in Everyday Exchanges

Our core sensitivities can be tapped when we least expect them to rear their heads. Here are examples of common statements another person might make and how you might respond—internally—depending on your core sensitivity.

Prompt: "You wouldn't believe what just happened to me. I just got another promotion, my second in the past six months—I'm now officially the new assistant manager at the bank, and I'm thinking they might be preparing me to be full manager at the branch office opening next year."

Internal response—Separation: "That will never happen to me. Never. I'm such a loser! That's all anyone thinks of when they think of me. Someone who will never make anything of herself."

Internal response—Esteem: "She's so full of herself. It's not like she doesn't kiss everyone's butt all the time trying to climb the corporate ladder. Who does she think she is? She's not so special."

Internal response—Safety: "Her enthusiasm has nothing to do with me. She's holding me hostage. I can't leave. But I can't stay. But I can't leave. And she just keeps going on and on and on."

Prompt: "Who do you think you are? You have no right to say that to me!" (Furious)

Internal response—Separation: "She's right. Who do I think I am? I should never have told her I disagreed. Take it back. Tell her I'm wrong. Tell her it's all my fault."

Internal response—Esteem: "I have every right to say what I want. This isn't my first food fight, and it won't be my last." Or "She's my boss. It's my job in life to keep her thinking she's awesome and special and the one who knows what's important. Get back on the same page."

Internal response—Safety: "I'm not willing to step into her movie. I'm not even willing to stay around for her movie. One more time it's clear I'm not cut out for whatever it is that people seem to need from me."

Prompt: "Why can't you just stay here for a few minutes? Why can't you help me?"

Internal response—Separation: "Serves you right. You sure weren't there for me last week when I was falling apart. This time I'm going to make sure you get what it feels like to be left in the dark."

Internal response—Esteem: "I thought we had a lot in common, but maybe not. I thought you had it together. Your going all tragic is not working for me. I'm looking for friends who are more like me than you are."

Internal response—Safety: "I don't want to stay for 2 seconds. I know we're friends, I know you need help, but I'm not able to do this. Every time you look at me I'm just backing 3 feet farther away."

Prompt: (Someone talking with a harsh look of devaluation/rolling of the eyes.)

Internal response—Separation: "Don't make her even more upset. She's already mad at you. You pushed too hard. Stop pushing her."

Internal response—Esteem: "I am *not* wrong on this one. I did nothing wrong. You always take the high road. You are so arrogant. Get over yourself!" or "She's really mad now. Remind her she's perfect. Tell her she's the best. Make her think she's always right. Perfection solves every problem."

Internal response—Safety: "Hmmmm. Whatever she just did I'm not OK with. I think that look on her face just made it clear why I don't stick around."

YOUR CORE SENSITIVITY IN ADULT RELATIONSHIPS

What do the relationships you've had as an adult tell you about your core sensitivity?

❑ <u>Do you tend to worry about your spouse/partner leaving you?</u>

❑ *Are you often concerned about what your friends, neighbors, and acquaintances think of you and your partner as a couple?*

❑ **Have you been comfortable with long-distance relationships (even if your partner was not)?**

❑ <u>Does relying on your partner to take care of things make you feel closer to him or her?</u>

❑ *Have you broken up with a partner because the other person kept being critical of "every little thing"?*

❑ **Have you had relationships end after you've been accused of being cold, withholding, commitment phobic, or simply not present?**

❑ **Do you see your best friends only every few months?**

❑ *Is your social life centered on a tight group of friends who all think alike?*

❑ <u>Do you count on the advice of your close friends to help you make your decisions?</u>

❑ *Has it been important for you to be elected or appointed the captain of your sports teams, the chairman of your volunteer committee, or the leader of your social group?*

❑ <u>Do your friends think of you as easygoing because you're OK with going along with whatever they want to do when you get together?</u>

❑ **Have you lost friends after being honest even when you knew it would hurt them?**

❑ **Are ethics and integrity more important to you on the job than relationships?**

❑ *If you're not the top performer at work, do you feel like a failure?*

❑ <u>Do your annual reviews usually say you're a good team player but don't take enough initiative?</u>

❑ <u>Do you tend to take jobs where you can rely on your boss to mentor you?</u>

❑ **Do you prefer work that focuses on the product and doesn't involve a lot of interaction with others?**

❑ *Do you believe that even though you're not necessarily the best, this can be remedied by being around those who are?*

Scoring

Now add up the number of items you checked that are **bold**, <u>underlined</u>, and *italic* and enter each number below.

Bold: _____ <u>Underlined:</u> _____ *Italic:* _____

OK, we mixed it up a bit just to try to get at your less conscious, less analytical answers. In this case, **bold** indicates safety sensitivity, <u>underlining</u> indicates separation sensitivity, and *italic* indicates esteem sensitivity. As before, these "scores" aren't definitive. The questionnaire is supposed to give you a few ideas of what types of responses we have in our adult relationships, from intimate partnerships to friendships to work. Do your results gibe with your results from the Shark Music Checklist? Looking at your core sensitivities from all these different angles may point you directly to a single conclusion, but they may not. The workings of procedural memory and implicit relational knowing are complicated; see the box on the facing page.

The Crucible of Core Sensitivities: Your Childhood

"To look at where all those things are on the Circle related to your upbringing and how you want them to be the same or different is very eye opening—and empowering that you can change it."
—Susan Pinnock, Washington County, Oregon

Now we come to what, for many people, is the hard part. One of the richest sources of information about your core sensitivity is your own childhood. And yet delving into your attachment bonds during your earliest years can be uncomfortable. It's not easy to look unflinchingly at the pain you felt when certain needs went unmet. So don't force yourself—go ahead and flinch, then back away if memories are too hard to bear. But you might try to give yourself permission to let procedural memories rise to the surface of your mind, where you can let them inform your understanding of yourself and how you became the person you are today.

Most people find that, once they've been introduced to the Circle of Security, memories of attachment interactions from childhood start popping up unbidden. You may already be experiencing that. Some of these memories may be wonderful to revisit—moments in time when a parent or other caregiver seemed to know exactly what you needed and provided it, freely and lovingly, with no words necessary. Others may evoke some sadness or even anger. You might be surprised that you haven't thought of these incidents in years, or that you've never thought of them in the context of attachment. But as you read about

Not So Fast . . .

Entire books could be written on the core sensitivities, and people sometimes spend a long time in therapy trying to sort out their attachment styles, usually those few who are experiencing a variety of problems that can be traced to their original attachment bonds. Our goal in this chapter is to stimulate your own reflection by giving you different ways of looking at your core sensitivity, but not to be completely definitive. The goal here is reflection, not having the right answer. You'll know you're grasping the complexity of this subject if you end up seeing two possible core sensitivities in statements like these:

"My earliest memories are of my father telling me that the Bible says we must be perfect, not just try. And before I was born, I was the child who was supposed to be special for God. That's been a big weight. Keeps me trying all the time. I can never relax. I never really have time for anything or anybody." **Here's somebody who feels lots of pressure from a caregiver, either pressure to be perfect or pressure to comply in order to keep the caregiver at a safe distance.**

"To be different feels like I'm no longer connected to my family. I'm just afraid I'll find out I'm wrong. The truth is that I'm no longer connected to my family; I'm just not the person they thought they raised. Which puts me on the outside. I don't know why I want to get back in, but I do. It makes me feel so isolated and alone." **This person seems to have a hard time being herself but also a hard time being connected, which could indicate safety sensitivity. It could also be an expression of having lost the one-mindedness that esteem-sensitive individuals seek and wanting to find a way back to that. Then again, it might mean that she is separation sensitive and struggles with the risk of having her own thoughts and feelings.**

"It just doesn't seem right that my parents would reject me for growing up. What did I do wrong? What's so bad about just trying to do something that is a little different? I actually like my parents, at least some of the time. But they want me to be a carbon copy of them. Especially my dad; he wants me to think like him. When I don't, I start to feel weird and nervous." **The key theme expressed here is the person starting to differentiate from his parents. This could indicate any of the three sensitivities: Separation-sensitive people get very nervous when stepping away from the important other person. Esteem-sensitive people who feel they're losing one-mindedness with the other person can be thrown off balance. And if this person went on to say, "I never was just like him; I just pretended I was," he could be safety sensitive.**

the different core sensitivities, incidents that fall into one category or another are likely to come up. Again, try to give yourself permission to hear what they have to tell you without forcing yourself to do so.

These spontaneous revelations might be enough to fill in the picture of your childhood attachment—how your core sensitivities were born in the caregiving environment you grew up in. If you had a parent who seemed to be esteem sensitive, you may have become what is called in attachment language avoidant in relationships—avoiding needs (your own, your partner's, your child's) on the bottom of the Circle because they set off shark music that warns you away. If your caregiver leaned toward separation sensitivity, you might have formed an anxious attachment style—anxious about being left and therefore about needs (your own, your partner's, your child's) on the top of the Circle. If you had a caregiver who was manipulative or who seemed not to be able to make sense of your need for distance or separate space, you might have developed what we can call a self-protective attachment style—one in which you're on guard against intrusion, manipulation, unpredictability, or meanness. There are no universal, straight paths from one generation to the next, however, as you'll soon read. All of this information about your childhood caregivers amounts to clues about where you might struggle in parenting your own children.

The insights that come to you naturally may be enough for you. If you're interested in further exploration, some ideas for gathering additional information follow.

Let's start with a couple of simple questions:

- What part of the Circle were your parents most comfortable with (top or bottom)?
- What part of being the hands on the Circle were your parents most comfortable with (bigger, stronger, wiser, or kind)?
- Were your parents likely to move toward mean, weak, or gone?
- What clues does this give you to your own core sensitivity and attachment style?

Tolerating the Full Spectrum of Emotions

How emotions were treated in your family of origin provides a good clue to your parents' core sensitivities and the attachment bonds formed in your childhood home. Think of emotions as existing along the full spectrum of the rainbow. If your parents or other caregivers were uncomfortable with certain emotions and did not seem to be able to help you organize these experiences, you were in essence being asked to live without these feelings. Imagine living your life without green or red or blue. What would that do to your view of everything else? Or what if you were entirely color-blind? Picture going through life trying to avoid red or green or another color because it scares you or otherwise makes you feel bad. That's what it's like to be taught, implicitly, that certain emotions are unacceptable. Having a full range of emotional capacity is key to having good relationships. If you'd like to look at your caregivers' emotional capacity—and get some clues to your own—try filling in the Being-With Circle in Chapter 5 if you haven't already done so.

To oversimplify, if your parent was separation sensitive, you might have written in "curiosity" or "anger" way out at the edge of the paper. If your parent was esteem sensitive, perhaps you wrote "fear" or "sadness" or "anger" outside the Circle. If your parent was safety sensitive, maybe you wrote "joy" or "sadness" on the far edge of the Circle. Ask yourself these questions about your diagram:

- What emotions were your caregivers able to fully help you with?
- What emotions were your caregivers partially able to help you with?
- What emotions were your caregivers not able to help you with?
- How has all of this affected you as an adult?
- If you have children, how do you think this affects how you are currently Being-With your child?
- How might your choice to do things differently impact your Being-With your child?

We always tell parents that Being-With your child even 30% of the time is "good enough." (This, of course, doesn't give a parent permission to disregard Being-With the other 70%!) That goes for *your* parents too. What this means is that offering your child the knowledge that each of the core emotions is fully acceptable at least some of the time—all the way inside the Being-With Circle—makes a huge difference for the security of a child.

The Legacy of Our Parents' Core Sensitivities

Do any of the following statements about childhood ring a bell for you?

"It was like I really wasn't there in her eyes, like all she wanted to see was my brilliance and future as the one she could be proud of."

"Sometimes I feel like I'm going to disappear into an empty black hole that will swallow me up. But as I started to look into the hole, it turned into the voice of my mother, a voice that I don't remember hearing but was actually the look that would suddenly appear in Mom's eyes the moment I did something that didn't make her think I was the most remarkable child in the world."

"Who am I when I'm not trying to be brilliant? Who am I when I'm not trying to be perfect? I'm afraid nobody wants to see me, just for me."

"Now that I'm not 'somebody' at work, I feel like I'm nobody at all."
                    —Reflections from esteem-sensitive adults

"Whenever my mom would seem to care, I'd be suddenly terrified that she would reject me. My fear has always been 'If I let my fear be known, they will punish me.'"

"Every time I start to think about friendship, I'm afraid of what might happen or that whoever it is wants something from me. It's as though they won't just let me be. I'm concerned they will take control. If I'm ever going to have a relationship, it is going to have to be one where I can have my own thoughts."
                    —Reflections from safety-sensitive adults

"I look inside to see what is me—but there is no shape, no real definition of what that is."

"Being me means being alone. If I give up on you, you will give up on me."

"Part of what I struggle with is resenting being treated like a child almost everywhere I go. But at the same time I don't want to give up being treated like a child and start taking responsibility for my life."
                    —Reflections from separation-sensitive adults

Like Parent, Like Child?

Not necessarily. Via the straightest possible path, an esteem-sensitive parent might raise an esteem-sensitive child simply because of the mis-cue phenomenon: Your mother turns away (literally or metaphorically) when you're sad and need comfort, so when you need solace you show her a drawing you made or your A+ from that day's schoolwork, know-ing that she'll stick around to applaud you and her being close (at least physically) will make you feel better. Your procedural memory of all this give-and-take leads you to discourage bids for comfort in your own child because shark music tells you that the rejection of those bids hurts—a lot—and you don't want your child to be hurt the way you were. And the wheel keeps on turning.

But there are other possibilities too:

We've known many esteem-sensitive parents who end up with one esteem-sensitive child, à la the route just described, and one who becomes more safety sensitive because the one-mindedness demanded by the parent feels too intrusive.

Likewise, in our experience, separation-sensitive parents may tend to have separation-sensitive children, especially daughters. But some-times a separation-sensitive parent is superproud of her "little man" of a son, but doesn't want him to leave home, and he becomes esteem sensitive: He sticks around, but he also thinks of himself as God's gift to the world. Or a separation-sensitive parent who is very clingy might end up with a safety-sensitive child. A parent who is intrusive can produce a child who does everything possible to separate himself. We know one boy, for instance, who insisted on being a die-hard Green Bay Packers fan in the midst of a Dallas Cowboys family. He did this on purpose.

A safety-sensitive parent, fearing intrusion, might keep her child at a distance, which in turn makes the child desperate to stay close—separation sensitive. When a safety-sensitive parent ends up learning to fear intrusion and control, you might see a parent–child dyad that is friendly but cool, choosing to spend time reading books together instead of doing something more interactive. A safety-sensitive parent could have an esteem-sensitive child if, for instance, the other parent is esteem sensitive and the child finds more availability with him or her. Or if the safety-sensitive parent needs distance and constantly feels like the child is too much for her, the child could end up feeling criticized and rejected. As stated in the example above, esteem sensitivity in the other parent would likely become the source of a way to find more access through either one-mindedness or joint goals toward perfection. (We have more to say about choosing security within two-parent families in Chapter 8.)

Security and Insecurity, Then and Now

If you're starting to get to know your core sensitivity, you may have an idea of whether your attachment to your first caregivers was primarily secure or primarily insecure. Keep in mind that security exists along a continuum. Our degree of security may vary, but it's quite likely that when under stress we demonstrate a tendency to be either avoidant or anxious or self-protective in our relationships. Fortunately, there's hope for all of us. As we've said, even the most insecurely attached individuals we've met have shown the ability to earn security. The Circle of Security as a map can be for a parent like the sextant that guides a sailor. Developing your reflective functioning can turn sharks into minnows and bring security into your life. In fact, John Bowlby defined health as the ability to update old internal working models with more current ones. Honing your ability to reflect via the Circle of Security can take you a long way toward relationship health. So can forming relationships with secure others throughout your life.

Here's what earned security can look like for each of the three core sensitivities:

● **Esteem sensitive.** Trusting relationship without conditions: "I can be average, make mistakes, not share your mind and still feel welcomed, cared for, and connected. When ruptures inevitably happen, I can express my vulnerability (sadness, anger, and fear) and request comfort, trusting you care. Imperfection is acceptable after all."

● **Separation sensitive.** Trusting in four truths: (1) I am capable; (2) life isn't easy; (3) I'm going to have to do a lot of heavy lifting by myself, but only with important others caring in the background; and (4) I have thoughts, feelings, and capacities I avoid at great cost to myself. I can also step away from relationships that do not support me supporting myself. ("I can finally stop going to the hardware store hoping to find milk. I can quit choosing relationships that simply repeat my negative certainty. The choice is always mine.")

● **Safety sensitive.** Trusting relationship as negotiable: "I can come and go, tell you the truth, have my own experience, and you won't try to change me or control me. When I start to feel too close (smothered, intruded upon, controlled), we can talk about it. Eventually I can admit my longing for safe connection, and I won't be too much for you. I'll need you to stay honest, available, and steady."

Fortunately, when we have our own children, we have an excellent "lab" for learning and earning security—for ourselves and for the next generations. In Chapters 8 and 9 we illustrate the "full catastrophe" of attachment relationships and show you ways to become attuned to your child's needs, to Be-With your child even when you'd rather be anywhere else, to be alert for typical situations and events that trigger shark music, to repair the inevitable ruptures, and to foster and sustain the kinds of relationships that dreams are made of.

We do not learn to greet our feelings, especially the difficult ones, alone.

We learn to greet them in relationship.

TESTING NEW WATERS

Choosing Security

I f you've read this book from the beginning, by now—or at some point—you may have felt like you know yourself, the attachment style that childhood bestowed on you, the unique resonance of your shark music. Perhaps you've sighed with relief, confident that your child is securely attached, or felt a momentary panic, worried that your child is completely insecure.

Reflection is always helpful. But life is never cut and dried, and as we stated unequivocally at the beginning of this book, secure attachment is relative. It's not even a case of there being an attachment continuum, with each of us falling somewhere along it between completely secure and totally insecure, as if attachment were a condition or a trait. **We all have insecurities.** Even the most securely attached among us will lose our bearings when under unusual stress or when the shark music that each of us hears swells in the background. It's just a matter of how much, how often, and how strongly our core sensitivities and attachment foundation guide our parenting and other interactions.

The protocols by which the three of us and many other scientists assess the attachment bond between a particular caregiver and child are research tools. Their original purpose was to help theorists gain a better understanding of attachment patterns among large populations. They are not designed to "diagnose" individuals, and our Circle of Security relationship assessment is not meant to label parents and children with a particular brand of attachment but to discover where a parent and child struggle most around the Circle. In helping each pair try to approach security in their interactions, we focus, in fact, on what we call a "linchpin" struggle. Similarly, this book is not intended to reassure you that you or your children have secure attachments (or, conversely, frighten you that you do not) but to help you identify where you're most likely to struggle with your child so that you can be alert for your shark music, not automatically run from your discomfort, and choose security in any given moment.

> *"What has helped me the most is using the language for both my child and myself: 'I love watching you go out to explore and play, and I will always be here to welcome you back in.'"*
> —Tina Murray, Australia

Secure attachment is not a contest or a goal. It is an ongoing process that unfolds before us day after day. Some days we make more ruptures than repairs. Some days our interactions with our child could serve as a public-service-message model of secure attachment. Other days we've not only taken our hands off the Circle but left the building. It happens. That's why it can help to gather more and more insights into shark music triggers, typical struggles, developmental challenges, and obstacles to security that every relationship between human beings presents. This chapter is full of illustrations that might help and suggestions for how to meet the challenges of creating security in the midst of the rush of daily life.

The Two-Parent Family: Sometimes a Mixed Blessing

Throughout this book, we've mainly spoken to individual parents with an individual child. That makes sense in attachment terms since attachment is formed between two people, not between one person and several. It also acknowledges the prevalence of single parents in modern society. But what happens when two parents (or more) are raising a child?

A child can't have too many caring adults in her life. And although having two adults available to raise a baby can be a blessing in many ways, it also requires a different kind of attention to attachment issues. Namely, every individual has his or her own core sensitivity and shark music. It makes sense to have some idea of where each of you stands in attachment styles if your child is being raised by two parents, so that you can anticipate the possibility that your child will miscue the two of you differently. Here are a couple of examples:

Twenty-seven-month-old Markus has a ready-to-greet smile to match his ready-to-discover sense of curiosity. He loves new things: toys, friends, climbing that new structure in the park, events that might seem daunting to some other children his age. When Markus ventures into the world alongside his mother, it's as though everything makes him happy. He simply can't wait to try that next adventure. "What do you see over there?" she whispers in response to his clear focus on something he's just noticed on the playground. Immediately, Markus runs off to discover the sense of surprise that awaits him.

But this very same Markus seems almost like a different child when he visits the same park with his dad. Shawn (his father) is anxious in social settings, and he's also worried that Markus may hurt himself if he takes too many risks. As they enter the play area, Markus continually looks back to see just how worried his father's face seems. For a moment, Dad seems fine and Markus begins to move toward the climbing structure. Then he hears "Markus, be careful." Immediately the little boy slows, then stops, then turns and returns to his father's rather fragile orbit. Dad quickly pulls a toy from the bag he brought with them and they begin to focus on play that keeps Markus close and, as the father says, "safe."

Richie seems to think he can do anything. At 2½ years old, he runs, jumps, and—on many occasions—attempts to fly. Climbing on every table, chair, and tree stump within sight, Richie does everything he can to launch himself toward the sky. Of course, this means that he often falls to the ground, crashing without a hint of a soft landing. Scrapes lead to tears, and tears lead to his mother, who reaches out to honor both his bravery and his sadness. "That was a hard fall, kiddo. A hard fall. [She pulls him in, holding him close for a few moments.] Maybe you can try jumping from this lower spot next time. I'm sure it will still be fun."

Richie and Dad have a different dance. Richie has just as much interest in reaching for the moon when they are together. But when Richie inevitably crashes to the earth, he doesn't cry. He glances. Which is to say that he quickly looks toward his father, who gives a well-worn look of disapproval, a signal that—in the past—included words like, "That's what happens when you climb too high." Those words are no longer spoken, only implied. Dad's look tells the whole story, and Richie finds a way to hold back his hurt and "suck it up," as his father has mentioned on more than one occasion.

Markus and Richie are each being raised by mothers and fathers who hear different renditions of shark music. Children find a way to internalize and then live out (in varying degrees) whatever state of mind their parents offer, and it's certainly possible for a child to bring the security of one parent and the insecurity of another parent into his own sense of how to navigate the world. There's never an exact one-to-one correlation or direct road map for how a child will turn out when asked to mix and match differing states of mind, however. What is clear is that all children find a way to incorporate their parents' strengths and struggles into what becomes their own unique personality. This doesn't have to be seen as a problem. Throughout time, all children have been asked to somehow make sense of the multiple influences that surround them during their formative years.

That said, problems inevitably arise when a child is asked to incorporate shark music (from one or both parents) that is clearly intense and teaches her to significantly deny her needs on the top or the bottom of the Circle or to be vigilant (fearful) regarding a caregiver who is chronically mean, weak, or gone. (This is, of course, why the Circle of Security protocol was designed as an intervention to help parents make sense of their shark music and work to find another, increasingly secure option for their children.)

Here's the hard news: Parents with a high level of shark music intensity *who also cannot reflect* on the problem this presents for their child are likely to pass a similar intensity of shark music on to their child. Through our years of working with families this is, painfully, a common result.

The good news: As parents are offered a clear road map of what their children need and a way of understanding their own shark music about some of those needs, their positive intentionality and innate willingness to *reflect and change* is an equally common result.

The Challenge: Many parenting books stress the importance of maintaining a united front with children. Whole books could be written on dealing with attachment differences between partners (including the common circumstance of two parents with separate households between which the children travel). Here we can only say that it doesn't make sense to ask one of you to give up your defensive strategies or mute your shark music to yield to your child's other parent. The challenge, instead, is to try to stick to developing an understanding of your own shark music and struggles and choose security for your child yourself. Whatever you believe you know about the other parent's struggles and their effect on your child, we recommend exercising empathy and trying to Be-With the other parent in his or her attachment needs as much as you can.

Danielle is too young to make sense of how much her parents fight. Whether the focus is which movie to watch, what to have for dinner, or how to raise a child, Danielle's parents are, much of the time, in a state of conflict.

"You just don't listen."
"You just don't care."
"You never pay attention."
"You never cared."

And so, at 4, Danielle has learned to spend increasing amounts of time in her room watching TV or playing with imaginary friends. Feeling as though she doesn't even show up on the radar, Danielle is slowly learning to become a stranger in her own home.

The Challenge: It's important to recognize when your marriage/partnership is undergoing a heightened period of stress and conflict, because it will obviously raise the potential for taking your hands off the Circle. And even when you're trying to stay on the Circle with your child, stress increases the likelihood of shark music–driven ruptures. Are there any "spare" caregivers who can lend a hand (on the Circle) while you address your relationship conflicts? If there are signs that your child is disappearing from the "and" with you, would seeing a counselor help?

Dealing with Your Struggles Around the Circle

Just recognizing that you've heard shark music and knowing where your core sensitivities lie will take you a long way toward Being-With your child all the way around the Circle. But this doesn't mean the process will be trouble free. Here are some common pitfalls you can watch out for when you know you tend to struggle on the top of the Circle, the bottom, or with keeping your hands on the Circle.

"The great way to think about the Circle is once you have been on it you can always find your way back if you fall off it. It doesn't matter where you get back on; you just have to find an opening somewhere and jump straight back on . . . you can go right back to the beginning and start again."

—Tina Murray, Australia

Managing Struggles on the Bottom of the Circle

Parents who struggle mainly on the bottom of the Circle, meaning those who tend toward esteem sensitivity and safety sensitivity, may feel more comfortable when their child is on the top, but favoring the top of the Circle can create problems of its own.

Fusion, One-Mindedness, Intrusion, and Too-Precious Parenting

It's hard to imagine a child more interested in tractors than 4-year-old Jeffrey. Everything he sees is either a tractor or something that reminds him of a tractor. Cars, trucks, boxes, even trash cans bring tractors to mind for young Jeffrey. And none of this is apparently problematic for his mother, Erin. She loves his interest in tractors. She also loves asking him about tractors. She's all about tractors.

Erin is, in reality, simply *too* into tractors. Enough so that she has made Jeffrey's obsession her obsession. He doesn't really ever get to have his own experience without her full-on involvement. What appears to be her strong interest and enthusiasm is actually her need to be of one mind with her son. Because his mother seems unable to allow him to be different from her (often called "healthy differentiation"), Jeffrey doesn't actually get to experience his own enthusiasm. Instead he's always having to incorporate his mother's mind and energy into his own. Sadly, Jeffrey is getting lost in their sameness.

Because everything he chooses ends up being claimed by his mother, Jeffrey increasingly loses his enthusiasm for tractors and is even beginning to withdraw his enthusiasm for other things. It's not that he doesn't still have interests, but he has chosen not to make them known to his mother.

This is a problem that comes when a parent seeks to be *fused* or *one-minded* with a child, a common issue, mentioned in Chapter 5, that can often show up with esteem-sensitive caregivers. Their child's achievements and talents, and everything else about the child, reflect on them, and sometimes it becomes hard for them to accept any differences. Greg is great at sports because Dad is great at sports; Carly can't stand certain foods because, according to her mother, "We don't like the taste of those things." Like parent, like child: this "mini-me" approach can feel cozy and reassuring to the parent, but it limits the child's opportunity to build a unique experience of self. Some children not only are expected to take on the family hobby, but are also raised with the assumption that they will take on the educational or vocational aspirations of their parents. The pressure, often unspoken, can be remarkably intense.

One mother described a wake-up call she got when she realized that, despite avoiding the trap of forcing her children to equate affluence with success as she had done while growing up, she had still become a parent who forced her way into her child's playing and interests. In essence, she wanted to be part of her little girl's world, to fuse with her at least in this one arena. Realizing that she was taking away her child's self-determination on the top of the Circle made her step back. She suggested that if parents could just recognize their "tendency" to try to direct or control their child's future, especially if it's in the direction of perfectionism or being exceptional, they would have already gone a long way toward stopping themselves from interfering.

The Challenge: Can you step back and let your child be on the top of the Circle without your following too closely? Can you meet your child's "delight in me" need without turning it into "delight in us"? Can you step back without checking out and leaving your child feeling alone in her authentic exploration? Children need a little space to test out their autonomy when on the top of the Circle, but they still need to know we're nearby and available as needed. If you tend to praise your child for whatever she's doing, try narrating descriptively instead. If you jump in and instruct, try turning this into a "watch over me" moment: nod, smile encouragingly, but keep verbalization to a minimum, following your child's need by stepping in when she asks for that. Children who have developed a pattern of miscuing their parents to step in because they've learned that's what their parents want will need a little time to adjust to your participating less, but stick with it.

It can be a challenge to keep "delight in me" from turning into "delight in us."

Engaging in "too-precious" parenting is another form of one-mindedness on the part of some esteem-sensitive caregivers. The "too-precious" approach is most common when a parent has a need to see her child as "uniquely different" or "exceptional" or "standing out from other children." This is, of course, not welcomed by other parents, but strangely, the parent with the "too-precious" child is often unaware that he's unintentionally devaluing the other children his child associates with. The underlying message isn't so much "You are exceptional," but rather "We are exceptional, together." Another way to say it is that "Your remarkableness makes me remarkable because our specialness is fused." This can sometimes show up with parents who need their child to stand out in terms of being uniquely talented or intelligent. It can also be seen when the parent of a child with special needs or a troubled child begins to see his child as "unique" and "amazingly rare" in her special needs or dysfunction, thus becoming a "special child with special needs" or "the most troubled in town." The hidden need remains the same: to stand out from others.

The Challenge: Can you remind yourself that all children are special to their parents? Delighting in your child is a great gift to him. Try to offer it without the comparatives and superlatives: Your child can be wonderful without being more wonderful or the most wonderful.

Cultivating Awesomeness

As mentioned earlier in this book, recognizing an alarming trend toward overvaluing our children in many developed countries moved a group of researchers to come up with a scale to measure this attitude and the parenting practices that accompany it. Overvaluing our children can lead to problematic (potentially narcissistic) personality traits, whereby the child feels superior to peers but also needs constant validation from others that this is the case, and when the inevitable humiliations or rejections of childhood occur, the child can't handle it, often reacting with aggression toward others or himself.

If you find yourself concerned about your child's self-esteem to the point of praising him constantly, using phrases like "Good job" and "You're awesome" for everything he is doing, you may be developing an inclination to overvalue/overpraise your child. Self-esteem is the result of a relationship that says in countless (often nonverbal) ways: "I like being with you because you're you, no matter what you do." Self-esteem is more a by-product of Being-With than the result of constant praise. Of course it's wonderful and necessary to let our children know that we're proud of them, but when they pick up our not-so-hidden anxiety that their self-esteem is constantly on the line, they will likely end up just as nervous about their sense of worth and value to others as we are.

Self-esteem is built not from praise but from acceptance.

Cultivating Self-Sufficiency

You read this scenario in Chapter 6:

"What's so hard about trying to fix that by yourself?" asks Eric's father. "If you keep coming to me, you'll never figure anything out on your own."
Eric is 3.

Obviously there are times when a parent needs to encourage self-reliance in a child. But forced competence can often lead to self-blame and self-sufficiency. And in this case, it's the tone of Eric's father's response that is most problematic. Rather than encouraging his son's competence, he's chiding him for needing a connection with Dad while he attempts something new.

This is why esteem-sensitive people are often referred to as "dismissing"—their shark music tells them to dismiss the importance of vulnerable feelings (a sign of "weakness" or "being soft") and so they avoid giving comfort to their children on the bottom of the Circle.

On the other hand, Eric's father may be safety sensitive. His response would still be labeled "dismissing," but it would have a different meaning. Rather than in some way devaluing or even shaming his son's need for comfort, his words would be intended to teaching his son to be self-sufficient and without a need to come close to his father, something that makes his dad uncomfortable.

Take-home lessons:

- If your child is playing happily, let her do it by herself. Watch for her need of your participation, or your filling her cup so she can comfortably go back to what she was doing, but otherwise, let her enjoy "being alone in your presence."

- Take a break from praise if you find yourself issuing it all the time.

- Learn more about the concept of "scaffolding"—offering just enough help that a child has the experience of doing it on his own. Encouraging self-reliance in your child is done best within a context of scaffolding. Being-With while supporting increasing self-reliance is precisely what children need. If your push for competence is actually a message to your child that she needs to take care of herself, your shark music is likely driving the message you're offering. This message may be somewhat esteem sensitive or may be more safety sensitive. Either way, be alert for when this happens again and see if you can notice a not-so-hidden bid for comfort or connection or closeness to you. Take a quiet breath and simply offer some of what your child needs.

Managing Struggles on the Top of the Circle

Maggie loves being a mother, except for the times when she doesn't. "I've never felt more fulfilled than being a mom," she'll often say. But, often, in the next sentence she'll utter something to the effect that she wishes her two children, Gary and Francie (ages 7 and 3, respectively), would give her some space. "I love them to pieces, but it's almost like they won't let me out of their sight."

As a single parent, Maggie feels the burden of "having to do it all." How could she not? She works full time, coming home, in her words, "exhausted and lonely." She adds, "Just wish I had a partner, someone who would share the wonderful yet unending tasks of being a parent with me. Thank God for my kids. They mean the world to me. I don't know what I'd do without them."

Once home, Maggie has a hard time allowing her children to play or do much of anything without her involvement. She makes sure they help her with dinner and the dishes and then proceeds to be a part of every game they play. She is also very uncomfortable whenever they ask to play with the neighbor children. "What's wrong? Am I not good enough for you?" she whimpers. "Come on, let's have some ice cream, and then we can choose another cool game." The children always agree, but they also get frustrated with each other and their mother, with all three of them disagreeing and even being angry much of the time. "I don't understand. Why aren't they more grateful?" asks Maggie. "I'm all but giving them my life."

This is a scenario that often emerges when parents seek to limit their experience of separation with their children, an issue that can typically show up with separation-sensitive caregivers. The parent works hard to be available for her children without realizing that (1) she is actually being too available, and (2) her intense focus on her children is sadly more about her need than theirs.

Given the issues discussed above regarding struggles on the bottom of the Circle, Maggie is not being one-minded, nor is she focused on her children's self-esteem. While she may often tell her children they're doing a great job at something, she's actually not that concerned about how they perform or the need for them to be special. She just doesn't want them to be away from her. She has actually blurred the boundaries of her relationship with both children to the point of all but assuming they're being "best friends" together. Even though she is still able to be the one in charge when it comes to doing the dishes or bedtime, it's not a surprise that when they're playing that they all can fight like siblings.

Protection versus Clinging

Maggie is quick to frame the issue as her need to protect her children. "It's just not a safe world anymore. I don't feel good about their being out playing with other kids. [Note: This family lives in what would be considered a middle-class neighborhood in our community.] A loving parent should be willing to give up some of her own happiness to stay focused on the needs of her children." Many separation-sensitive parents hold to this line of thinking. In the name of safety they keep their children close to home and close to themselves. While it can often be true that the world is not as safe as we'd want it to be for our children, a parent's insistence that her children remain close with limited external exploration (with other children or outside adventures) can be a sign of a caregiver who is actually uncomfortable with having the relationships she considers essential move toward autonomy.

The Challenge: Can you remind yourself that autonomy does not equal abandonment? Can you recognize that unsaid, but somehow always felt just beneath the surface, is the shark music message "Once you leave, you may never come back"?

Uncomfortable with Not Being Needed . . . but Also with Being Needed Too Much

Yet another issue emerges with Maggie that is common with separation-sensitive parents. Her statement, "I love them to pieces, but it's almost like they won't let me out of their sight," followed closely by "I'm all but giving them my life," indicates her ambivalence about the nature of need. While it's apparent that she needs to be needed, she also struggles with the neediness that is the obvious result.

The Challenge: If you're separation sensitive and you're beginning to see your difficulty allowing autonomy, can you consider the possibility that you struggle equally (although less obviously) with intimacy? At first glance, this may not make sense, but as it turns out, insecurity is an equal opportunity employer. When I'm not particularly good at supporting your (or my own) bids for self-support on the top half of the Circle, I'm also going to have a hard time allowing the intensity of self-support needed for genuine vulnerability on the bottom half. Autonomy and vulnerability are something of a matched set. As we increase in our capacity for one, we deepen in our capacity for the other. Knowing (and trusting) that you can be in a relationship with someone who clearly has his own mind and his own needs for experiencing the world on his own terms (including spending time away from you) is fertile ground for knowing and trusting that core feelings can be experienced and shared, sometimes with intensity. The more secure we are with a unique sense of self (our own and that of those around us), the more comfortable we can be with the needs and closeness that two separate-yet-equal selves can offer each other. So, the deeper the autonomy, the richer the vulnerability. And, when this isn't the case, a separation-sensitive person clings (thus blocking autonomy) to avoid abandonment and in so doing doesn't allow the separation necessary for true intimacy. As the saying goes: "How can I come home if you never let me go?"

Take-home lessons:

- If your child is playing happily, let her do it by herself. Watch for her need of your participation, but be aware that what she likely needs most at this point in your relationship is ongoing support for increased exploration *on her own*. Your quiet, noninterfering presence will likely begin to look more like availability in the background—someone she can turn to when she needs to but also someone not overly involved in what she is doing.

- Stay present, stay interested, stay focused on your own interests as well. Children of separation-sensitive parents need to know they have their own lives, with their own interests that are not child based.

- At the same time, be clear that you don't go "hot and cold"— available one moment and then apparently disinterested the next. Separation-sensitive parents can come across as inconsistent, something that makes their children feel vigilant—"If you're here, then gone, it's up to me to stay focused on you in case you start to leave again." That anxiety is likely something you knew growing up and may inadvertently be passing on to your children.

- When you offer welcome and support on the bottom of the Circle, enjoy the pleasure and the gift of being available to the feelings of your child. Simply be aware of how your shark music may encourage you to overplay her needs here, pushing for more feeling-oriented discussion than she may need. All children need to explore their feelings, but they don't need to swim in them. And they certainly don't need us to swim in their feelings with them.

- Honor both the top and the bottom of the Circle. Support your child's strong desire to find his own passions and explore the world with increasing interest while you're welcoming his need to be close and fill his cup to the top . . . but not to the point of overflowing!

Managing Struggles with Keeping Our Hands on the Circle

Soren wasn't sure about being a dad, but once he realized that Missy was pregnant his enthusiasm grew day by day. Now, 6 years later, Soren and Missy are at odds about how to parent. Missy doesn't want to see her son, Zak, spoiled. Soren, raised by a stern, distant father, feels ner-

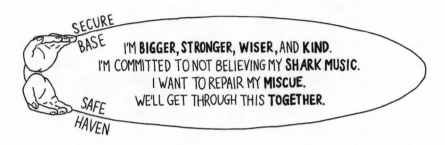

Repair: Keeping our hands on the Circle.

vous every time he needs to discipline Zak. Lately, when it comes time for Zak to go to bed or clean up his room, he comes to his father, all but certain that he'll give in. This makes Missy furious, at both her husband and her son. She typically lets the full force of her upset end up being focused on her son.

The pattern repeats itself almost daily: Zak does something that pushes the limits his mother has set for him, and he turns to his father for a reprieve. Soren frames his son's behavior as "not that bad" and steps in to intervene with Missy. Missy finds herself being more exasperated and becomes increasingly critical of her son. Soren feels he's doing his best to protect Zak from a harshness he remembers being so difficult to deal with in his own childhood. The gentler Soren becomes, the more intense Missy seems. Missy feels alternately ashamed of her anger and furious at how she's been put in the role of what she calls "the family tyrant." Soren feels confused and unclear about what to do. He's frightened for his son, and he's increasingly afraid of Missy.

We've seen this scenario, in one of its many manifestations, dozens of times in our work with families. The "bigger, stronger, wiser, and kind" paradigm isn't recognized as central, and parental roles begin to solidify in the direction of one parent attempting firmness with limited emphasis on understanding and the other parent acting on the belief that understanding needs to outweigh a need for someone in charge. The farther one parent goes on his or her side of the balance beam, the farther the other parent walks, in almost equal proportion, to the opposite side. The tension can be palpable and seemingly without resolution, in ways that eventually bring parents to seek help for "this impossible situation."

Losing Balance

Missy, Soren, and Zak are obviously not alone when it comes to living inside a family system that struggles with hands on the Circle. Adopting the "bigger, stronger, wiser, and kind" phrase as a guiding principle has helped a wide variety of parents we've worked with. It's certainly not a magic wand, but it's a simple and realistic way to know precisely what your child needs and also a road map that lets you know the dangers on either side of the balance beam (when the other side is either forgotten or underused). A simple refresher: Bigger and stronger without kind becomes mean. Kind without bigger and stronger becomes weak. And we always need wisdom to know the necessary balance, especially as this needed balance is never a cookie-cutter, easy-to-apply formula available in each new circumstance. Wisdom is what we need to tap into as we balance the appropriate intensity of firmness with the needed commitment to caring and understanding.

> *Bigger and stronger without kind becomes mean.*
>
> *Kind without bigger and stronger becomes weak.*

As was the case with Missy and Soren, simply understanding where they were struggling and having clarity about what was missing for each of them began the necessary shift. Soren initially looked at his own growing up with a "mean" father and began to see his unwillingness to risk taking charge as his fear that he would become like someone he had once hated. This allowed him to see his son's need for a father who was indeed strong and in charge while also being kind. He committed to this choice.

Likewise, Missy named her resentment toward Soren for putting her in charge of all family discipline. She was also able to name how much she wanted to participate in being kind and supportive of her son but felt she couldn't in the face of his "always having an escape hatch opened by his father." Once she could clarify her grief, she was able to openly claim her place as a mother who wanted to offer kindness while remaining strong.

With this relatively simple understanding, this family made quick and remarkable strides in the direction of bringing their hands back on the Circle in a balanced way. Zak, who at first seemed puzzled by the obvious shift his parents had made, soon relaxed and found himself feeling more secure and without a need to push limits.

The Challenge: Can you avoid the blame game? Pointing fingers at your child's other parent takes the focus off yourself, when understanding yourself is exactly what you need to aim for. But that also takes self-compassion. Can you extend kindness to yourself for the pain that created your defensive strategies long ago? Any significant history of mean, weak, or gone leaves memories and feelings that can be hard to face. Honoring that pain will greatly alter its impact on your family now.

Who's the Parent Here?

Another common theme, especially for parents who struggle with taking charge, is the unconscious shift that can be made when a parent feels overwhelmed and asks a child to become the designated "bigger, stronger, wiser, and kind" person in the family. At its extreme, especially if it is ongoing, this can cause significant emotional difficulties for a child being asked to function as the parent in the family. But there are often instances when, for reasons due to a family crisis or period of grief or depression on the part of the parent, roles unintentionally shift and the child is asked to become the strength for the parent. While this can be framed to the child as positive and worthy of praise, role reversal is always confusing for a child, disorganizing her internal world. In terms of attachment research it is never supportive of security.

Children, even into their teen years, need to remain in a relationship with someone (or several people) who always maintains the position of being bigger, stronger, wiser, and kind. Even into early adulthood, it is helpful and necessary for children to have someone to turn to who isn't a peer and isn't needy, but rather available with support, wisdom, and compassion.

Within the context of the core sensitivities, role reversal can have a different "tone."

- Separation-sensitive parents who reverse roles are typically looking for someone, in this case their child, to "take care" of them. The message: "I'm not capable. I need you to be bigger than me."
- Esteem-sensitive parents will tend to idealize their child, claiming that he is "wise beyond his years" in ways that are framed as being unique and special. Unfortunately, praise in this form can feel somewhat good (a "positive" within a context of obvi-

ous confusion), and the child will then actively seek out ways to be of further support for his troubled parent, garnering more praise.

- As it turns out, role reversal is far less common with safety-sensitive parents. One way it can show up is as a parent who withdraws and simply requires her child to take charge. In every case, the child is no longer allowed to be a child and, developmentally, is required to pretend to have strength and wisdom that is simply not yet available.

The Challenge: As children begin to recognize their bind they will begin to find ways to extricate themselves from this assigned role. When that happens, if you're separation sensitive, can you avoid using guilt as a way to bring your child back in ("I'm not asking for much; I just need your help here")? If you're esteem sensitive, can you resist using shame ("That's OK—you just worry only about yourself. I'm just fine")?

Let's Be Friends

Another common theme, closely related to role reversal, has to do with parents attempting to live on the same level of maturity as their children. This is most often associated with a fear of being rejected (esteem sensitive) or being abandoned (separation sensitive) regarding taking charge. "If I stand up to you, you won't like me, so I'll find a way to make sure we are friends who get along with each other." A simple rule of thumb in healthy parenting is that it's never helpful to define a family as a democracy. Someone needs to be in charge. Hierarchy is a very good thing. So, when a parent is afraid to claim her necessary role as the one in charge, but rather ducks that responsibility, the child can feel adrift. Role distortion—especially when it's seductively presented as "friendship"—is always significantly confusing to a child: "The very person I need most is now the person I can't trust because (1) she refuses to function in the bigger, stronger, wiser, and kind capacity I still need; and (2) she's pretending to be someone I know she's not. I don't need a 'best friend'; I need a parent."

The Challenge: Can you keep in mind that the opposite of mean is not "BFF"? If you had a parent who was bigger, stronger, and unkind, you might be tempted to go too far in the opposite direction, remembering how much it hurt to be treated harshly. It's understandable, but it's easier to resist this if you think of the urge to do so not as avoiding repeating your parent's mistakes but as shark music. When you understand your shark music, you can make other choices that include kindness and wisdom only with strength.

I Need My Space (or, Don't Need Me Too Much)

This is a common theme for safety-sensitive parents who struggle with feeling intruded on by the needs of their children. Always being busy, "disappearing" into your kitchen, study, television, cell phone, or computer; blaming your child for being "too needy"; or intellectualizing your child's feelings when Being-With is needed are typical ways of keeping a distance. The sad irony is that with many children keeping a distance actually creates a more demanding child. With other children, a parent's unavailability is taken to be a sign that closeness isn't to be considered safe or a viable option. These children can often keep their bottom half of the Circle needs hidden because they have learned they won't be responded to.

The Challenge: Can you put on the brakes when your shark music tells you to run away? Try to remind yourself that providing what your child needs can keep the demands from increasing.

A filled cup in time saves nine.

Take-home lessons:

- If your child is being asked to take the position of the caregiver in your relationship, find a way to return to being bigger, stronger, wiser, and kind. While it's fine for an older teen to periodically offer advice or support, it's problematic when a child living at home is asked to carry the weight of your struggles or feelings. Rule of thumb: If the circumstance is too big for you to make sense of or deal with, it's too big for your child to carry. **This is a circumstance where finding outside support is essential. Friends, support groups, or professional advice are all helpful options.**

- If you can see that you've asked your child to become your favorite buddy or best friend, find a way to shift the focus back to your being the parent. Children need parents who are friendly but not equals (or anywhere close to being equals). Shared hobbies, shared sports, and shared fun are all wonderful options. But if this sharing moves in the direction of one-mindedness and fused thinking ("We totally agree on everything" or "We absolutely love the same things"), then it's time to consider finding ways to encourage different minds and different experiences some of the time. Honoring differences is an essential aspect of security. In practical terms, do what you can to increase adult friendships in your life.

 • If you realize that you're often "gone" and that this comes from your safety sensitivity, do your best to remember that the issue here isn't that your choices are "bad" or that you should feel ashamed of wanting to make them. The issue is that they tend to leave your child feeling like his parent is often "gone." Simply be aware of your child's legitimate needs, especially on the bottom of the Circle, and offer a little more availability each week until you can, on a regular basis, allow an extra few minutes of your presence. No quick changes are required. Take it slow. And remain committed to finding a way to recognize (1) the genuine need in your child's requests for Being-With you, even when those needs require more closeness than feels currently tolerable; and (2) the gift of understanding the Circle and how when needs are met on the bottom a child naturally welcomes returning to his own adventures on the top. He wants you, yes, and he also wants to know a world that includes so much more than you.

Reflection on Reflection

Derek knew that he was esteem sensitive. His first clue came in realizing that he was all but requiring his 5-year-old son to think like him and have exactly the same interests in sports. He even began to realize that he had hopes that Reece would grow up and become a coach, which just so happened to be Derek's chosen profession. His second clue was that he found himself both furious and withdrawn when his wife, Wanda, would comment in an even slightly negative way about his parenting. He was loath to experience any form of criticism, especially about something so important to him as parenting.

Derek was proud of himself as a father. Coming from a family where his own father had been distant and critical, he was pleased with how he'd taken the responsibility of parenting as part of his life purpose. He read a ton of books on the subject, he attended a variety of parenting classes, he could say with satisfaction that he was the kind of father he had missed as a child.

So, when he learned about the Circle, he was surprised to notice that his vehemence in cheering his son's accomplishments was actually an additional pressure he was placing on Reece. He was also intrigued to notice his subtle, yet consistent, hints that sadness, fear, and anger weren't worth paying attention to. While not quite in the "suck it up" category, Derek was teaching his son that "trying harder" and "succeeding in spite of pain" were actually ways to stay away from these important feelings.

Derek began to recognize and name his esteem-sensitive miscues. He noticed his pressure to achieve, as well as his focus on one-mindedness. He was, indeed, reflecting. He was, however, unaware of the subtle sense of superiority this reflection gave him. He was limited, yes, but he somehow felt better than those who couldn't admit their limitations. What he had yet to notice was that he was often teaching other parents and remarking about how his knowledge of the Circle made him unique and special. What he also had yet to notice was his hair-trigger response to criticism.

Esteem-sensitive individuals often live with a kind of edge in their relationships. Often friendly up front, there can be a "Don't push me or I'll bristle" attitude just below the surface. Children can be very aware of and nervous around this implied threat. So, it was an important day when Reece came rushing into the house, upset and crying, only to find his father quick to admonish him for being "over-the-top dramatic." Wanda stepped in and asked her husband to settle down and reconsider what he was saying. Derek exploded. "Who do you think you are to tell me how to parent?" Within seconds, Reece was running to his room.

To use Derek's words: "Things would never have gone well, except—within minutes—I was able to realize that Wanda was right. I had stepped off the Circle and I'd done it by shaming Reece for being sad but also by blowing up at Wanda in front of him. My recent pride in being a great dad showed up for what it was, somehow accurate and somehow an elaborate cover-up for how much I hate to be less than perfect, how much I hate to be criticized."

Derek was reflecting on his lack of reflection, on how he'd begun to see his struggles on the Circle, but how he'd also blunted a further step. Yes, he was clearly a better father than his own father had been, but he had been unwilling to look at the tension his entire family was being asked to live in regarding his underlying (and always pending) reactivity when it came to criticism. As Derek allowed himself this deeper level of reflection (and how he chose to limit this newfound skill), he found himself feeling increased sadness about his own upbringing. In almost direct proportion to his new experience of vulnerability, he noticed Reece coming to him more often for moments of comfort and soothing. Reece seemed less anxious and more playful with his father. Derek's edginess had noticeably begun to soften.

We've been talking a lot about the power of self-reflection, the capacity to stand back and recognize common patterns on the Circle. What psychotherapists have noticed through the decades is that the more we can reflect on what we're currently doing (the positive stuff) and not yet doing (the negative stuff), the healthier our relationships turn out to be. The future of a family with caregivers who can reflect on their strengths and struggles on the Circle turns out to be more secure than for a family where the caregivers (especially when they struggle in significant ways) don't choose to notice where problems keep turning up.

The Nine-Dot Trick

Have you ever been exposed to the nine-dot trick? The challenge is to connect nine dots in the following configuration without using more than four straight lines or lifting your pencil from the paper.

People often struggle to come up with the conventional solution, which looks like this:

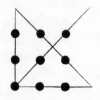

But, as it turns out, there is more than one way to solve this puzzle. Here's one:

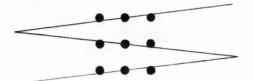

The way this puzzle is understood in the field of psychology is that a problem can't be solved as long as it remains stuck on the level or in the box where it was created. We literally have to "think outside the box," and, in fact, the phrase comes from this exercise. In terms of attachment, we need to stand outside the patterns or beliefs (shark music) that we've always taken to be "just the way things are" and begin to see some of our current behavior as being controlled by patterns and beliefs that limit us and those around us. When we do begin to see our "inside-the-box reality" as both understandable (blame is never useful) and limited, we can open into new possibilities. As we realize that our past choices to stay inside the box are based on moments in our life lived within a less-than-secure environment, we can find it easier to welcome new options offering greater security for ourselves and others.

Making parenting choices other than reflexively responding to our shark music requires us to think outside the box.

From the perspective of our work with parents using the Circle of Security, reflection is always a healthy option. This book has clearly been written with the goal of building reflection in those who read it. By now you've likely discovered a variety of patterns—secure(ish) and insecure(ish)—that have been a part of your parenting. Hopefully, the outcome of this reflection hasn't increased shame, guilt, or fear. Our hope has been that as you stand back and see patterns that limit your parenting and choose new options, you also begin to see genuinely beneficial shifts in all of your relationships. This has consistently been the outcome we've observed over time with the families we know and the research we've conducted.

And yet, an additional, helpful step within the reflective process remains. It can best be described with a question: "Can I reflect on my reflection?" Which is to say, "I know I'm considering these issues, but can I stand back and notice the ones I'm still not quite willing to make sense of or allow to impact me?" Or, "Which theme on the Circle or aspect of a core sensitivity am I currently thinking I fully understand when, just below the surface, I'm probably keeping it at arm's length?"

As described in the story about Derek, Wanda, and Reece, in our experience, when a parent is willing to reflect on his or her reflective process, new considerations emerge. New doors open.

The more deeply we can reflect, the more secure our relationships can become.

Handling Common Core Sensitivity/Shark Music Triggers

Some things set all of us off and make it hard to Be-With our children. Distractions, stress, exhaustion, illness, hunger, depression, anxiety . . . the list goes on. But your core sensitivity can make you vulnerable to certain situations or factors and make ruptures more likely. The more we know now, the better off we'll be when the times of inevitable stress and difficulty suddenly show up. Check out the following lists of typical triggers for each sensitivity and the types of thoughts that usually arise with the triggers. Some of these thoughts could come up in parent–child interactions with children of varying ages and others more commonly in adult–adult interactions—or maybe in both. These are followed by thoughts you might have if you recognize your vulnerability, take a time-out as needed, and practice Being-With.

Separation Sensitive

When you've asserted yourself:

- "I'm sure he's mad at me now. Take it back, take it back."
- "OMG, it's all over. She'll just turn and walk away. She always does whenever I tell her what I think."
- "I hate these tantrums. Picking up his toys right now isn't that big a deal."
- "I'll bet I can get her to mind me if I'm just nicer when I ask."

What you might say once you've recognized your shark music:

- "He may be mad at me, but I actually said what's true for me. Stay with yourself. He's not always right."
- "It's not over. Even if she walks out, she'll come back. Or not. If I keep giving myself away, there won't be anyone here to come back to!"
- "I hate these tantrums. I actually hate having to take a stand with her. But picking up her toys right now is a genuinely big deal. If I don't, she's the one who will pay the price. Well, both of us will."
- "I want to give in right now. But being 'nice' like I've always done is letting her down. She needs me to be firm *and* kind. Not just kind."

When you have to do something on your own or support yourself:

- "I can't stand not hearing from him—I'm texting again."
- "I'm probably making a big thing out of nothing. My idea isn't that important."
- "What was I thinking? I'm not someone who can figure this out. I know Roger will have the answer. He always knows more about children than I do."
- "If I give in to how he wants to handle things with the baby, I know he'll soften. I'll do anything, just take care of me."

What you might say once you've recognized your shark music:

- "I really worry when I don't hear from him. He's so new at driving. But if I keep texting him, he'll just push me back. Plus it's not safe for him. I just need to settle myself down here."
- "Who am I kidding? My idea *is* important!"
- "Roger is a good parent. So am I. Now is my time to figure things out."
- "If I give in, I know he'll be happier. But I always give in. That's bad for him. It's really bad for me. I need to trust my point of view here."

When you feel lonely:

- "This is freaking hell. I'm so lost without her. There's got to be something I can do to bring her back. I'm just too pushy."

- "No one likes me. No one will ever like me. I'm just in the way."
- "I feel so guilty. I should never have told him what I really think."
- "I'm sure he's safe, but I'm just going to call to make sure."
- "I love it when she snuggles like this. I wish she'd never grow up."

What you might say once you've recognized your shark music:

- "Whenever I stand up for myself I feel guilty. Then I give in. Then I don't feel lonely. Which is nuts, because that just keeps a hole in my bucket, and no matter what anyone does, it just empties out and I keep needing more."
- "It's time I start liking me. If I don't step up, I'm not in the way, I'm not even here!"
- "My fear isn't helping him or me. The more I try to reassure myself, the worse everything gets."
- "I love it when she snuggles like this, but I think this is more my need right now than hers. If I keep pulling her in every time I start to feel lonely, she'll never learn the top of the Circle."

Esteem Sensitive

When you feel vulnerable:

- "This beyond sucks. I can't believe I'm starting to cry in front of her. That's just going to make me look weak. How can anyone love weak?"
- "I hate it when he gets all the praise. Why does he get all the attention? He's just so full of himself. It's always Wesley, Wesley, Wesley."
- "When she talks about her daughter I always feel so bad as a parent. Like I'm second-rate. No, like I shouldn't even be a parent. What makes her so special?"
- "Who does she think she is? I'm the one with the child who is dealing with the most difficulty. Are you kidding me? If there is a child with special needs who deserves extra special attention, it's Donnie."

What you might say once you've recognized your shark music:

- "These tears aren't a sign of weakness. They're a part of me that

I've kept hidden my whole life. Now is as good a time as any to quit hiding them."

- "I feel insignificant right now. That's about me. Putting Wesley down won't help that feeling one bit."
- "There I go again. Whenever she talks about Jamie's latest accomplishment I start to feel like a second-rate parent. That's crazy. Jamie is Jamie. And Tanya is Tanya. They are both delightful children. Childhood isn't a beauty contest!"
- "My Donnie does have a ton of special needs. But so does Tasha. It's not like Donnie's needs have to take precedence over every other child. Plus I like Tasha so much. I think it's time I let her mom know that."

When you feel you might be imperfect:

- "I did *not* forget this meeting. He always says it's me. He's the one who screwed up. I didn't even know I was supposed to show up until an hour ago. I'll get him."
- "How dare she imply that my child was wrong! Angie did everything perfectly. It's her little freak show of a child that should be called out for what just happened."
- "She's spoiled rotten. She deserves that timeout. Maybe then she'll decide to work harder."
- "There's nothing wrong here. I'm awesome. Just because the boss is mad doesn't make me any less fabulous. I just need to remind myself how amazing I am and I'll be fine."
- "This is terrible. I'm so ashamed. I always screw up. I'm such a failure. I'm sure everyone is talking about me right now. Yesterday I was sure I was the best one here. Now it's clear that I shouldn't even be on the team."

What you might say once you've recognized your shark music:

- "Once again, I'm getting defensive the moment I feel criticized. I hate being criticized, but that didn't start here. Take a breath. Now take another. See if you can calm down enough to show some kindness in what you say next."
- "Yikes. She tells me Nicki is acting up in class and I start to blame her approach to teaching. I've got to calm down right now and listen to what it's like to be Nicki's teacher."
- "She's not spoiled, she's really confused right now. If I pull back

right now and send her to her room she's going to keep feeling upset and she's going to feel alone."

- "I succeed. I fail. I'm human. It's time I quit seeing my only options as either being special or being nobody. It's time I find a friend who will see me as OK, flaws and all."

When you're disappointed:

- "I'm not angry. I'm disappointed. I just thought you were better than that."
- "He looks bummed. Smile. Smile big. Tell him he's awesome. Make sure he thinks he's the best. Tell him it was all your fault."
- "Don't give me that 'We all make mistakes' crap, lady. You're the one who didn't come through . . . again! I'm the one with the awesome child, and your child is a total screw-up. And yet yours is the one who gets all the extra attention."

What you might say once you've recognized your shark music:

- "Yes, I'm disappointed in what she just did. Yes, I want to punish her right now. But that's exactly what Mom always did to me. Give me that cold shoulder and change the subject. I'm going to slow this whole thing down and ask her to talk this over."
- "He's hypersensitive about how he's perceived, and there's no need to humiliate him. But there's no need to humiliate yourself either. Find a way to be respectful and say what you think needs saying."
- "When she makes excuses for her child like this, I want to scream. But it's time I start thinking about the pressure she's under. I doubt I even have a clue what it's like to parent with what's going on in her home."

Safety Sensitive

When you feel intruded on:

- "He's so needy. He's always crying and wanting something from me. This feels horrible to even think, but I just wish he could take care of himself."
- "Smile, but step back a bit. Keep smiling, seem interested. Step back a bit further. This conversation is going to go a lot better from this distance."

- "What makes her think I agree with her? That's not something that even makes sense. It's like she thinks we're on the same page!"
- "I'm lucky. Rosie really does know how to handle herself without whining and hanging all over me. I don't know what I'd do with a clingy child."

What you might say once you've recognized your shark music:

- "I don't like this neediness. It's freaking me out. But he really does need me right now, and if I push him away, he'll only feel worse. So will I. Just remember what you've been learning: 'Fill his cup and he gets less needy, not more.'"
- "It's fine to step back and claim my own distance. Nothing needs changing in me right now."
- "It's just fine to claim difference. No need to be harsh. And no need to join in as though you're the same."
- "There it is again, me thinking Rosie can do everything by herself. That's what I want, not what she really needs. Just take a breath and then ask her to come on over and sit close for a few minutes. We'll both feel better (as long as it's only a few minutes!)."

When you feel exiled (not belonging or not being normal):

- "What am I supposed to do here? I never know what is expected. I'm just strange. I never fit in."
- "Why is everyone so interested in their child being exceptional? That's nuts. Every child is just who he is. What's with all this 'special, special, special' stuff?"
- "If she tells me that she understands me 'perfectly' one more time, I may just walk away."

What you might say once you've recognized your shark music:

- "I may not feel like I belong in this group of parents, but that's not true. We're all trying really hard. We all make mistakes. I can live with that."
- "There she goes again telling me how Brian is so exceptional. That's clearly something a bit sad for her and for Brian. I can either feel totally annoyed or just wish them both well."

- "I don't need her total approval. I don't even want it. Find a way to move this discussion away from you and on to something more neutral."

When you feel controlled:

- "Why do I have the child who won't even let me go to the bathroom without freaking out? No wonder I'm always pushing him away!"
- "Why are parent meetings always run by people who worry about their child's self-esteem? It's like a religion."
- "I love my children, but I love myself too. Sometimes I think there's something wrong with me, because I never hear other parents say what I feel: 'I'm just as important as my child.'"

What you might say once you've recognized your shark music:

- "Jessie really needs me right now. I feel like I need to hide. That's the simple truth of it. But it's not the only truth. Right now, for Jessie's sake, I'm going to pick him up and cuddle for at least a minute. Hopefully that will do it. If not, I'll take a breather and then offer again."
- "These meetings are just meetings. I'm here because I love my daughter, and I have no obligation to agree to everything that is being said. Paloma will be just fine."
- "I just started resenting him because I thought he was the only one with needs here. I'm not buying into any parenting approach that tells me I'm supposed to adore my child and center my life around him. That's just goofy. I count. He counts. As long as both are true I can focus more on him."

The thoughts you might have after learning to recognize your shark music show what increased reflective functioning can look like and how it might boost your ability to Be-With your child (and others in your life who are important to you). But Being-With your child is an ongoing (never-ending) commitment, and of course you have to be prepared for all the changes in the ways your child's Circle needs manifest as your child grows. Being open to reflecting on your reflection can be helpful from this point forward. Chapter 9 will help you choose security for your children at different ages.

STAYING AFLOAT

Choosing Security Over and Over as Your Child Grows

In raising our children from birth to adulthood, it helps to know that there is a somewhat predictable developmental trajectory that most children follow. We can also be guided by the knowledge that our core sensitivities are shared by many other parents who are struggling with the same types of shark music we hear—and that there are ways all of us can respond to choose security for our children. But Being-With a child and establishing a secure attachment means connecting with that individual child and knowing our own unique state of mind. Always remember that you know your child best—and will know your child better and better if you can Be-With your child through all the trials and tribulations of growing up.

Infants

Most of what you've read in this book is about infants and toddlers, because that's the age group we work with most often in our Circle of Security work—that's when attachment bonds are first formed. So we've devoted most of this chapter to showing what it looks like to choose security and Be-With your child beyond the first few years. But first, a few tips on Being-With your baby that are worth keeping in mind. Don't miss the box on pages 241–242, which offers a little Being-With insight into the perennial question about how to get babies to go to sleep.

• *The eyes have it.* Babies are all about looking Mom and Dad in the eyes. But when your baby looks away, that doesn't mean anything is wrong or you should force eye contact. When babies get overaroused, they often look away briefly. It's important to let them do this, because it's an early form of self-regulation. If you and your 4-month-old are playing and he looks away, wait there with him, maybe murmuring softly, while he calms himself. In a few moments he'll welcome coming back to looking at you again. That's how he begins learning to coregulate emotion. Out. In. Out. In. Your only task: Follow his need.

• *Moment-to-moment: OK or not OK?* Babies change emotional states more quickly than we might imagine. They go from feeling OK to not OK to sort of OK to not OK to OK—all within a few moments' time. This is why we as parents do not label our babies as "good babies" or "difficult babies"; babies are simply living in a moment-to-moment world all of the time. Once again, your task is to simply Be-With your baby in whatever emotion she is currently experiencing. Rather than showing undue concern each time your baby is upset and trying to bring your child back to happiness, let yourself experience some of what your baby is experiencing and stay with her—allowing your face, breathing pattern, words, and gentle tone of voice to reflect that you share some of her experience. Of course, this doesn't mean that when her upset continues and there is something that needs to be done (change her position, pick her up, feed her, etc.) you only continue to join her emotional state. But some of the time babies need opportunities to learn about emotional regulation with us, and our Being-With both positive and negative emotions without trying to emphasize one feeling (usually toward happiness) over the other is how this happens.

• *You can't spoil an infant.* Parents worry about spoiling, but it's simply not a possibility in the first year of life. Current research in fact suggests that being delighted in during the first year is a central building block for secure attachment. Research has shown spoiling to be associated with being unable to say no or set limits as children get older, but infants don't know anything about limits, so they certainly aren't going to push them and put you in the position of "spoiling" them. What they are learning in their first year when you do what you

Being-With a Baby Who Doesn't Want to Go to Sleep*

Getting babies to sleep when we want them to is an age-old problem and a subject of constant debate. Should we let babies sleep when they want to or push them to sleep for a prescribed amount of time per day at specific times of the day? Is it OK for your baby to cry himself to sleep, or should you try to soothe him until he's calm enough to fall asleep? Should babies sleep by themselves or in your room or even in a family bed?

Our current society values sleeping babies, but because babies naturally wake often parents may be tempted to rush babies into sleeping for longer periods before they are ready. Babies will ultimately sleep for longer periods as they mature, but along the way they may just need a little gentle guidance in finding sleep. Whatever your preferred method, remember that babies are experiencing their world in each moment, as it happens, so be considerate of your baby's feelings in the process of looking for a particular outcome.

A few suggestions for you to consider:

1. The normal adjustment to parenthood often leaves us feeling anxious about sleep. Babies naturally pick up on how we are feeling, so the issue of sleep often turns out to be more about our state of mind when we are settling our child than about what we are actually doing. Keep in mind that, as babies mature, sleep comes more readily if they feel they have someone who cares and is able to calm her own distress as she is offering to calm their distress.

2. Give yourself the next week to just Be-With your baby without "trying" to get him to sleep. Watch your baby, and once he is calm, allow him to have a moment where he can simply be in your presence; you don't need to do anything except be there. This allows your baby to also Be-With you in a calm, quiet, enjoyable time together, before sleep time.

3. The best time for babies to sleep is when they are tired, so watch for tired signs so you can support your baby in a manner that is in synchrony with the baby's body.

4. Calm your baby as much as you can when he cannot settle for sleep. Sleep happens more readily from a calm state.

*With thanks to Helen Stevens.

5. If you are trying new ways to help your baby sleep, monitor two things: First, what's your gut feeling? If it feels wrong, it probably is wrong for you and your family. Second, watch your baby's response. If he is terribly distressed, comfort him and try again another time.

6. Don't be in a rush to "make" sleep happen; babies don't naturally have routine sleeping patterns when they are tiny, but you can be comforted by the fact that, as they develop and mature, so does their capacity for sleep.

7. If your baby's sleep patterns are bothering you, listen to advice from others with your "bigger, stronger, wiser, and kind" filter on, so you can decide what would suit your baby, because nobody knows a baby like the parent. Honor your own wisdom to help you decide what is best.

---

can to Be-With your baby and respond to her needs all around the Circle is "When I have a need, it will likely be met. There's no second-guessing, no fear that what I need isn't available. My security is based on trusting that the goodness I require is here with me."

• *Talk and talk and talk.* At about 6 months, your baby will increasingly show interest in the world beyond your face, and the joy of exploring the top of the Circle outside of your little internally shared experience will increase. As he does so, he wants you to talk to him about what's out there. Don't hesitate, even if it makes you feel silly to narrate his actions ("Are you going to grab your little toe?") or describe what he might be seeing ("Oh, yes, that's a really big teddy!"). Your talking sets your baby on the road toward learning language. And when your baby is on the bottom of the Circle, your tone of voice as you're talking to him about his emotions will help him understand that all of his feelings are safe and that, whatever they are, they're normal and acceptable to you. In this way, each of his emotions also becomes acceptable to him.

Now let's look at how you might respond to a developmentally typical situation at different ages of your child depending on your core sensitivity—and how you would respond if you were to choose security over "your current version of *Sharknado*."

3-Year-Olds

Shelby is 3 going on 35. She thinks she owns the world, runs to her own tune, and has a hard time taking "no" as an answer. Her famous meltdowns are known well throughout the neighborhood. But nothing upsets Ms. Shelby more than being told that she needs to share her toys with a friend.

Esteem Sensitive

"Shelby, You're a big girl, a good girl. But if you don't share that toy, I am going to take it away and give it to a little girl who knows how to not be so selfish. If I have to ask one more time, you are going to your room."

Sometimes our esteem-sensitive shark music leads us to shame our children, punishing them for not meeting our expectations and embarrassing us.

"Honey, it's not right for you not to share. We love sharing in this house. I know you want to be just like Mommy and be nice to Kelly. She's a guest, and she wants to play too. Please don't make such a fuss. You're just embarrassing yourself. You want to be a big girl, don't you?"

Sometimes our esteem-sensitive shark music triggers fear that our taking charge will break the fusion. So we plead and hope for the best, but in these moments we've given up being bigger, stronger, wiser, and kind.

Separation Sensitive

"Shelby Jane, I just don't know what to do with you. Every time I try to make you share I just can't. You've got a mind all your own, and I've tried everything under the freaking sun. Now if you don't mind me this time, I'll just have to tell your father when he gets home. He won't like knowing that you're trying to run the show one more time. He won't like it a bit."

"I totally give up, Shelby. I don't know what to do with you. I can't seem to get through to you. We're not going to play with anyone anymore if you can't listen to me. What am I going to do with you? I'm out of ideas."

Our separation-sensitive shark music can leave us feeling alone, with no sense of self-support or capacity as a caregiver. Feeling helpless, we resort to threats and messages of helplessness.

Safety Sensitive

"This is just getting out of hand. I'm not going to put up with this, Shelby. You are not the boss here. I asked you nicely to share with Kelly. She's such a nice friend, and I'm tired of asking you to be kinder. Either give her that toy or go to your room."

Concerned about being enslaved and without power, our safety-sensitive shark music triggers anger and fears of being out of control. In these moments we lose touch with our sense of how relationship can be positive.

Secure

"Shelby, I know you remember what we talked about this morning. You really don't like to share when you have a new toy. And I know this doll is your favorite. Come over here with me and I'll get Kelly to join us. Then you can tell Kelly why you like your new doll so much. We'll figure this out together." (The tone is firm and caring, said in a way the child definitely knows the parent is fully in charge.)

"Shelby, I know this doll is your favorite and it's especially hard to share your most special toys. Let's work this out. Why don't you see if Kelly would like to play with some of your other dolls? Could you get some other dolls for her?"

When we choose security, we acknowledge our child's feelings and also offer to deal with this need together. Three-year-olds are just starting to learn to play with other children, and it's difficult for them to negotiate peer relationships at first.

Secure responses begin with accepting the child's
experience as real and worthy of shared focus.

Only then does a shift to solving the problem offer new
options for change.

*"When my 3-year-old becomes angry, I now stay near him and talk
out loud/organize his feelings: 'You're angry with Mummy because she
asked you to stop hitting your brother. You feel that's not fair because
your brother did some hitting too.' The limit is still the same—hitting
is not OK—but I'm now staying with my 3-year-old's feelings of anger
and frustration and supporting him to make sense of this and express it
in more useful ways. I have noticed that my 3-year-old has been more
affectionate again toward me, he chooses to sit near me on the couch,
and asks me to rub his back before he goes to sleep, where previously
he was becoming 'Mr. Independent' and didn't like me doing these
things so much."*

—Cheryl Lowe, Adelaide, South Australia

5-Year-Olds

Kamal is having a hard time adjusting to kindergarten. He's already
struggling with the full days away from home, and it's showing up
with an uptick in his defiance when asked to do something around the
house. Kamal's latest outburst about being rushed to get in the car for
school included his new favorite phrase, "I hate you," no fewer than
five times (in less than 2 minutes). His second favorite phrase, "You're
mean," showed up twice.

Esteem Sensitive

"Young man, you will never, and I mean *never* talk to your father that
way again. It's time you learned to be on time! I can't tell you how
many times we have been over this! Get in that car now! If I hear one
more word from you, there will be no video games for a month!"

When we're esteem sensitive, we often resort to teaching as a
medium for our relationship with our child, especially when emotions
run high. Disappointed and furious, the teaching tone of this father
isn't able to mask his outrage. As is often the case, the child will likely
feel ashamed, blocking any sense of new learning.

"Kamal, I don't have time for this. I'm late. If you'll get in the car now, I'll let you play a game on my phone the whole way to school. For now we need to be on the same team."

In this case, Kamal's father hears shark music that reminds him of his own father's anger and begins to anticipate his child's tantrum if he takes a stand. Continued one-mindedness always worked with his father, so this now becomes the goal with his upset child. The father uses bribery as a practical strategy, while also appealing to the child to be "on the same team."

Separation Sensitive

"Kamal, we agreed you'd never say those mean things to me again. It's not right to hate your mommy. It hurts my feelings. You're my little man, and I need you to listen so you can help me get to work on time. I've told you before that I'm having a hard time at work. Please understand."

This parent's separation-sensitive shark music tells her that her son will leave her if she takes a stand, so she uses guilt and her own helplessness as a way to coerce her son to cooperate.

Safety Sensitive

"I don't think I ever gave you permission to talk that way to me. I'm sure not doing it now. I, for one, have had it with your attitude, young man. The door is right there, and the car is outside. I need you to find your way to both. Now!"

Instead of focusing on the relationship and how the parent and child can work together around this child's need, this safety-sensitive parent resorts to concepts he's comfortable with—strict boundaries and firm clarity.

"I wish you didn't have such an attitude. I'm just not sure what you want from me. If you go to the car, you can play on the tablet all the way to school."

Lost and without a sense that she can be the resource to regulate her child, this mom shares her confusion and assumes an external object will bring the calm she's hoping for.

Secure

"Kamal, you know and I know that this last week has been really tough for you. We also know that when you use those words nothing works right. I know you're upset, and I know you don't want to go to school right now. I also know that I've got to get to work. So, whether you want to or not, you're going to get in the car. And we're absolutely going to have an important talk about all of this tonight. I promise we'll find a way for you to feel better than you do right now."

This parent is exemplifying being bigger, stronger, wiser, and kind, with a focus on strength, kindness, and a commitment to work together about his upset. Notice that he doesn't try unrealistically to resolve the whole situation or to teach a lesson. There is also no overreaction to the word "hate"—because part of what our children need is to know they can have such moments and we'll survive them without panic or overreaction.

7-Year-Olds

Samantha is feeling stressed by all the new homework being assigned at school. On top of her already busy schedule of dance lessons, music lessons, and soccer, she's always afraid she is falling behind. At night she worries and has begun to struggle getting to sleep.

Esteem Sensitive

"Sammy, you're the smartest child in the class. You know that. Everyone knows that. You don't have a thing to worry about. You're so obviously in a league of your own it almost makes me laugh that you'd be concerned. Now stop your little meltdown, finish your homework, and you can have that bowl of ice cream you mentioned at dinner."

Esteem sensitivity can make our child's perceived superiority a burden. Attempting to bribe her daughter to live up to her own achievement-oriented agenda, this mother also devalues her daughter's worry.

"Sammy, honey, it's going to be OK, I promise. I used to be exactly like you, and it worked out perfectly for me. I did great in school, and you will too. There is absolutely nothing to worry about. You have something special that most children don't have; this worrying is actually kind of ridiculous."

Besides dismissing her child's upset, this parent's shark music is telling her to comfort through one-mindedness, assuming that being "exactly the same" will feel supportive to her daughter. Rather than listening to her daughter's feelings, this mother uses a mix of praise and shame in an attempt to stay away from the vulnerability required to navigate the bottom of the Circle.

Separation Sensitive

"Sammy, school is hard; they ask so much of you. Maybe you're in the wrong class. Maybe we should talk to your teacher about giving you less work. I think this is just too much for you. I'm sorry, honey. I wonder if we should just keep you home a day a week so you can rest. Do you think that would help?"

Separation-sensitive shark music triggers defenses that always imply being left alone. Thus this mother unconsciously tries to limit her child's competence and foster an increased sense of helplessness so she'll stay close. Likewise, this parent overidentifies with her daughter's anxiety instead of just Being-With her.

Separation-sensitive shark music warns us to defend
ourselves against being left alone.

Safety Sensitive

"Samantha, I'm sorry that you feel so much pressure. It makes a lot of sense. But if you want anything in life, you have to learn how to work hard and make it happen for yourself. Education will make all the difference for you. So I want you to go back in your room and try just a little harder."

Safety-sensitive shark music warns that need will lead to too much closeness. So the task orientation of this parent is used to avoid feeling more empathy and increased connection on the bottom of the Circle.

Secure

"Sammy, you're feeling way too much pressure, and we've got to figure out what needs to change. Would you like me to sit with you while you go to sleep tonight? Your dad and I will talk this over later tonight, and then we'll sit down with you tomorrow and figure out what needs to shift. I want you to know I'm sorry you're going through this, and I want you to know we will get this figured out together. There is a solution, and we'll find it."

The secure parent shows empathy but also models shared responsibility, with a clear focus and confidence in finding a new option.

9-Year-Olds

Kira is always having her feelings hurt. She is sure that her brother is always teasing her. Lisa, her best friend, is her "worst enemy" every other day. "She used to like me. Now all she does is text Jodie. I hate Rand. I hate Lisa. Doesn't anybody care anymore?"

Esteem Sensitive

"Kira, it's not that bad. You're just making so much out of so little. I've had enough! This world does *not* revolve around your every whim and upset. I don't know if you've noticed, but you can be so full of yourself. Why don't you start thinking of others for a change?"

For esteem-sensitive parents, what appears to be commonsense and practical thinking is often a form of shame. Shame has been known to inspire a change in behavior, but it doesn't bring a change in attitude. In this case it just pushes feelings of anger and sadness further down, away from the very relationship that can help this child resolve her pain.

"Kira, I don't even know why you care about those girls! We both know they are not nearly as mature and cool as you. Just forget them. Why don't you and I go out on a special date tomorrow?"

Esteem-sensitive parents often resort to encouraging fusion as a way to resolve negative feelings. Joining forces with someone "bigger" can appear helpful. But when the one who is bigger is unwilling to Be-With a child's feelings, the underlying learning is that dismissing feelings on the bottom of the Circle is the only way to find resolution.

Separation Sensitive

"If you don't quit complaining, I think I'll scream. I'm so tired of your going on and on about every little thing. Can't you see that I go out of my way for you all the time, but all you seem to care about is your friends? I even picked up your clothes and did your chores for you yesterday. [Tears.] Where's my thanks?"

In an attempt to keep her child close, this parent uses blame and guilt as a way to keep her daughter focused on Mom. The issue becomes the mother's sense of being overwhelmed, and the child is left without a way to make sense of her own feelings.

Safety Sensitive

[Walking toward the door and away from Kira.] "I'm not sure what to say. I can see you're upset, but so is every other girl your age. Have you considered going out for a bike ride? You know how well that has worked in the past."

This safety-sensitive parent isn't comfortable with his daughter's upset, so he gives her a practical way to let off steam—one that, not coincidentally, puts distance between his daughter and himself while also encouraging self-sufficiency.

Secure

"Kira, I'm not going to pretend I fully know what's going on inside. But you're clearly feeling like you're on the outside of things these days. Let's talk some of this out together. Maybe talking out loud with me will help you come up with some ideas about how to help this situation. We can do this now or we can wait a bit. Either is fine with me."

This parent is simultaneously encouraging coregulation of feelings and the daughter's capacity for self-support.

If this sounds a little too easy . . . keep in mind that secure responses like this one will be much more effective if they have been used over the years. When a pattern of secure interactions is deeply ingrained, this type of response takes much less effort on the part of the parent and elicits a trusting response with much less effort from the child.

"Before I took the Circle of Security class, I was definitely not comfortable with my children's negative emotions. My daughter, in particular, frequently had tantrums that made me feel anxious because I considered them dramatic and unreasonable. My usual tactic was to push her away—either by sending her to her room or by trying to persuade her that she was wrong, which all too often just ended up in a tearful shouting match.

"In class, I learned about 'Being-With' your child, and I tried to practice these strategies. My first few attempts, however, felt awkward and didn't seem to be particularly effective.

"Finally, about a year after taking the class, something seemed to click with me. My daughter was in rare form. She stormed off to her room shouting, 'Everyone hates me! No one understands me!' Sobbing and flailing her arms, she threw herself on the bed.

"I followed her in and began to rub her back. I started saying things like 'You feel like no one understands you. You feel like everyone hates you.' It was as if I had found the 'tantrum off' switch. Almost immediately, my daughter's tears shuddered to a halt and she gave me a big hug.

"Later, she reported to my husband, 'I was really freaking out and Mommy came and it was like she had these magic words that made me feel instantly better!'

"Magic! I felt better about myself as a parent, and my daughter felt better about herself as a person. It was a major victory and hopefully the beginning of a whole new way of being with each other. Thank you, Circle of Security."

—*Sarah Sanderson, Spokane, Washington*

"Being attuned does *not* mean giving in or lavishing our children with 'things.' It does *not* mean letting them rule the roost or get everything they want. Somehow it does seem that when they want something we don't want to give them for whatever reason, be it materially or emotionally, we make them feel wrong or bad or guilty or selfish. Perhaps this is to deflect our own guilt when we disappoint them, or to protect us from feeling inadequate, or to avoid our own deeper feelings of despair that we did not get what we needed as children. So instead of us being able to bear the child's disappointment with regulated equanimity—'I'm sorry you are disappointed, honey. I know how much you want that. But the answer is no'—we are tempted to respond with defensiveness and judgment, as in 'I can't believe you are asking for that. You are always wanting something more! Seriously? It's never enough for you.' What does this teach our child?

"We are miscuing them to not ask via shame, teaching them to act like they don't want something because it makes us (parents) uncomfortable."

—*Judy Fiermonte, Santa Rosa, California*

11-Year-Olds

Emily "totally loves" her best friend, Jenn. Like many of the 11-year-olds they know, Emily and Jenn seem to be on their phones most of the evening—texting, talking, conversing in a world that has, until recently, kept everyone else on the outside.

But this inseparability has begun to shift.

Jenn has a boyfriend. And Jenn's boyfriend doesn't want her so focused on Emily. "Emily, I'm still your best friend, but I can't let Brian go. I love him. Why can't you see that?"

Emily is devastated and for the past 2 weeks has been sulking through dinner, sitting alone in her room, unwilling to discuss what she calls "the end of my life." When she does speak, the message is always some variation on being worthless, "a total loser," someone who no one will ever like. "I'm such a geek. No one cares. What's wrong with me? Maybe I'm getting fat."

Esteem Sensitive

"You're making a big thing out of nothing. I'm not even sure Jenn is worth all of this. You're so out of her class in terms of almost everything: your looks, your intelligence. Trust me, there are a lot more fish in the sea."

Devaluing needs on the bottom of the Circle is a tactic that often squelches their further expression. This parent begins with dismissing need, then assuming that praise will make his daughter feel better. Then he devalues his child's relationships by implying that people are interchangeable.

"Sweetie, you're beautiful. You're the most beautiful girl in your class. And how could you say no one loves you? Since the day you were born I've always known you were the most perfect child on the planet."

The underlying assumption of many esteem-sensitive parents is that praise always trumps emotional pain. In this case the parent is complimenting her daughter and claiming that love and perfection (one based on comparison to the less beautiful girls in class) are connected. For children, the implication can become be perfect or else lose affection.

> **Esteem sensitivity tells us that praise always trumps emotional pain.**

"I know just how you feel. The exact same thing happened to me when I was your age. It's almost like we're the same person. And look at me now. It's all going to work out perfectly for you, just like it did for me."

This parent turns to fusion and ideal outcomes as a way to block her daughter's (and her own) feelings of vulnerability.

Separation Sensitive

"It's not fair that Jenn would treat you this way. Best friends don't do that kind of thing, playing you off against someone else. I hope you know that I'm always willing to be your best friend."

This parent drops all claim to hierarchy and offers "best friendship" and blame of others as a way to guarantee ongoing closeness.

"Honey, when you say you're fat, that worries me. You're not fat. I hope you don't start making me a nervous wreck always thinking you're going to be one of those girls who starves herself just to fit in."

In an attempt to block her child's distress, this mother attempts to "one up" her daughter's upset by promising to be overwhelmed should the daughter continue to have problems. The assumption is that guilt can control emotional distress.

> *Separation sensitivity tells us that guilt can control emotional distress.*

Safety Sensitive

"I wouldn't worry if I were you. This isn't the end of the world. You've got a lot of years ahead of you, and you will find more friends. For now, why don't you zero in on your studies? Now's as good a time as ever to start getting ready for college. You'll find plenty of friends there."

Safety-sensitive parents often have a "go-to" plan and it often includes self-sufficiency as a means to ending emotional difficulty. Focus on the mind or the body (exercise) is a common theme through which distancing from feeling is accomplished.

> *Safety sensitivity tells us that self-sufficiency can resolve emotional pain.*

"This kind of thing happens all the time. To be honest, I was getting concerned that you were spending too much time with Jenn. She's a good girl, but you've got school to focus on. I'd rather see you doing your homework than always being caught up in having a best friend."

The not-so-subtle message from this safety-sensitive parent is that relationships may not be as important as a child seems to think they are. The implied goal is doing well in school as a way to manage the need for others rather than doing well in school for its own sake.

Secure

"Emily, I'm so sorry. I'm not sure what's going on with Jenn, but I know it really, really hurts. You've been friends for such a long time.
"I also know that this is just the kind of stuff that can make us

feel, well, almost worthless. And maybe like no one likes us or ever will like us again. I sure know I've had those times. And I hated the whole experience.

"For now, I don't have any kind of an answer. But I do know that it's never good to deal with such big feelings alone. So, now or tomorrow or sometime soon, let's spend some time with how you're feeling about what's going on. Just know I'm here when you need me."

This parent keeps the focus on the child's own experience while giving the message that she is available to Be-With whatever the child is feeling. No pressure. No solutions. No teaching. Just simple presence.

13-Year-Olds

Nick has, until recently, kept to himself. But in the past few months he's begun to (1) notice girls and (2) hang out with a new group of guy friends. His new favorite pastime? Texting about girls with his new friends—day and night.

It's not uncommon for Nick to get five or six texts during dinner. Another three dozen before bed. And that's on what he calls an "off" night. It's also not uncommon to hear the "dings" coming in at 2:00 or 3:00 A.M.

Esteem Sensitive

"I did not buy you that phone just so you could blow off the rest of us. You have a responsibility to your family. We're not here to be an audience to your newfound hobby. Now put that damn thing away during dinner. I'm not telling you again."

Esteem-sensitive parents when feeling angry often use pronouncements about what is happening with an underlying message of devaluation and shame. The mistaken and sad assumption is that the best way to put out a fire includes a value judgment about the one who apparently started it.

"Nicky, I don't think my parents would have allowed me to do what you're doing right now. It's totally awesome that you have these new friends. I remember what it was like for me when I got new friends. It's the best feeling ever. I'll allow one more text and then, please, put your phone away until after dinner."

This esteem-sensitive parent seems unwilling to set boundaries because it might jeopardize the assumed togetherness of their fusion. The hope is that praise and one-mindedness will negate the need for hierarchy. They won't.

Separation Sensitive

"Nick, what happened to you? You used to belong to our family. Now all you think about is everyone except us. Why can't you be the boy you used to be—polite, easygoing, always around? I've done so much for you over the years, and now it's like I'm a piece of dust to you. What do I have to do to make you come back to us?"

Sometimes the fear of losing a child to independence leads a separation-sensitive parent to apply guilt in the service of keeping him close. This often includes a message of helplessness with a dose of either begging or bribery.

Safety Sensitive

"You've got plenty of time in the day to be texting with those guys. I'm glad you've got new friends, but for the love of God would you put that thing away during dinner? It's noisy enough around this place without that thing going off all the time."

Safety-sensitive parents often aren't comfortable negotiating emotions, but with anger they can maintain both a comfortable distance and some semblance of control.

Secure

"Nick, we've got some serious talking to do. Something is very wrong here, and it begins with us finding a way to figure this whole thing out. For starters, I'm taking charge of the phone every night at 9:00. No calls, no texts until after breakfast. Second, we are a family, which means that mealtimes are sacred. No texts during dinner. This isn't to say that you don't get to spend a lot of time with your friends. That's utterly fine with me. But family time is family time. And sleep time is sleep time. And, as always has been the case, anything about what I'm saying is open for discussion. I'm glad to hear your point of view as long as you know that these boundaries I've just drawn remain as stated and aren't open for negotiation."

Being the Hands on the Circle for Your Teenager

In June 2015, psychologist Gretchen Schmelzer* wrote a fictional letter to a parent from a teenager that went viral in social media shares. The hypothetical teen's missive that he wished he could write obviously struck a visceral chord with parents struggling to understand and connect with adolescents who might very well have become defiant or withdrawn, angry or sullen, mystifying or aggravating—or all of these. The teen described how much he (or she) needed the fight he and his parent were in at the moment, even though he couldn't express his feelings or thoughts about it. The letter stressed that it wasn't the subject of the fight that mattered but just that "I need to fight you on it" and that the teen needed his parent to stay strong in the face of it. The teenager then made a heartfelt plea that sticks with parents who read this letter: "I desperately need you to hold the other end of the rope. To hang on tightly while I thrash on the other end—while I find the handholds and footholds in this new world I feel like I am in," and "I need to see that no matter how bad or big my feelings are—they won't destroy you or me. I need you to love me even at my worst, even when it looks like I don't love you. I need you to love yourself and me for the both of us right now."

In the almost impossible, heat-of-the-crazy moments we find ourselves in with our children, especially as they are making the harrowing journey through adolescence, it's possible to tell ourselves: "My child, in this freaking, overwhelming, close-to-unbearable moment, has innate wisdom. Under the surface of what's going on—including this behavior that currently makes no sense to me—my child is waiting for me to return to my best version of bigger, stronger, wiser, and kind. Thankfully, I'm committed enough to find my way back onto the Circle and make clear that somehow, some way, we'll get through any ruptures that happen, together. I will be the Hands you need."

*Gretchen Schmelzer posted this moving hypothetical letter at www.emotionalgeographic. com/parents-corner on June 23, 2015.

15-Year-Olds

Marney is a 15-year-old who has recently discovered the excitement of Snapchat on her phone. She has a new boyfriend, and they have found ways around their parents' "open-bedroom-door" policy. One night, Marney's mother happens to peek into her room to say good night and catches Marney not only breaking the no-phone-in-bed rule, but also Snapchatting her boyfriend sexualized pictures of herself.

Esteem Sensitive

"Marney!! What are you thinking?? I thought I raised a girl who thought more of herself. That's what silly girls do who have no self-esteem. Give me that phone right now. I'm so disappointed in you. It's going to be months before you get this back. Go to bed."

For this esteem-sensitive mother, anger is the immediate and lasting intervention of choice. While shaming her child, she is also punitive and blocks access to an open discussion about the dangers of what her daughter is doing. In this case anger and shame overwhelm any options that might lead to future healthy self-regulation.

"Marney? Honey, I remember the thrill of first loves, and he is really cute. My parents were way too strict with me, and I never got to date at your age. Now tell him good night. And, I'm going to trust that you won't text him those pictures anymore—boys never value a girl who is too easy."

This mother fears the loss of fusion with her daughter, so she compromises hierarchy and becomes overly identified with her child's fantasy life. Her child is clearly left to fend for herself in very dangerous waters.

Separation Sensitive

"Put that phone down right now. I never should have let you have a phone or date in the first place. It's like you have forgotten you even have a family who cares about you and a mom who lets you do cool things. I am so nice to you, and all you do is take, take, take. How about some gratitude, or at the very least listening to the rules I'm trying to enforce for your own good."

A Quick Quiz: What If Your Teen Withdraws?

Alex is 14 years old. She's entered the "dark-side-of-the-moon" phase that many teenagers can inhabit for months . . . or years. Talkative and playful only a year ago, her responses to any questioning now mostly consist of shrugs and one- and two-word answers: "Yeah." "Maybe." "Not sure." "I guess." While not being rude, Alex is traveling that fine line between distant and disrespectful.

At the same time, Alex can be needy. Two hours after not wanting to stay at the dinner table 4 seconds after she's finished her meal, she's back in the kitchen wanting to figure out if she's really as ugly as she's sure everyone thinks she is. That's what brought her in to talk just now.

What do you think you would say, depending on your core sensitivity? Jot down your answer before reading our examples.

Separation Sensitive

Esteem Sensitive

Safety Sensitive

Secure

Now compare your answers with our examples:

Separation Sensitive

"Alex, honey, you're really upset, aren't you? It's been so long since you've told me you feel bad. Remember when we used to feel close? You know I'm right here for you. Maybe it's time we become friends again. Let's talk."

Esteem Sensitive

"Alex, I totally get what you're going through. Trust me, I've been there. When I was your age, I felt exactly the same way. What you need to know is that this will pass. Totally go away. Someone as beautiful as you will get beyond this in no time."

Safety Sensitive

"I think I know what's going on here. But I don't think it's anything to really worry about. I want you to think this through, because thinking you're ugly isn't really accurate. I think you are quite nice looking. I know your father and I are so glad you are doing well in school. I think this will pass."

Secure

"Well, this makes sense. Feeling attractive is really important, and feeling you're not sucks. I've sure had my moments. What I hope you know is that there will be times when you feel this way and probably want to talk about it and times you'll feel this way and want to stay far away from even mentioning it. My biggest hope is that when you want to talk you know I do too. If this is one of those times, I'm right here."

This mother asks her daughter to stop dangerous behavior by focusing on the needs of the parent. In the short run, her daughter may comply (or rebel), but either way she learns a dangerous lesson: protection isn't available, guilt motivates, but at the expense of building a healthy sense of self and healthy boundaries.

Safety Sensitive

"Marney, I get that this is what teenagers do, and it's all about fitting in, but this kind of behavior is not going to happen under my roof. I made the rules about your phone and dating pretty clear, and it's like I spend my whole life having to monitor whether or not you are following them. You just keep pushing it. I'm so tired of it. Give me your phone."

While maintaining hierarchy, this mother forgoes any chance for a deeper experience of relationship as her daughter is entering young adulthood. The focus is on the parent's perceived enslavement to her daughter rather than her daughter's need to learn new relationship skills.

Secure

"Marney, what you are doing is out of bounds. Completely! This is remarkably dangerous. Hand me your phone, now! I'm not sure what you were thinking, but sometime soon I'll be willing to listen. The rules I've set about your phone and dating are boundaries that have been set for a good reason. They've just gotten much, much tighter. We've got some real talking ahead of us. Right now I'm freaked out. Tomorrow we are going to talk about this, and somehow we'll figure this out . . . together."

This parent uses honest (not overdramatic) anger and simple, clear boundaries with genuine concern for her daughter while promising to help her make sense of what's just gone on. The mother uses no blame, no shame, no name calling, no guilt, while honoring her daughter's need to build new skills that she clearly doesn't have yet. Her implied parent–child contract is that they will, together, find a way to build those skills. Secure parents of older teens know that the days of being "in control" are over. (The harder they try to maintain control, the greater the push-back and ensuing chaos.) Instead they recognize that their primary option and gift is ongoing influence. Influence—when offered from a position of being bigger, stronger, wiser, and kind without threats, bribes, devaluation, or guilt—scaffolds a teen into young adulthood with ever-increasing capacity for healthy decision making.

It's not always easy to look at how we respond to our children and commit to making conscious choices. And of course our daughters and sons will keep changing over the years, presenting us with a new playing field again and again. When in doubt, remember this:

Just Be-With your child. If you can do that,
everything slows down and things tend to get better.
Sometimes sooner. Sometimes later.
When fully chosen, security happens.

And when shark music causes you to make ruptures that you regret—taking your bigger, stronger, wiser, and kind hands off the Circle—remember that each rupture is an opportunity to repair, and each repair reinforces security for your child. Also keep in mind that the more you choose security, the easier your relationship will get over time.

> *"I have four children, which gives me a lot of practice at reading cues and looking for those moments when things are starting to escalate, or 'go bad,' as I always think of it. On one particular evening, I was with my kids at their school Christmas concert. I could see by the look on my 9-year-old's face that while he was having fun at the moment, a meltdown was forthcoming. I also knew that a meltdown in the school, in front of all of his friends and their families, would cause him more embarrassment than one in the car or at home would.*
> *"I quickly gathered up the kids, without causing a stir. I knew that calm in that moment was going to get me through whatever was coming. As we began to leave the school my son became more and more angry and agitated. I left the building before he really began to let me have it. By the time we got into the car my son began to cry and yell at me. He was so angry that we had left! My first reaction, before I learned all I now know about attachment and the Circle of Security, would have been to get really angry at him for causing a scene and for being disrespectful to me. He was saying horrible things to me that he had never said before! Instead of reacting, I took a deep breath and realized that I had a good opportunity to practice Being-With him. For the next 30 minutes he raged in the car and I stayed right there with him. When we got home, I told him that he could be mad and upset but that we were going to stay together until he felt better . . . and his 'tantrum' lasted another 20 minutes or so. He cried and yelled and I stayed and listened and empathized. Eventually his anger began to deflate like a balloon. He calmed down and still we sat. Then he began to cry again. When I asked him why he was crying now, he told me it was because he felt so bad for the things he had said to me. I got him a glass of milk and sat next to him on the couch for a talk and*

a cuddle. Of course, I forgave him for the things he said! He wasn't trying to be mean or disrespectful; he was angry and overstimulated and didn't know what to do with all of that. I felt like not only had I done the right thing, but that my son had learned that Mom would not get mad or abandon him when he was upset or when things were not going right for him. He also knew that he could get through those tough moments and that he could repair relationships when he needed to. I know that if I had followed my usual formula, he would have gone to bed angry and feeling justified in that anger. Instead, my son went to bed that night knowing that his mom loves him.

"One day, I will have four teenage boys, all at once. I know that there are many more moments like this one to come. I also know that the Circle of Security is going to help us get through those moments and make our relationships stronger for it."

—Erin Vandale, Winnipeg, Canada

On the Road to Security

Here's the hope and the wonder: Your child, once so tiny and seemingly fragile, will transform the secure attachment you have lovingly created (with no small amount of hard work along the way) into a lifelong experience of being a trusting, loving, confident adult. When you think about it, this is the inheritance we most want to pass along to our children and the generations beyond.

Throughout these pages we've been implying that the key ingredients of this inheritance are, fortunately, not all that complex:

1. We need access to a simple road map.
2. We need to believe in our deep intention to do the best we can.
3. We need an awareness of where we tend to get lost along the way.
4. We need to give ourselves permission to make mistakes and find our way back to what's needed.
5. We need to trust that shared goodness is both the means and the end of all that we hope to share.

As legacies go, our children's resulting capacities for caring, self-reliance, and resilience are as good as we could hope for. Because, as we know, life is guaranteed to provide circumstances that we would never choose for them. Some of these circumstances may happen when they are in our direct care, some may not happen until years after they have left the orbit of our influence. Regardless of what may be, our deepest intention is that our children will be able to meet all circumstances with both grit and grace: the necessary capacity to stand firm in the face of difficulty and the trust that allows a willingness to ask for and provide support when it is needed. As it turns out, what they learn from us and with us is how they will build the capacities most necessary for their future.

We all love.

We all struggle.

"And" is always hidden in plain sight.

RESOURCES

Additional Reading

The following selected books and articles may be of interest to those who want to explore the history of attachment theory, some of the major research studies that have informed the Circle of Security, and learn more about infant and child development and specific topics mentioned in this book.

Bowlby, J. (1973). *Attachment and loss: Vol. 2. Separation.* New York: Basic Books.

Bowlby, J. (1980). *Attachment and loss: Vol. 3. Loss, sadness and depression.* New York: Basic Books.

Bowlby, J. (1982). *Attachment and loss: Vol. 1. Attachment* (rev. ed.). New York: Basic Books.

Bowlby, J. (1998). *A secure base: Parent–child attachment and healthy human development.* London: Basic Books.

Bowlby, J., & Ainsworth, M. D. S. (1951). *Maternal care and mental health.* Geneva, Switzerland: World Health Organization.

Bretherton, I. (1992). The origins of attachment theory: John Bowlby and Mary Ainsworth. *Developmental Psychology, 28,* 759–775.

Cassidy, J., & Shaver, P. R. (Eds.). (2016). *Handbook of attachment: Theory, research, and clinical applications* (3rd ed.). New York: Guilford Press. (Excellent compilation of attachment research, theory, and clinical applications.)

Cooper, G., Hoffman, K., & Powell, B. (2009). *Circle of Security parenting manual for use with COS-P DVD.* Unpublished manuscript distributed as part of COS-P training.

Cooper, G., Hoffman, K., & Powell, B. (2009). *Circle of Security parenting: A relationship based parenting program* [DVD]. Available at *http://circleofsecurity.com*.

Fraiberg, S., Adelson, E., & Shapiro, V. (1975). Ghosts in the nursery: A psychoanalytic approach to the problems of impaired infant–mother relationships. *Journal of the American Academy of Child and Adolescent Psychiatry, 14*(3), 387–421.

George, C., Kaplan, N., & Main, M. (1984). *Adult Attachment Interview.* Unpublished document, Department of Psychology, University of California, Berkeley.

Goleman, D. (1995). *Emotional intelligence: Why it can matter more than IQ.* New York: Bantam Books.

Goleman, D. (2006). *Social intelligence: The new science of human relationships.* New York: Bantam Books.

Karen, R. (1990, February). Becoming attached. *The Atlantic.* Retrieved from *www.theatlantic.com*.

Karen, R. (1994). *Becoming attached: First relationships and how they shape our capacity to love.* New York: Oxford University Press. (Good introduction to attachment theory.)

Lieberman, A. F., Padrón, E., Van Horn, P., & Harris, W. W. (2005). Angels in the nursery: The intergenerational transmission of benevolent parental influences. *Infant Mental Health Journal, 26*(6), 504–520.

Lyons-Ruth, K., & Process of Change Study Group. (1998). Implicit relational knowing: Its role in development and psychoanalytic treatment. *Infant Mental Health Journal, 19*(3), 282–289.

Masterson, J. F. (1985). *The real self: A developmental, self, and object relations approach.* New York: Brunner/Mazel.

Masterson, J. F. (1993). *The emerging self.* New York: Brunner/Mazel.

Powell, B., Cooper, G., Hoffman, K., & Marvin, B. (2014). *The Circle of Security intervention: Enhancing attachment in early parent–child relationships.* New York: Guilford Press.

Powell, B., Cooper, G., Hoffman, K., & Marvin, R. S. (2009). The Circle of Security. In C. H. Zeanah, Jr. (Ed.), *Handbook of infant mental health* (3rd ed., pp. 450–467). New York: Guilford Press.

Schore, A. N. (1996). The experience-dependent maturation of a regulatory system in the orbital prefrontal cortex and the origin of developmental psychopathology. *Development and Psychopathology, 8*(1), 59–87.

Schore, A. N. (2002). Dysregulation of the right brain: A fundamental mechanism of traumatic attachment and the psychopathogenesis of posttraumatic stress disorder. *Australian and New Zealand Journal of Psychiatry, 36*(1), 9–30.

Shonkoff, J. P., & Phillips, D. A. (Eds.). (2000). *From neurons to neighborhoods: The science of early child development.* Washington, DC: National Academy Press. (Excellent overview of the first 5 years of life; full text available at *www.nap.edu*.)

Siegel, D. J. (2012). *The developing mind: How relationships and the brain interact to shape who we are* (2nd ed.). New York: Guilford Press.

Siegel, D. J. (2014). *No-drama discipline: The whole-brain way to calm the chaos and nurture your child's developing mind.* New York: Bantam.

Siegel, D. J. (2015). *Brainstorm: The power and purpose of the teenage brain.* New York: Tarcher/Perigee.

Siegel, D. J., & Bryson, T. (2012). *The whole-brain child: 12 revolutionary strategies to nurture your child's developing mind.* New York: Bantam.

Siegel, D. J., & Hartzell, M. (2004). *Parenting from the inside out: How a deeper self-understanding can help you raise children who thrive.* New York: Penguin.

Sroufe, L. A., Egeland, B., Carlson, E. A., & Collins, W. A. (2005). *The development of the person: The Minnesota Study of Risk and Adaptation from Birth to Adulthood.* New York: Guilford Press.

Steele, H., & Steele, M. (2008). On the origins of reflective functioning. In F. Busch (Ed.), *Mentalization: Theoretical considerations, research findings, and clinical implications* (pp. 133–156). New York: Analytic Press.

Stern, D. N. (1977, 2002; with a new introduction). *The first relationship: Infant and mother.* Cambridge, MA: Harvard University Press.

Stern, D. N. (1985). *The interpersonal world of the infant: A view from psychoanalysis and developmental psychology.* New York: Basic Books.

Stern, D. N. (1990). *Diary of a baby: What your child sees, feels, and experiences.* New York: Basic Books.

Stern, D. N. (1995). *The motherhood constellation: A unified view of parent–infant psychotherapy.* New York: Basic Books.

Stern, D. N., & Bruschweiler-Stern, N. (1998). *The birth of a mother: How the motherhood experience changes you forever.* New York: Basic Books.

Tronick, E. (2007). *The neurobehavioral and social–emotional development of infants and children.* New York: Norton.

Articles and Chapters about the Circle of Security

Avery, L., Matthews, J., Hoffman, K., Powell, B., & Cooper, G. (2008). Project Same Page: An evaluation of an attachment training seminar. *Journal of Public Child Welfare, 2,* 495–509.

Blome, W. W., Bennett, S., & Page, T. (2010). Organizational challenges to implementing attachment-based practices in public child welfare agencies: An example using the Circle of Security model. *Journal of Public Child Welfare, 4*(4), 427–449.

Cassidy, J., Woodhouse, S. S., Cooper, G., Hoffman, K., Powell, B., & Rodenberg, M. (2005). Examination of the precursors of infant attachment security: Implications for early intervention and intervention research. In L. J. Berlin, Y. Ziv, L. Amaya-Jackson, & M. T. Greenberg (Eds.), *Enhancing early attachments: Theory, research, intervention, and policy* (pp. 34–60). New York: Guilford Press.

Cassidy, J., Woodhouse, S. S., Sherman, L. J., Stupica, B., & Lejuez, C. W. (2011). Enhancing infant attachment security: An examination of treatment efficacy and differential susceptibility. *Journal of Development and Psychopathology, 23,* 131–148.

Cassidy, J., Ziv, Y., Stupica, B., Sherman, L. J., Butler, H., Karfgin, A., et al. (2010). Enhancing attachment security in the infants of women in a jail-diversion program. In J. Cassidy, J. Poehlmann, & P. R. Shaver (Eds.), An attachment perspective on incarcerated individuals and their children. *Attachment and Human Development, 12*(4), 333–353.

Cooper, G., Hoffman, K., Marvin, R., & Powell, B. (2007). Clinical application of attachment theory: The Circle of Security approach. In K. Golding (Ed.), *Attachment theory into practice* (Briefing Paper No. 26, pp. 38–43). Leicester, UK: British Psychological Society.

Cooper, G., Hoffman, K., Powell, B., & Marvin, R. (2005). The Circle of Security intervention: Differential diagnosis and differential treatment. In L. J. Berlin, Y. Ziv, L. Amaya-Jackson, & M. T. Greenberg (Eds.), *Enhancing early attachments: Theory, research, intervention, and policy* (pp. 127–151). New York: Guilford Press.

Hoffman, K., Marvin, R., Cooper, G., & Powell, B. (2006). Changing toddlers' and preschoolers' attachment classifications: The Circle of Security intervention. *Journal of Consulting and Clinical Psychology, 74,* 1017–1026.

Page, T., & Cain, D. S. (2009). "Why don't you just tell me how you feel?": A case study of a young mother in an attachment-based group intervention. *Child and Adolescent Social Work Journal, 26*(4), 333–350.

Powell, B., Cooper, G., Hoffman, K., & Marvin, R. (2007). The Circle of Security project: A case study—"It hurts to give that which you did not receive." In D. Oppenheim & D. F. Goldsmith (Eds.), *Attachment theory in clinical work with children: Bridging the gap between research and practice* (pp. 172–202). New York: Guilford Press.

Powell, B., Cooper, G., Hoffman, K., & Marvin, R. S. (2009). The Circle of Security. In C. H. Zeanah, Jr. (Ed.), *Handbook of infant mental health* (3rd ed., pp. 450–467). New York: Guilford Press.

Zanetti, C. A., Powell, B., Cooper, G., & Hoffman, K. (2011). The Circle of Security intervention: Using the therapeutic relationship to ameliorate attachment security in disorganized dyads. In J. Solomon & C. George (Eds.), *Disorganized attachment and caregiving* (pp. 318–342). New York: Guilford Press.

Sources of Additional Information and Support

Circle of Security International

www.circleofsecurity.com

Our website offers free downloads, animations, and educational video clips for parents. This includes referrals to professionals and facilitators throughout the world who have been trained in the *Circle of Security Parenting* protocol should you need further information and support.

Zero to Three: National Center for Infants, Toddlers, and Families

www.zerotothree.org

This nonprofit organization provides parents, professionals, and policy makers the knowledge and know-how to nurture early development, with the mission of ensuring that all babies and toddlers have a strong start in life. This site offers a wealth of reading material, referrals, training opportunities, and a national conference. Zero to Three is a pioneer in the field of early childhood development and intervention.

INDEX

Note: *f* following a page number indicates a figure.

ABOUT THE AUTHORS

Kent Hoffman, RelD, has been a psychotherapist since 1972. Certified in psychoanalytic psychotherapy by The Masterson Institute in New York City, he has worked with prison and homeless populations as well as adults seeking psychoanalytic psychotherapy. His primary focus since the 1990s has been working with and designing treatment interventions for street-dependent teens with young children. The underlying theme of his life's work can be found in a TEDx talk titled "Infinite Worth." Since 1985, Dr. Hoffman has had a shared clinical practice in Spokane, Washington, with Glen Cooper and Bert Powell. Together, they have created and disseminated the Circle of Security, for which each has received the New York Attachment Consortium's Bowlby–Ainsworth Award, among other honors. They are coauthors of *The Circle of Security Intervention* (for mental health professionals).

Glen Cooper, MA, has worked as a psychotherapist with individuals and families in both agency and private practice settings since the 1970s. He has extensive training in family systems, object relations, attachment theory, and infant mental health assessment. Mr. Cooper also works as a treatment foster parent and long-time Head Start consultant.

Bert Powell, MA, began his clinical work as an outpatient family therapist in a community mental health center, where he helped a broad range of families find and use unacknowledged strengths to address their problems. Mr. Powell is certified in psychoanalytic psychotherapy by The Masterson Institute in New York City. He is Adjunct Assistant Professor in the Graduate School of Counseling Psychology at Gonzaga University and serves as an international advisor to the editorial board of the *Journal of Attachment and Human Development.*

Christine M. Benton is a Chicago-based writer and editor.